This book is d   ꞌ to
Hamish Canham's wife and children—
Hazel, Mabel and Oliver.

CONTENTS

ACKNOWLEDGEMENTS

Thanks are due to the following:

Random House Books for permission to use the phrase "acquainted with the night", from the poem of the same name by Robert Frost, as the title of the current volume;

Carcanet Press for permission to reproduce "The Broken Bowl" by James Merrill;

Bloodaxe Books for permission to reproduce "A Surprise on the First Day of School" and "Vertigo" by Anne Stevenson, and "Between the Lines" and "Passed On" by Carole Satyamurti;

The *Journal of Child Psychotherapy* (http://www.tandf.co.uk) for permission to reprint Priscilla Green's article, "The Poet and the Superego";

Faber & Faber for permission to quote from *Collected Poems* by W. H. Auden and from *Death of a Naturalist, Seeing Things, The Spirit Level, North, The Haw Lantern*, all by Seamus Heaney.

SERIES EDITOR'S PREFACE

S ince it was founded in 1920, the Tavistock Clinic has developed a wide range of therapeutic approaches to mental health that have been strongly influenced by psychoanalysis. It has also adopted systemic family therapy as a theoretical model and a clinical approach to family problems. The Clinic is the largest training institution in Britain for mental health, providing post-graduate and qualifying courses in social work, psychology, psychiatry, child, adolescent, and adult psychotherapy, as well as in nursing and primary care. It trains about 1,400 students each year in over 45 courses.

The Clinic's philosophy is aimed at promoting therapeutic methods in mental health. Its work is founded on the clinical expertise which is the basis of its consultancy work and research. This series aims to make available the clinical, theoretical, and research work that is most influential at the Tavistock Clinic. It sets out new approaches in the understanding and treatment of psychological disturbance in children, adolescents, and adults, both as individuals and in families.

While this book was in the final stages of preparation, Hamish Canham fell ill. He died on 5 July 2003. His death is an immense loss to everyone who knew him.

The papers in *Acquainted With The Night*, each in its instructively thoughtful, scholarly, and subtle way, elaborate various contemporary perspectives on the relationship between psychoanalysis and poetry. As the editors make clear, the aim is not to psychoanalyse poets, but rather to examine the ways in which each medium, whether clinical or literary, explores and expresses the symbolic process as a means of understanding psychic reality.

Both generally and specifically in relation to individual poets, the authors illuminate the role of some central psychoanalytic concerns—those of containment and reparation, for example, and of mourning and loss—in furthering reflection on the psychic determinants of the nature of imaginative life and of creativity. All the papers are lodged in the practice or experience of psychoanalysis or psychoanalytic psychotherapy rather than simply the theory, and dreams and children's play are drawn on, as are the details of the way language is used—that is, the meaningfulness of language itself. At once challenging and enriching, this volume takes its place in a long tradition within the Tavistock Clinic of drawing together aspects of cultural life with the working life of the Clinic.

Margot Waddell
Series Editor

FOREWORD

Al Alvarez

P sychoanalysis and literature have been close partners from
the start, not least because Freud himself read widely and
wrote compelling prose. Both these accomplishments were
unusual in a scientist and they generated in him an even more
unusual respect for the arts. When, during the celebration of his
70th birthday, one of his disciples hailed Freud as "the discoverer of
the unconscious", he answered, "The poets and philosophers before
me discovered the unconscious. What I discovered was the scientific
method by which the unconscious can be studied".

Freud, with his interest in archaeology, worked like a novelist to
recreate the past. The patient told his story from his point of view
and the analyst told it back to him, using his interpretations to give
it new meaning, and creating form and significance out of the chaos
of the unconscious, especially as it expresses itself in dreams. And
because dreams, in their loopy way, seem creative, this led to a
fundamental misunderstanding of the nature of art, particularly in
the early days of psychoanalysis, when the idea of sexual
symbolism was still fresh and exciting and subversive. Instead of
reading, say, a poem as a work of art with a life of its own
independent of the creator—as something which, in Coleridge's
words, "contains in itself the reason why it is so and not

otherwise"—psychoanalysts with a taste for literature often used it as though it were mere dream-stuff, welling up uncensored and unbidden, another "royal road to the unconscious" of the unfortunate author.

A century later, psychoanalysts tend to be less interested in weaving stories and digging up the past. They concentrate, instead, on the transference and counter-transference—on what is happening between the patient and the therapist in the here-and-now of the consulting room, where the story matters less than how it is told. Instead of looking for clues, they are listening, like critics, to the overtones and undertones, alert to false notes, monitoring when and why they are moved and—equally important—when and why they are bored. It's all about nuances—about body language and tone of voice, about what is said and what is left unsaid.

Thanks to this shift of focus, the contributors to this book have not fallen into the trap of treating poetry as though it were clinical material. They see it, mostly, as a kind of parallel universe that they can use to illustrate and illuminate states of mind they must deal with in their work. This makes good sense, since the business of poetry is not just to express thoughts and feelings in the purest, most concentrated form, but also to think about them or even, as Bion put it, to make them thinkable. Psychoanalysis tries to do the same and, at their best, interpretations can sometimes be as intuitive and creative as a work of art.

As an art-form, however, psychoanalysis has very little to do with imaginative writing and a great deal in common with literary criticism. Or rather, with criticism as it used to be in the days before it was hijacked by extra-literary preoccupations, such as theory, gender, politics, race and, indeed, psychoanalysis. True criticism, the kind practised by masters like Coleridge and Eliot, comes without theoretical baggage and with nothing to prove. In order to find out what is going on in a work of art, the critic must let go of his own sensibility and immerse himself in that of the artist, without theories and without preconceptions. All that is required of him is attention and detachment—listening, thinking, and giving himself up all at the same time. And that, I assume, is much the same as the "evenly suspended attention" with which, said Freud, the therapist listens to a patient.

It is here that the analyst and the critic join the creative artist.

Like psychoanalysis, the arts are complex disciplines, crafts that take years to acquire. But once this long apprenticeship is over and the technical skills are so perfected that they have become instinctive, a strange transformation takes place: as the artist becomes absorbed in the practical details of his craft, his personality recedes and the work cuts itself free of its maker, acquiring a separate life of its own. Coleridge put it best when he described Shakespeare in full flow:

> himself meanwhile unparticipating in the passions, and actuated only by that pleasurable excitement, which had resulted from the energetic fervour of his own spirit in vividly exhibiting what it had so accurately and profoundly contemplated.

Coleridge's word for this style of creative detachment was "aloofness" and it doesn't come easily or often. But when it does, the effect on both writer and reader is strangely liberating.

This is why D. H. Lawrence was wrong when he wrote, "One sheds one's sicknesses in books—repeats and presents one's emotions to be master of them". Art is about more than compensation and self-therapy, just as psychoanalysis is about more than relieving symptoms, and cure is too narrow a concept for what either can do at its best. Repeat, best. A good poem is as hard to find as a good analysis but, once found, the effect of both is to make you—the reader, the patient—more fully and pleasurably alive. This oddly invigorating relationship between psychic reality and aesthetic pleasure is, I think, the underlying theme of this book.

CONTRIBUTORS

Kate Barrows is a child psychotherapist, trained at the Tavistock Clinic, and a training psychoanalyst for the British Psychoanalytical Society. She lives and works in Bristol. She has a background in the study of literature, and writes and lectures on a variety of psychoanalytic and literary topics.

Ronald Britton is a training analyst and currently President of the British Psychoanalytical Society. He is the author of *Belief and Imagination: Explorations in Psychoanalysis* (Routledge, 1998) and *Sex, Death and the Superego* (Karnac, 2003). He is co-author, with Michael Feldman and Edna O'Shaughnessy, of *The Oedipus Complex Today: Clinical Implications* (Karnac Books, 1989).

Hamish Canham (1962–2003) was a Consultant Child and Adolescent Psychotherapist at the Tavistock Clinic, and was Joint Organizing Tutor for the clinical training in child psychotherapy. He was Joint Editor of the *Journal of Child Psychotherapy*. He also taught in Bologna, Italy on the Tavistock model child psychotherapy training there.

Judith Edwards is a consultant child and adolescent psychotherapist working at the Tavistock Clinic, where she teaches on several courses and is Course Tutor for the MA in Psychoanalytic Studies. Apart from publications in academic journals, her most recent published work includes chapters in *Autism and Personality* (Alvarez & Reid, Routledge, 1999) and *Personality Development* (Hindle & Smith, Routledge, 1999). She collected and edited *Being Alive: Building on the Work of Anne Alvarez* (Routledge, 2001), and until 1999 was Joint Editor of the *Journal of Child Psychotherapy*.

Priscilla Green is a child and adolescent psychotherapist. She works at the Tavistock Clinic where she is a tutor and Assessment Tutor for the Psychoanalytic and Observational Studies Course, and where she also specializes in work with parents whose children are in intensive treatment, particularly in association with the autism team. She also works at the Marlborough Family Service in St John's Wood, where she sees individual children and young people for long term therapy, and she has a small private practice in Hampstead. After reading History, and then working as a solicitor, a writer, and a civil servant, she trained as a child psychotherapist at the Tavistock Clinic, where she wrote her MA dissertation on the Book of Ezekiel.

Michael Maltby is a clinical psychologist and group analyst. He is the Clinical Director of a doctoral programme in Clinical Psychology at Salomons, which is an associate faculty of Canterbury Christ Church University College. He also works clinically as a consultant clinical psychologist in the NHS, specializing in psychotherapy with adults and older people. Over the last few years he has developed a particular interest in the nature of creativity in the arts and therapeutic practice with a particular focus on the use of creative writing in personal and professional development. He is currently undertaking research into the relationship between poetry and self-experience from a psychoanalytic perspective.

Carole Satyamurti is a poet, and a sociologist with a particular interest in psychoanalytic ideas. She teaches at the University of East London and at the Tavistock Clinic. She has published four collections of poetry, of which the most recent is *Love and Variations* (Bloodaxe, 2000). She received a Cholmondeley Award in 2000.

Graham Shulman read English at Oxford, and later trained as a child psychotherapist at the Tavistock Clinic. He has a particular interest in the links between literature and psychoanalysis. He has written a review of the poet Carole Satyamurti's volume of poetry *Striking Distance*, and a psychoanalytic commentary on two novels of the Scottish children's fiction writer Des Dillon, and recently had a paper on Henry James's novel *What Maisie Knew* published in the *Journal of Child Psychotherapy*. He was Joint Guest-Editor of an issue of the *International Journal of Infant Observation* on the subject of autism. He is a consultant child and adolescent psychotherapist and Senior Tutor on the Child Psychotherapy Training and the Therapeutic Skills with Children and Young People course at the Scottish Institute of Human Relations.

Margot Waddell is a psychoanalyst and a consultant child psychotherapist in the Adolescent Department of the Tavistock Clinic. She took a PhD in English Literature at Cambridge and has explored literary perspectives in relation to clinical theory and practice in many publications over the years. A new edition of her most recent book, *Inside Lives: Psychoanalysis and the Growth of the Personality*, was brought out by Karnac in 2002.

Introduction

Hamish Canham and Carole Satyamurti

T he title for this book, *Acquainted with the Night* is taken from a Robert Frost poem. We have chosen it because it captures something of the overlapping areas of interest shared by poets and psychoanalytic psychotherapists. It hints at the hidden recesses of the mind: imaginative possibilities; a familiarity with the more shadowy aspects of personality and life; the adult intimacy of the bedroom and the childhood feelings of exclusion from it; awareness of death but also the excitement and intensity of experience and feeling that the night can bring. Both poetry and psychoanalysis seek to help poet and reader or therapist and patient become more closely acquainted with these aspects of experience and mental life.

"Acquainted with the Night" also represents the way in which a few words, in either poetry or psychoanalysis, can contain so much through the images they conjure up and the associations they lead to. This is also true of a dream image, or a portion of a child's play. It is these reverberations that give each poem or dream its particular and private meaning between the poetic or psychoanalytic pair— poet and reader or therapist and patient. Indeed it is this condensed use of imagery and the extent to which it succeeds in communicating subtlety of meaning that determines the success of a poem or results in understanding through interpretation.

There are many similarities between poetry and psychoanalysis. Both depend on paying unusual attention to nuances of language—to the precise sense in which words are used, and to the range of associations they carry. Both operate in the realm of the symbolic. Both are concerned with condensation, with the way meaning is compressed—in the poem and in the dream. Both invite us to look differently at the world by challenging our taken-for-granted perceptions and assumptions. In the quality of attention that is paid by practitioners of each at a certain stage in the process, there are also similarities. There is a link between, on the one hand, Freud's idea of the analyst maintaining "free floating attention" to the material brought by the patient, or Bion's recommended absence of memory and desire on the analyst's part, and, on the other, Keats's concept of Negative Capability, a state "without any irritable reaching after fact and reason", which he thought desirable in the poet. In each case, the ability to tolerate uncertainty, to refrain from comfortable but premature closure, is central.

The psychoanalyst, Thomas Ogden (2001), has written about the similar functions of poetry and psychoanalysis.

> We are known as we had not known ourselves because, up to that point, we had not been ourselves as fully as we are becoming in experiencing the poem and as the poem experiences us. Similarly in the analytic relationship, patient and analyst as individuals each read and are read by the unconscious of the other. [p. 177]

Ogden is one of a small number of analysts and analytic therapists who have turned their minds to poetry. Two of the authors of chapters in this book have already made contributions to the application of psychoanalytic theory to literature: Waddell (with Williams) in *Chamber of Maiden Thought* (1991) and Britton in a series of papers in *Belief and Imagination* (1998). Here some of their ideas are developed further. Some chapters in this book examine individual poets and try to illuminate certain aspects of their work through the application of psychoanalytic theory. Others look more generally at the relationship between psychoanalysis, poetry, and the creative process.

It should be clear that what we are not attempting to do here is psychoanalyse poets. As Carole Satyamurti makes clear in her chapter, poetry should not be read as literal biography. It is an expression of certain aspects of the poet's imagination and experience that can help the reader to understand better, perhaps, their own feelings. This way of viewing experience has been at the heart of psychoanalytic theory since Freud's relinquishment of "seduction theory". The emphasis in contemporary psychoanalytic thinking is on understanding the way in which psychic reality shapes our perception. It may be of interest briefly to trace the development of some of the key concepts that inform the thinking in this book.

Freud was not much interested in aesthetics, i.e., in what makes the difference between good and bad art—indeed he confessed himself more interested in the content of a work of art than in its form. This tended to lead to a rather reductive account of what creative activity is about—seeing it in terms of sublimation, of unconscious phantasy and of symbolism conceived in a somewhat literal way. These concerns resulted in a preoccupation with the psychology of the artist, and gave rise to a long tradition of studies in which the inner world of the artist was "read off" from the work, the perceived task being to distinguish between manifest and latent content and to bring the latter into view. But such writing can tend towards too simple an equation between the work of art and the biography of its creator—as though the work were (nothing more than) an equivalent[1] of a factual account, or even of a lived life. Furthermore, it does not address the *art* aspect of a work, nor account for why we should derive profound pleasure/satisfaction from an encounter with a great painting or poem. It does not illuminate the way in which a successful work of art addresses aspects of the human predicament which are universal—what the Kleinian writer on art, Adrian Stokes (1947), called "the themes of human nature".

In a number of books and essays written between 1932 and the 1960s, Stokes addresses these questions. Following an analysis with Melanie Klein, his writing on art (on painting, sculpture, and architecture) is often infused with psychoanalytic ideas—and particularly with Klein's formulation of the paranoid–schizoid and depressive positions. The distinction between carving and modelling is central to Stokes's thinking—treated, at one level, as the familiar difference between art that is "excavated" from its medium, and art that is built up into its final form—as with stone sculpture on the one hand and bronze casting on the other. Stokes took the distinction further, however, and thought of carving and modelling as not only literal artistic processes but also as metaphors for two basic orientations that artists might bring to their medium. So, in his view, there is a correspondence between the love of stone (in the carving tradition) for its particular qualities, potential, and richness, and the love of colour exhibited by such painters as Vermeer, Piero della Francesca and Cézanne.[2]

> On the artist's side, there is the outward thrust of fantasy, the projection of this onto stone, and parallel to this, there is ... the way in which the stone, in the hands of such an artist, pushes itself forward on to the surface. The stone blooms ... [Wollheim, 1972, p. 14]

while at the same time it retains its integrity. Stokes seeks to relate the carving orientation to Klein's depressive position, in which the integrity and otherness of the whole object is respected, and the spectator is faced by something separate from her or himself.

The modelling orientation, in which the work of art is characterized by sharp disjunction and differentiation, an accumulation of disparate elements, is held by Stokes to correspond to the paranoid–schizoid position. The spectator is brought into what Stokes calls an "enveloping relationship" with the work—in which, presumably, he or she has to wrestle with something unresolved, where that unresolvedness can be seen as the subject matter of the work, rather than as a lack of artistic achievement. Art of this kind, "enables its objects to epitomise both the part-objects of early relations and the still inchoate ego which enters into such relations" (Wollheim, *ibid.*, p. 28).

Although Stokes originally valued work in the carving tradition more highly, he later altered his view and came to recognize the qualities of the "enveloping relationship" as integral to the aims of art and, indeed, as the essential counterpart to the response engendered by "carved" works of art.

One can see that, although Stokes's interest was in the visual arts, his ideas can illuminate our thinking about poetry, and might be borne in mind when reading the various contributions to this book. Engaging with the medium of language, with all its specific qualities and associations, the poet seeks to give expression to aspects of the internal world, and looks for a way of handling that medium which will best serve his or her vision.

A number of papers in this volume show a clear debt to the ideas of Hanna Segal, who has perhaps contributed more than any other contemporary psychoanalytic thinker to an understanding of creativity. For her, too, the starting point is the inner world of the artist. She asks,

> Can we isolate in the psychology of the artist the specific factors which enable him to produce a satisfactory work of art? And, if we can, will that further our understanding of the aesthetic value of the work of art, and of the aesthetic experience of the audience? [Segal, 1986, p. 186]

For Segal, the capacity for symbol formation, inherent in the creation of a work of art, originates in the infant's attempt to deal with anxieties stirred by his relations with his object. In earliest experience, the infant is aware only of "part-objects", not of whole people, part-objects whose idealized or persecutory character derives from the way in which feelings of pain, rage, pleasure, etc. are projected into the object. Given adequate containment, the infant comes to recognize the people who care for him as real people, each of them associated with both "good" and "bad" experiences. The infant introjects the whole loved object but, since he is still liable to experience devouring and destructive impulses when thwarted, in phantasy he attacks and destroys the object, now seen to be the source of goodness as well as of frustration. This sense of damage done, the fear of loss, and a growing sense of responsibility for that damage and loss, give rise to an urge to repair and restore a unified world and, in the right circumstances, to a growing confidence in his ability to do so—the depressive position.

It is, thus, out of the experience of mourning that the urge to create is born. As David Bell points out (1999, p. 9), Freud had already made this link in his discussion of the way the human mind responds to the fact of transience, but it was left to Segal, following Klein, to arrive at a coherent theoretical account of creativity. For in the depressive position the struggle to overcome the effects of destructiveness, and the fear of loss, is never-ending. Death—and

the death instinct—is part of life. Only in relatively rare circumstances—and the creation, and apprehension, of a successful work of
art are two of those—can there be a (temporary) sense of resolution.

> Restated in terms of instincts, ugliness—destruction—is the expres-
> sion of the death instinct; beauty—the desire to unite into rhythms
> and wholes—is that of the life instinct. *The achievement of the artist is
> in giving the fullest expression to the conflict and the union between these
> two.* [Segal, 1986, p. 203; our italics]

The spectator, reader, or listener experiences unconsciously the
artist's engagement with these conflicting forces, forces with which
we are all familiar. It is the apprehension of the artist's ability to
bear the pain of a fractured inner world and of his or her
achievement in depicting it and, sometimes, unifying it, that makes
for a satisfying aesthetic experience. We could say that it is the
degree to which the artist achieves this that makes the difference
between good and less good art.

This experience, amounting at times to consolation, may consist
in feeling recognized, feeling less alone. As Wallace Stevens puts it,
"... the imagination is the power that enables us to perceive the
normal in the abnormal, the opposite of chaos in chaos" (Stevens,
1960). Successful work achieves this through the specific balance it
strikes between the particular and the universal—between the
unique experience or imagination of the artist and the pool of
experience common to all of us. The work of art also offers a place
for painful experience to "be", and to be thought about, in the
widest sense of "thinking". And it is proof that pain is survivable.
Even where the work is very bleak indeed, as Hamish Canham
shows in his discussion of Larkin's poem "Aubade" (2002), the
existence of the work is evidence of the artist's ability to give form
to despair, and thus to put him or herself at some remove from it,
rather than being engulfed.

Notes

1. For a discussion of the distinction between symbolic equation and
   symbolic representation, see Hanna Segal (1950).
2. See Wollheim (1972). Introduction.

References

Bell, D. (1999). *Psychoanalysis and Culture: A Kleinian Perspective*. London: Duckworth.

Britton, R. (1998). *Belief & Imagination: Explorations in Psychoanalysis*. London: Routledge.

Canham, H. (2002). Group and gang states of mind. *Journal of Child Psychotherapy, 28*(2): 113–127.

Ogden, T. H. (2001). *Conversations at the Frontiers of Dreaming*. London: Karnac.

Segal, H. (1950). Some aspects of the analysis of a schizophrenic. *International Journal of Psycho-analysis, 31*: 268–278. In: Hanna Segal, 1986, *The Work of Hanna Segal*. London: Free Association Books.

Stevens, W. (1960). *The Necessary Angel: Essays on Reality and the Imagination*. London: Faber and Faber.

Stokes, A. (1947). *Inside Out*. London: Faber and Faber.

Waddell, M., & Williams, M. H. (1991). *Chamber of Maiden Thought: Literary Origins of the Psychoanalytic Model of the Mind*. London: Routledge.

Wollheim, R. (1972). *The Image in Form: Selected Writings of Adrian Stokes*. Harmondsworth: Penguin Books.

CHAPTER ONE

The vale of soul-making

Margot Waddell

T here are many affinities between the poetic process and the psychoanalytic process. The value of engaging with inner and outer experience and their meeting ground, and of finding some way of communicating that experience is the stuff of each. I shall constantly be drawing on the one to illuminate the other, while not wishing to blur distinctiveness nor to oversimplify similarity. But I have a specific focus: that it is this very engagement with experience, the capacity to suffer it and to think about it, that is essential to the growth of the mind. The vale of soul-making of my title was Keats's metaphor for the life of the mind, one that is lived through creative psychic activity (Williams, 1991, pp. 109–125). In Keats's journal-letter to George and Georgiana Keats (*Letters*, 1819: p. 249) he offers a wonderful description of the process which has become intrinsic, implicitly, to the contemporary psychoanalytic picture of human development: that development is rooted in the capacity to undergo experience, neither evading it nor being defeated by it, and that psychic growth only occurs in so far as a person's experience makes sense by having been worked on truthfully internally. This picture underlies my central concern with the nature of meaning, how meaning is generated and registered.

The congruencies between poetry and psychoanalysis have long been recognized. Finding symbolic form for elusive and possibly as-yet-unknown emotions or psychic states—the power that Shakespeare ascribed, in *A Midsummer Night's Dream*, to the "poet's pen" to give to "airy nothing" a "local habitation and a name"—this process is shared by poets and psychoanalysts alike (Williams, 1991, pp. 8–52). Psychoanalyst Thomas Ogden (2002) writes as follows:

> Perhaps what is most fundamental to both poetry and psycho-analysis is the effort to enlarge the breadth and depth of what we are able to experience. It seems to me that both poetry and psychoanalysis at their best use language in a way that encom-passes a full range of human experience—as Jarrell (1955), speaking of Frost, put it—from "the most awful and the most nearly unbearable parts to the most tender, subtle, and loving parts, a distance so great" (p. 62). Both poetry and psychoanalysis endeavour to "include, connect, and make humanly understandable or humanly un-understandable *so much*" (p. 62). [p. 113]

Writing explicitly about the relationship between the poet and the psychoanalyst, in this case, T. S. Eliot and W. R. Bion, Anna Halton (1980) notes a striking comparison:

> When an analyst describes an interpretation like this:
>
> > "I was listening to the silence; I was listening to the interference; I was listening to what came between him and me; I can now draw you a picture in words ... a representation of what I intuited during so many minutes, or weeks, or years," it reminds us of a poem.
>
> When a poet describes poetry like this: "... the abstract conception of private experience at its greatest intensity, becoming universal", it reminds us of an interpretation. This is Bion and Eliot attempting to communicate something of the nature of the complex task they have set themselves. [p. 25]

Reaching within, the poet distils emotional states, finds expression for them and makes them, thus, available for thought. So often poems express the extraordinary in the ordinariness of human emotion. Drawing on Heaney, Hamish Canham describes how "detailed and honest description of a moment, or a memory, can open it up ... subjecting this moment or memory to such scrutiny can be both transforming and liberating" (this volume, p. 190). This is precisely the process to which Hanna Segal draws attention in her discussion of Proust (1991, pp. 86–89). Familiar to psychoanalysts will be this urge, particularly in twentieth-century writing, to establish the significance of the apparently mundane and the value of engaging with all experience.

It is in the understanding of dreaming, and in the role of dream interpretation, that the psychoanalytic and the poetic become especially close. The contemporary view of dream-life is that it is the product, as Donald Meltzer (1984) puts it, of "the meaningful core of the experience which requires transformation into symbolic form in order for it to be thought about and communicated to fellow creatures" (p. 27). This way of seeing things construes the metaphors of dream-work as tracing and communicating inner reality, a process which is made possible by the prior containment of the raw sensa of emotional experience within a psychically "holding" relationship—whether this be between mother and baby, between therapist and patient, or between artist and art-object. These are loose analogies rather than exact parallels, but such relationships can each bring about a kind of "realization" which lies outside the realm of consciousness. The medium is symbolic form. In the language of poetic diction, "the metaphor attempts to arouse cognition of the unknown by suggestion from the known" (Barfield, 1928, p. 110), or, as Shelley put it, effectively defining the essence of poetry: "Metaphorical language marks the before unapprehended relations of things" (quoted by Barfield, p. 67).

The way in which the meaning of a dream emerges in the shared work of analyst and analysand is a rather wonderful experience, akin to the dawning recognition of what a poem is actually *about*. In the contained and structured space of the analytic setting those "unapprehended relations of things" become apparent, just as literary form captures and yields up the experience which underlay the creative act itself.

And yet psychoanalysis is not poetry. Certainly the poet's task of being true to the self and of communicating to others through words is related to the task both of the patient and of the analyst, yet the poet's talent, as I hope to show, condenses and builds on what the analyst tries to do and, in more publicly shareable ways, "moves" in Dryden's words, "the sleeping images of things towards the light". As Carole Satyamurti puts it:

> ... poetry, like psychoanalysis, is centrally concerned with the way language behaves; ... the poet and the analyst share an acute attentiveness to the precise and multiple meanings and associations that words may have, and to the way they are transformed by the specific context in which they are used ... [this volume p. 32]

> ... what the language of an achieved poem does is to transform experience, not merely provide a verbal equivalent of it ... the making of the poem is ... just as much "life itself" as life itself ... The form—the language—is, in part, the content. [p. 36]

Barfield (1928) stated that "meaning can never be conveyed from one person to another; words are not bottles; every individual must intuit meaning for himself, and the function of the poetic is to mediate such intuition by suitable suggestion" (p. 138). This description of the poetic encapsulates rather beautifully and specifically something essential to the developmental process. In my exploration of meaning, I shall be touching on the complexities of the psychoanalytic interpretative function as mediating "intuition by suitable suggestion", especially in relation to the interpretation of dreams, and the deep affinity both between that process and the role of the poet, and also between dreaming itself and the making of the poem.

In Bion's later work, the problem of how to engage with meaning, to express it and to elaborate it becomes central. It becomes central in ways which often evoke quite arresting resonances with the preoccupations and dilemmas of creative artists over the years— especially of the poets and, of those poets, perhaps most of all the Romantics—to be later echoed and re-echoed by many others, but stated with particular force in the poetry and reflective prose of T. S. Eliot.

Throughout his life, and perhaps more than most psycho-analysts, or at least more explicitly than most, Bion struggled to find language for his clinical insights; some way of conveying the immediacy of experience without reducing its impact and sig-nificance and without de-limiting the relationship and shared perceptions which were precariously in the process of becoming. He, like many others, was acutely aware that words, indeed, "are not bottles", that words belong in the particularities of the analytic relationship, itself highly structured by the setting. Here, too, words are finely wrought, culled from the shared relationship and having a particular specificity of tone, pace, and temperature. The issue of at what point, and why, words may be registered as meaningful in a transformative, or perhaps catastrophic, way, commands continuous attention, scrutiny, and debate.

Bion is at his most explicit in his final trilogy, *A Memoir of the Future*. Through dramatic fiction, rather than theory, he illuminatingly, though not wholly successfully, sought to express the meaning of the internal world. His endeavour was to find a way to avoid pinioning meaning by the discursive analytic mode. He was acutely aware of the predicament both of the psychoanalytic interpretation and of psychoanalytic theorizing more generally. "The words in which we dress ideas disguise, as readily as they display, the meaning to which we aspire" (p. 478). In the persona of PA, the psychoanalyst of the internal drama, Bion speaks challengingly and poignantly to what he felt to be his own plight: "Language ... as used by me, is a distorted, distorting, turbulent reflecting surface" (p. 490). "The 'pen' ... will imprison me and my meaning—inescapably" (p. 477). At this point, Bion was rejecting what he called the "Satanic Jargonieur" and was, with jokey seriousness, suggesting that "Disguised as fiction the truth occasionally slipped through" (p. 302).

A central tenet of this trilogy is the problem of ordinary language being inadequate to formulate thoughts which reach beyond the sensual for their formal structure and require, essentially, the evocative. The *Memoir* seeks to engage with the problem of how external world events are uniquely registered internally and how internal world events impinge back on external ones. Echoing Coleridge ("the chameleon darkens in the shade of him who bends over to ascertain its colours" [1839, p. 80]), Bion was quite clear that the thing itself is altered by being observed, and particularly by being articulated.

The constraining and camouflaging function of words, how they can reduce rather than enhance experience, is beautifully caught in two short, contemporary poems which, with extraordinary simplicity and clarity, evoke, respectively, a child and a young girl's sense of words being substituted for the immediacy of passionate involvement (limiting or foreclosing development), and of words being used to dissimulate, and so to confuse, mystify, and distort (also limiting and foreclosing development). Each poem describes the potential stultification of young experience and the road-blocks which words can pose when they are at odds with felt experience, when they lack the ring of truth. At the same time each one also demonstrates the developmental possibilities when words and felt experience coalesce. The first is by Anne Stevenson (2000), "A Surprise on the First Day of School".

> They give you a desk with a lid, mother.
> They let you keep your book.
> My desk's next to the window.
> I can see the trees.
> But you mustn't look out of the window
> at light on the leaves.
> You must look at the book.
>
> A nice-smelling, shiny book, mother,
> With words in it and pictures.
> I mostly like the pictures,
>   some of them animals and birds.
> But you mustn't look at the pictures.
> You don't *ever* read the pictures.
> You read the words!

The metric and rhythmic variations in this poem artfully catch the child's sensuous delight—enthusiastically attracted by sun on leaves and pictures of animals and birds—and starkly contrasts that delight with the reining-in of imaginative impulsiveness by the end-stopped lines of the school regimen. The poem suggests that that first day of school signals some kind of death to the spirit of childhood in a learning-about culture where words become privileged above all other aesthetic responses—words, here, signifying the loss of a whole world, the constriction of unfettered joy and freedom in favour of learning defined by externals, arresting emotional experience and setting the individual apart from his or her former self. It expresses the price to the personality of the exigencies of conformity, and succinctly evokes Bion's fundamentally important distinction, where personal development is concerned, between learning *about* things and learning from experience.

Yet so much more is embedded in the lines of this beguilingly simple poem. It offers a taut expression for all those life experiences which hold in precarious balance the possibility of genuinely moving on psychically, and the danger of living merely by the trappings of development, the external experiences concealing the internal lack. The poem's voice immediately establishes the tension between two worlds—the "they" of the external world and the "mother" of the internal. "They give you a desk with a lid, mother". That first line asserts the lure of *things*, of pride of possession, of *special* features, of status and position. One can sense the seductive power of those external-world values and, as the poem unfolds, the increasingly authoritarian hold they come to have on the personality. The lines, despite their straightforwardness, are by no means merely descriptive. In the slightly breathless tempo and tone there is a hint of the persuasive, the proud, but also of the tentative—as if the "child" persona senses, and struggles with, the betrayal of inner values. The poem is more than a statement of the hitherto untried blandishments of external reality, it is a statement ridden with conflict and uncertainty, as if with an unconscious awareness of seduction, and also of relinquishment—seduction and relinquishment, a painful duo which thereafter attends, or is at play in, every further step towards necessary social adaptation and away from the personal and, perhaps, too idiosyncratic links with inner reality.

The words also carry a hint of appeasement—registering the child's sense of the mother's loss, the loss of the child who is now making his/her way *away*—into the world outside, a world apart from the security of the known mother–child relationship. This child's account of the school-day suggests some feeling for the maternal wrench of yielding up her young one to the realities of life outside, unmediated and unmodulated by her. This element brought to mind the final lines of a much more explicit, perhaps too explicit, poem by C. Day Lewis—"Walking Away"—expressing a father's pride and anguish over his son's "eddying away / Like a winged seed loosened from its parent stem". He describes, "How selfhood begins with a walking away / And love is proved in the letting go".

Anne Stevenson's much more spare and suggestive lines capture the simultaneous excitement, and also the guilt, expectation, and disappointment of this point of transition, a stark representation of all such points to come; the mixed blessing of each "new experience" which both holds out so much to the novice but which may also ultimately offer so little; the external conditions which, too readily, contribute to the shut-down of the personality, to the fracturing or dispersing of the crucial links with internal objects in favour of belonging, belonging to the system and reducing the power of those early experiences which provide, as George Eliot put it, "the mother tongue of our imagination" (*The Mill on the Floss*, 1860, Ch. V).

In the second stanza the child/poet would seem to be casting the description of the new school book in language honed to appeal to sensual experiences hitherto shared with the mother, as if carrying a desire to remind and impress as well as to appease: "A nice-smelling, shiny book, mother".

There is a vivid evocation of the mutual pleasure of looking at pictures together—a child and a mother—the rush of re-engagement with that world, but with the sense of the enforced necessity to forego such childish things hard on its heels, the necessity to be a big, sensible boy or girl now, struggling with the weight of the loss of a former self. Defensively, too, there is a hint of triumph over the mother who is felt to be still identified with baby things, at a point where the child needs to be, and is ambivalently insisting upon, the backing of authoritarian identification to help bear the multifold anxieties which attend this so-called "step forward". Janus-like, the child is looking both ways, attempting to relinquish the old self and to embrace the new, struggling with bereavement, and also with wonder at novelty, with self-importance and also with littleness.

And we have the poet—the overseer of the process—so sparely articulating the pain and the excitement of development; the dangers of accommodation, the snares of the system that promises much in terms of status and achievement and may deliver little opportunity for genuine development; the challenge posed to imaginative and joyful capacities, at whatever stage or age, by the necessity to move away from base, to join in with the others. The poem suggests the repeated renewal of ambivalence towards the beloved internal object, to be relived at each and every potential point of departure from the known and the familiar, when that point precisely re-instigates the problem of embracing future possibilities while yet honouring the *lares and penates* of the internal hearth. This child loyally hangs on to mother. Later, perhaps as an adolescent, he or she may feel impelled psychically to "kill" her off in order genuinely to be him or herself—a crucial quandary for the creative spirit, so clearly described by Carole Satyamurti (this volume, p. 42).

This poem is *about* the conflict at the heart of development, full of irony, full of pathos. But it is also *itself* an irony—in the best sense—a poem which exquisitely draws on the medium of words to express the fearful limitations of that very medium. What it makes clear is that it is not words *as such* which are the problem, nor is it the painful and necessary process of learning to read *as such* which poses the difficulty. The issue, rather, is the purpose and function of the words for their user and purveyor—what they represent. While the *content* of the poem describes, in effect, how the tyranny of words (the knowing-about reality) can limit the personality, the *form* of the poem, by rhythm and arrangement, condenses and conveys the meaning. These two bare stanzas speak to the predicament of human development in an exceptionally evocative way.

The implication that words used in the name of knowledge, at the expense of imagination, to bind rather than to free, inhibit, even arrest, development, is also explicitly the subject of a poem by Carole Satyamurti, "Between the Lines". Again these "lines" are freighted with irony: the child is imprisoned by the family's culture, the vernacular of words drained of their meaning, or substituted by other words which obscure, distort, and conceal reality, consigning the developing child to an underground existence, "straining for language / That would let me out". The poem's rendering of the agonies of this young girl's experience, stranded in a world of suggestion, innuendo and denial, painfully convey the suffering of one who lacks any vestige of a container of meaning, while yet the poem in itself, as a poem, constitutes that very thing.

> Words were dust-sheets, blinds.
> People dying randomly, "for want of breath"
> shadowed my bed-times.
> Babies happened; adults
> buried questions under bushes.
>
> Nouns would have been too robust
> for body-parts; they were
> curt, homeless prepositions—"inside",

"down there", "behind", "below". No word
for what went on in darkness, overheard.

Underground, straining for language
that would let me out, I pressed to the radio
read forbidden books. And once
visited Mr Cole. His seventeen
budgerigars praised God continually.

He loved all words, he said, though he used
few to force a kiss. All that summer
I longed to ask my mother, starved myself,
prayed, imagined skirts were getting tight,
hoped jumping down ten stairs would put it right.

My parents fought in other rooms,
their tight-lipped murmuring muffled
by flock wallpaper.
What was wrong, what they had to say
couldn't be shared with me.

He crossed the threshold in a wordless
slam of doors. "Gone to live near work"
my mother said, before she tracked down
my diary, broke the lock, made me cut out
pages that guessed what silence was about.

This child, as so many, "grows up" without hope or expectation
that there could exist for her an answering voice that would make
sense of her world, her breathless curiosity and her anxiety. (She
"grows up", that is, on the outside, with little source of sustenance
for any kind of internal, psychic growth.) There was clearly no
access to the kind of emotional "common sense" that Bion describes
as giving a feeling of truth to experience—as establishing the basis
for psychic reality, just as the coming together of sense impressions
gives a feeling of coherence to external reality. And, as we learn at
the end, perhaps this child's saving grace has been that, despite
everything, she has found, in her own internal resources, some kind
of "container" for her feelings—her diary, her writing—the fruit,
perhaps, of her listening (the radio) and of her reading (the books).

Here, with great eloquence, words undercut words in the
description of how meaning is destroyed by euphemism, circum-
locution—and silence. Yet somehow the child's spirit has survived

to articulate the terror of sexual and emotional abuse; the knowing ignorance of the basic facts of life; the unspoken physical realities (pregnancy, birth, death); the emotional absences (stuck in the inadequacy and hypocrisy of the adult world). These are indigestible experiences, ones which tend not so much towards thought but towards action—the "slam of doors", the breaking of locks and the cutting of pages.

The description of this paring down of language, from nouns to prepositions, speaks to the thinness of emotional life in this household, to the lack of receptivity to a child's ignorance and anguish, in short to the reduction of potential meaning to meaningless detail.

And yet this child does register the significance of the silence, of the muffled murmuring, and with that extraordinary and mysterious human capacity to engage with experience and make something of it, however bleak the emotional wilderness of "home" may seem, the child/poet draws on internal resources to frame and contain her experience. The poem condenses and communicates the pain of unmanageable experience, even encompassing the parental intrusion and destructive violation of the child's (diary) privacy in that final act of abusive indignity. The mother enacts the feelings which she herself cannot contain emotionally: the primitive belief that in physically cutting out and disposing of the diary pages she would eradicate the child's knowledge, would eliminate, as if from her own mind too, the bitterness of the failed relationship.

In this poem, the evocative use of words to describe their own paucity or absence directly expresses the emotional paucity and absence of lives lived in shadow, drained of meaning, "under dust sheets", blind to the light. Again the peeling back of the surface simplicity of this child's account of girlhood experience reveals a highly articulated and dense understanding of the profound, yet not terminal, obstacle to development posed by the lack of a properly symbolic expression of human experience, itself rooted in the lack of containment for the emotional experience itself.

Aesthetic pleasure of the kind I have been seeking to describe arises from identification with the creative process—a kind of living with, or being inward with another's engagement with internal struggle—"... our power to concentrate is concentrated back on ourselves" (Canham, quoting Heaney, this volume, p. 205). The experience is more emotional, even physical, than intellectual: "feelings arouse feelings, with no other intermediary than the expression itself" (Dilthey describing his concept of *Nacherleben*, or "re-living", quoted by Steiner (2000), p. 236). Process, form and content are inseparable. As Clive Bell (1914) put it, "What orders the work of art is, I suggest, the emotion which empowers the artist to create significant forms" (p. 13).

Those forms, in the case of poetry the choice of word, the arrangement, the pace, cadence, rhythm, gaps, and silences, *hold* the emotion, and in so doing enable and convey the underlying meaning, bearing always in mind that the meaning *is* the making—το ποιειν, to do or to make, is the Greek root of "poetry". With Bion, as I have suggested, emotion is at the heart of the matter and experience becomes meaningful in relation to one's picture of oneself, in so far as emotion can be understood and thought about. The process of being receptive, of apprehending and then of giving verbal form, or representation, to the evidence of internal life (perhaps most available, in the psychoanalytic context, in a patient's dreams) is the therapeutic endeavour. Wilkinson (1957) speaks of a certain "psychical distance" based on the idea that "however much feeling is involved in a work of art, it is a feeling set before the eye of the mind sufficiently to be contemplated" (p. 43). This seems to me a good description of the interpretative moment in psychoanalysis.

This process of enabling experience to be known and to be thought about describes an aspect not only of the poetic but also of the parental function, as conceived by Bion, and of the therapeutic. The model is the infant–mother relationship: the mother's receptive capacity to think about her baby, unconsciously as well as consciously, her capacity for "reverie" (as Bion put it), enables her to take in communications about which the baby is not yet able to think. In making sense of these communications she becomes the container of the baby's emotional experience. Thus, she becomes a container of meaning. She enables her baby, in turn, slowly to acquire the internal resources *him/herself* to think about experience and thereby to engage with its meaning. For meaning is felt to be something which provides an internal coherence when a sense of disconnectedness is so persecuting and fragmenting. James Grotstein (1983) uses the analogy of the prism to describe the process:

the prism, which refracts the monochromatic scream of the infant into the differentiated color spectrum of meanings which can then be arranged into hierarchies of importance for mental deliberation and for action. In so doing the mother's container function has not only absorbed the impact of the baby's screams, but has also translated the infant's organismic panic into signal anxiety with definitive realistic transformations into realistic danger, and of need-satisfaction. [p. 20]

At this pre-verbal stage where no specific meaning is available, the sound, the pitch, rhythm, volume, and intonation can, nonetheless, "speak" volumes to the receptive ear. In this picture of things, meaning is embedded in the quality of the links of relatedness between self and other, and in how those links can be mutually communicated and sustained. To stir the capacity to think clearly and to feel deeply about the same subject simultaneously would seem to be the function both of the poetic and of the psychoanalytic process. Intrinsic to that function, one of promoting and enriching psychic development, is, as we have seen, the role of the art-object as a framer and container of meaning, in some sense the witness—albeit perhaps only fleetingly—to emotional chaos having been overcome: "... the general mess of imprecision of feeling / Undisciplined squads of emotion" (T. S. Eliot, "East Coker", 1963, ll. 181–182) are offered a shape and a form by being held up to the mind's eye; and (being the *Four Quartets*) also to the mind's ear:

> ... Words, after speech, reach
> Into the silence. Only by the form, the pattern,
> Can words or music reach
> The stillness ...
> ["Burnt Norton", *ibid.*, ll. 139–142]

thereby, to go back to Barfield (1928), mediating the intuition of meaning by suitable suggestion.

Mandelstam (1977) casts the relationship between word and meaning in different, but arresting terms:

Every word is a bundle and the meaning sticks out of it in various directions, not striving to any one official point. When we pronounce "sun" we are, as it were, making an immense journey ... poetry ... rouses us and shakes us awake in the middle of a word. Then the

word turns out to be far longer than we thought, and we remember
that to speak means to be forever on the road. [p. 13]

"Perhaps", suggested the friend who drew my attention to this
passage, "the word turning out to be far longer than we thought
might apply, mightn't it, to words spoken in an analysis?" (Martina
Thomson, personal communication).

A fragment of infant observation is suggestive of how these
aesthetic responses enable and contain incipient meaning from the
very first. Describing the "Beginning of the mind", Margaret Rustin
(1999) comments on an extract from an observation that beautifully
illustrates the way in which, as she says, "A mind lights up in
response to meeting another mind" (p. 4). Nine-week-old Jonah is
sitting, propped up in a soft chair by the fireside, with his parents.
His aunt comes into the room:

> ... he turned to look at her and gave her a huge smile as she greeted
> him. They began a reciprocal exchange of smiles as his aunt talked
> to him ... Jonah made little sounds, energetically waving his arms
> and clasping his hands together with apparent satisfaction. His
> "speaking" was in harmony with his movements. To match his
> broad smiles, his tongue darted in and out of his mouth in a rhythmic
> dance. Happiness and liveliness suffused his whole body. [*ibid*.: p. 5]

In Jonah we find the kind of integration of bodily experience and
emotion so characteristic of babies who, like him, have enjoyed, we
are told, his parents' passionate love for him, their constant and
deeply joyful way of relating, relating through the musicality of
voice, story, and song among the many other modes. Wordsworth
powerfully evokes this relationship in the *Prelude*—the autobiographical poem in which he traces his own development as a poet and
the forces that shaped his imagination.

> Blessed the infant Babe,
> (For with my best conjectures I would trace
> The progress of our being) blest the Babe,
> Nursed in his Mother's arms, the Babe who sleeps
> Upon his Mother's breast, who, when his soul
> Claims manifest kindred with an earthly soul,
> Doth gather passion from his Mother's eye!
> [1984, p. 398, ll. 237–243]

Such a relationship could be described as providing the prototype, or model, for the creation of emotional meaning. To the basic developmental axes of love and hate (L and H), Bion added "K", signifying what he regarded as the inherent need, or desire, for the kind of knowledge which links feeling with thinking and brings together experience of the internal and external worlds.

Carole Satyamurti's poem, "Passed On" (1998), both in content and in form, describes the process of the formation of a container of meaning a bit later on in life, while also, in itself, as in "Between the Lines", providing one.

Before, this box contained my mother.
For months she'd sent me out for index cards,
scribbled with a squirrel concentration
while I'd nag at her, seeing strength
drain, ink-blue, from her finger-ends
providing for a string of hard winters
I was trying not to understand.
Only after, opening it, I saw
how she'd rendered herself down from flesh
to paper, alphabetical; there for me
in every way she could anticipate
—*Acupuncture, conditions suited to*
—*Books to read by age twenty-one*
—*Choux pastry: how to make, when to use.*

The cards looked after me. I'd shuffle them
to almost hear her speak. Then, my days
were box-shaped (or was I playing safe?)
for every doubt or choice, a card that fitted
—*Exams, the best revision strategy*
—*Flowers: cut, how to make them last*
—*Greece: the men, what you need to know.*

But then they seemed to shrink. I'd turn them over,
find them blank; the edges furred, mute,
whole areas wrong, or missing. Had she known?
The language pointed to what wasn't said.
I'd add notes of my own, strange beside
Her urgent dogmatism, loosening grip
—*infinitives never telling love*
lust single issue politics when
don't hopeless careful trust.

> On the beach, I built a hollow cairn,
> tipped in the cards. Then I let her go.
> The smoke rose thin and clear, slowly blurred.
> I've kept the box for diaries, like this.

Between the bald, literal statement of the first line: "Before, this box contained my mother" and the simple metaphorical significance of the last, "I've kept the box for diaries, like this", we trace an internal odyssey of poignant and recognizable complexity. Herself frozen with the denial of anticipated loss, the poet/daughter states the urgency with which a mother, ambiguously aware of her own failing mental capacities, but clearly anticipating her premature death, seeks to "squirrel away" on index cards a future ABC for her young daughter. It is an ABC of whats and wherefores, of how to and how not to live when she, the mother, has "passed on". Now she passes on, nut-like, nuggets of advice and homily to nourish her daughter during the dark winter months of her impending bereavement, attempts to assuage her own anguish and that of her daughter with notes of dated instruction. There is a chilling obsessionality about this secret, written, and then scribbled, project. A touching yet dogged attention to fact and detail defends this mother from the pain of her own predicament, but also cuts her off from making the kind of emotional contact with her daughter which might have offered a more sustaining and genuine nourishment in the lonely shadows of life to come.

With a single word, or phrase, the poet powerfully conveys the daughter's nagging, but guilty, frustration, threaded with fearful anticipation, neither able, nor helped, to encompass the meaning of what is happening; turning the blind eye. She evokes the constrictions of a "box-shaped" life of bereavement as this daughter clings to the external, concrete representations of her mother—her sense of her own self lost, or in abeyance, wholly dependent, for the moment, on her mother's choice and recommendation. Only slowly does she allow herself to recognize the truth of things—the blanks and confusions of her mother's mind, standing also, perhaps, for those blanks and confusions which are bound to attend on the inevitable generational difference between one age and another. She struggles to regain or recover some vestige of her own thoughts.

We are involved in a painful process of mourning and working through, during which the external figure can eventually be let go and installed, instead, as an internal presence. With the growing acceptance that first her mother's mind, then her body, and then the import of the index entries have "passed on" the daughter discovers that what has also been "passed on" is a container for feeling.

The box can function finally not as the casket/container of the actual mother, as conceived at the beginning of the poem, but of a version of her which allows the daughter to become herself, to contain and express the meaning of her own life—"like this"— through poetry.

The final dream of a young model, Sarah, who was facing a premature interruption of therapy for external reasons, rather tentatively indicated that a similar, though perhaps less robust, introjective process was occurring. Sarah had sought help for her depression—desperate to break a pattern of relating to men through clinging dependency, masochistically unable to separate until, like a climbing plant, she had some alternative supporting structure to which to attach herself.

She had developed enormously in the course of her therapy and her pain and rage of relinquishment in the final sessions was acute. Being the fourth of six siblings, her life had, from the first, constituted a kind of group experience—family attitudes were stereotyped around notions defined either by acceptability or by opposition to the dominant culture of the group at the time. She had had little experience of her own private feelings being registered or thought about before embarking on therapy. Having to leave was yet another in a long series of premature weanings, evoking intense feelings of desolation, abandonment and anger, her early losses all too emotionally immediate. In this dream:

She found herself in the ante-chamber of a large and beautiful house. There were doors which opened into the interior, dark passages leading off, to which she felt she had access and was on the point of entering, but felt uncertain and apprehensive. This small room was itself lovely, paneled, as in her childhood home, with many recesses and alcoves in which there were exquisite, precious objects—china ornaments, glass, wood carvings. The room was pervaded by a smell of spices—myrrh and frankincense, she thought. Her eyes alighted on one object in particular, a blue glass bowl of special fragility and beauty. She gazed at it, half believing that it belonged to her and that she had the right to take it with her, yet feeling, too, that that might be to steal. A tall, dark woman entered, apparently the owner. As they looked at each other, Sarah "knew" that the object was indeed her own.

As therapist and patient explored this dream together its meaning began to take shape. The dream vividly conveys Sarah's anxiety and apprehension about standing alone on the threshold of life. It is as if she has Keats's "Chamber of Maiden Thought" in her bones. She is aware of the dark passages leading off this ante-chamber, but is frightened to move forward into them at this time when she feels so alone. The atmosphere is sensuous, redolent of past experiences and evocative (the frankincense and the myrrh) of both birth and loss—the birth of her fledgling self and the loss, externally, of so important a relationship. Despite that loss, an internal relationship with her own parents seems to have been secured. For the house evokes features of her parents' home, something which she could now savour and appreciate, when before she had only been able to envy and resent. The shadowy recollections, as Wordsworth put it in the *Immortality Ode*,

> Which, be they what they may,
> Are yet the fountain light of all our day,
> Are yet a master light of all our seeing;
> [1984, p. 301, ll. 153–156]

—those "memories in feeling"—were now available to be drawn on to sustain Sarah, rather than being bitterly recalled for their absence and inadequacy.

Despite being so angry and distressed about this premature ending, and fearful too that she has somehow brought it about, Sarah is also aware that the house-owner/therapist is nearby (has a place, that is, in her internal world). The felt capacity, on the one's part to make available, and on the other's to make her own, the emblem for the container of meaning—the blue glass bowl—stands as confirmation of the therapeutic work achieved, and of the internalization not just of the therapist but also of her function in having held mental states until they could find a shape or a form, as in the dream. The dream feels something like a gift—the expression of a willingness to repair the feared damage brought about by Sarah's grief-stricken rage and by her despair over being left too soon. It offers a metaphor for the internal establishing of a container of feeling. But perhaps the fragility of the bowl was some indication of the impact of prematurity, and of Sarah's uncertainty. It could also be that she feared that she had internalized less the strong, functional qualities of the therapist than some kind of non-functional preciousness and would soon be overcome with the fear of not being sufficiently equipped to enter the dark passages of life—Keats's Mansion of Many Apartments (Waddell, 2002).

What lay behind Sarah's developing capacities is beautifully captured in the compact and highly-wrought energy of James Merrill's poem, "The Broken Bowl" (see Carole Satyamurti, this volume pp. 33–4).

> ... A world in jeopardy. What lets the bowl
> Nonetheless triumph by inconsequence
> And wrestle harmony from dissonance
> And with the fragments build another, whole,
> Inside us, which we feel
> Can never break, or grow less bountiful?
>
> Love does that.
> [Merrill, 1996, p. 8, ll. 19–24]

That experiences of grief and loss, in particular, stir the creative impulse is widely recognized in Kleinian aesthetic theory. It is, perhaps, in suffering, enduring, and encompassing the experience of loss in poetic form, rather than succumbing to melancholia, that the poet both achieves, expresses, and evokes something of the growth of the mind, of the process of "soul-making". So too, enshrined in psychoanalytic thinking, is the crucial insight that the capacity for symbolic thought is lodged in the prior capacity to bear separation and to mourn loss, and in the recognition that the well-springs of creativity lie in a constant re-working of that most painful cluster of "depressive" emotions—those of love and hate, of guilt, remorse, anger, destructiveness, and also of reparation.

I shall conclude by linking poetry—two poems of loss but also of hope—with the work of the consulting room. The first, by Emily Dickinson, was given to me many years ago by a patient after her first summer break. It has come to mind ever since at times of "larger-Darknesses". It expresses much of what I have been struggling to say. The second, again by Anne Stevenson, compact and even more reticent than Emily Dickinson, often makes its appearance in my mind as I try to think about turbulent states of adolescent despair and to contain the anguished uncertainty of whether, and how, there can be a pull-back from the brink, in this case, of suicide.

We grow accustomed to the Dark—
When Light is put away—
As when the Neighbor holds the Lamp
To witness her Goodbye—

A Moment—We uncertain step
For newness of the night—
Then—fit our Vision to the Dark—
And meet the Road—erect—

And so of larger—Darknesses—
Those Evenings of the Brain—
When not a Moon disclose a sign—
Or Star—comes out—within—

The Bravest—grope a little—
And sometimes hit a Tree
Directly in the Forehead—
But as they learn to see—

Either the Darkness alters—
Or something in the sight
Adjusts itself to Midnight—
And Life steps almost straight.
[Dickinson, 1970]

Vertigo
Mind led body
to the edge of the precipice.
They stared in desire
at the naked abyss.
If you love me, said mind,
take that step into silence;
If you love me, said body,
turn and exist.
[Stevenson, 2000]

This chapter has been exploring different structures of contain-ment—the psychoanalytic and the poetic—which enable and communicate the meaning of emotional experience. The emergence of that meaning is embedded in a particular quality of relationship. To apprehend the poem the reader must put him- or herself in the poet's place, must make the poem an outgrowth of one's own mind as well. Coleridge compares the mind to a living plant that, absorbing into itself the atmosphere to which its own respiration has contributed, grows into its own perfection (*Statesman's Manual*, 1817, pp. xiv–xv). This would seem to me to describe the analytic process at its best.

References

Barfield, O. (1928). *Poetic Diction: A Study in Meaning*. London: Faber & Faber.

Bell, C. (1914). *Art*. London: Chatto & Windus.

Bion, W. R. (1975; 1977; 1979). *A Memoir of the Future*. London: Karnac, 1991.

Coleridge, S. T. (1817). *The Statesman's Manual, Lay Sermons*, R. J. White (Ed.) [reprinted London: Routledge, 1972].

Coleridge, S. T. (1839). *Church and State*, P. H. N. Coleridge (Ed.). London: Pickering.

Day Lewis, C. (1992). Conversations about Dante. In: *The Complete Poems*. New York: Sinclair-Stevenson.

Dickinson, E. (1970). *The Complete Poems*, Johnson, T. H. (Ed.). London: Faber & Faber.

Eliot, George (1860). *The Mill on the Floss* [reprinted Harmondsworth: Penguin, 1985].

Eliot, T. S. (1963). *Four Quartets*. London: Faber & Faber.

Grotstein, J. (1981). Wilfred R. Bion: the man, the psychoanalyst, the mystic. A perspective on his life and work. In: J. Grotstein (Ed.), *Do I Dare Disturb the Universe. Memorial to Wilfred R Bion* (pp. 1–35). London: Karnac, 1983.

Halton, A. (1980). W. R. Bion and T. S. Eliot. In: *The Tavistock Gazette*, No. 4, Diamond Jubilee edition, pp. 25–28.

Keats, J. *Letters of John Keats*, Gittings, R. (1987) (Ed). Oxford: Oxford University Press.

Langer, S. K. (1953). *Feeling and Form: A Theory of Art Developed from "Philosophy in a New Key"*. London: Routledge & Kegan Paul.

Mandlestam, O. (1977). *Selected Essays*, Sidney Monas (Trans.). Austin: University of Texas Press.

Meltzer, D. (1984). *Dream-Life: A Re-examination of the Psycho-analytical Theory and Technique*. Strathtay: Clunie Press.

Merrill, J. (1996). *Selected Poems*. Manchester: Carcanet Press.

Ogden, T. (2002). *Conversations at the Frontier of Dreaming*. London: Karnac.

Rustin, M. (1999). Beginning of Mind. In: D. Taylor (Ed.), *Talking Cure: Mind and Method of the Tavistock Clinic* (pp. 1–12). London: Duckworth.

Satyamurti, C. (1998). *Selected Poems*. Oxford: Oxford University Press.

Segal, H. (1991). *Dream, Phantasy and Art*. London: Routledge.

Segal, H. (1994). Salman Rushdie and the Sea of Stories: a not-so-simple fable about creativity, *International Journal of Psycho-Analysis*, 75: 611–618 [reprinted in *Psychoanalysis, Literature and War: Papers 1972–1995*, J. Steiner (Ed.). London: Routledge].

Steiner, R. (2000). *Tradition, Change, Creativity: Repercussions of the New Diaspora on Aspects of British Psychoanalysis*. London: Karnac.

Stevenson, A. (2000). *Granny Scarecrow*. Newcastle-on-Tyne. Bloodaxe Books.

Waddell, M. (1998). *Inside Lives: Psychoanalysis and the Growth of the Personality*. London: Karnac, 2002.

Wilkinson, E. M. (1957). *Bullough's Aesthetics: Lectures and Essays*. London: Bowers and Bowers.

Williams, M. H. (1991). Shakespeare: a local habitation and a name (pp. 8–52); Keats: Soul-making (pp. 109–125). In: M. H. Williams & M. Waddell, *The Chamber of Maiden Thought: Literary Origins of the Psychoanalytic Model of the Mind*. London: Routledge.

Wordsworth, W. *William Wordsworth*, Gill, S. (1984) (Ed). Oxford: Oxford University Press.

CHAPTER TWO

"First time ever": writing the poem in potential space

Carole Satyamurti

S oon after starting to write poetry, I had a dream: I climbed onto my desk in order to reach a door I had never noticed before, high up on the wall. I hauled myself in (a kind of reverse birth process) and found myself in a railway waiting room that looked as though it had been frozen in time. On the seats were a number of mummified old women, who had died waiting for a train that never came, and dried up where they sat. Thick china cups, stuck to tea-stained saucers, stood on a pine table. I passed through this room and into a light, large space beyond it, which was empty apart from a tapestry hanging on one wall.

I knew the tapestry was me in some way—it was like the painting in Dorian Grey, but also connected with a story I loved as a child, but can't identify now, in which a girl finds her way to an attic where she discovers a tapestry into which all her deeds, good and bad, are woven.

This tapestry represented not only me as I was, but also the colours and textures I had at my disposal from now on. The mood of the dream was one of joy, and of gratitude to these desiccated ancestors—for I knew they were that. There was a sense that I had arrived here at the expense of the dead women who had waited and never gone anywhere. The dream ended there—without my doing anything, either in the bright room, or in the gloomy waiting room. What I could do with these spaces and their content lay beyond the boundaries of the dream.

Of course this dream, like any other, is subject to a multiplicity of interpretations, even without the associations which would illuminate it in a therapeutic context. But I present it in order to set the scene for thinking about what is going on when a poet writes a poem. I want to try to make some links between the ways in which psychoanalysis seeks to understand the creative act, and my own experience as a writer of poetry. My interest in psychoanalysis stems from having myself had an "analysis (almost) interminable", and from drawing on psychoanalytic ideas in my teaching and academic work. But I come to the present topic as a practising poet, and what I offer here are some psychoanalytically informed reflections on the experience of writing.

Adam Philips (2000, p. 15) has recently discussed the question of why it is that in psychoanalytic writing, from Freud onwards, the poet has, more than any other kind of artist, been seen as a sort of alter ego, even an ego-ideal, for psychoanalysts. He suggests that for psychoanalysis, an activity which has language and almost nothing else with which to work (though this is not to underplay the importance of the setting), the poet is "a figure ... who can sustain our belief in the meaningfulness of language". One might add that poetry, like psychoanalysis, is centrally concerned with the way language behaves; that the poet and the analyst share an acute attentiveness to the precise and multiple meanings and associations that words may have, and to the way they are transformed by the specific contexts in which they are used.

In thinking about what is involved in the making of a poem, I will be drawing upon ideas derived both from the Kleinian tradition in psychoanalysis, and from the work of D. W. Winnicott. The two traditions share a certain amount of common ground. Both see the origins of creativity—in a wide as well as in a more specifically artistic sense of that word—as located in infantile experience. Both see the creative act as essentially object-related—that is, as originating in an inner world constituted by relationships with others and parts of others, notably the maternal figure. Both schools, too, see the process of maturation as having to do with the development of an authentic self, an authentic way of being in the world, which depends on the establishment of a relationship with truthfulness, centrally involving the capacity to acknowledge, and bear, loss. This kind of relationship is also the artistic project.

I want, first, to think briefly about the Kleinian concepts of reparation and containment as they illuminate different aspects of what it is to make a poem. And then to consider Winnicott's concept of "Potential Space" as having, I will suggest, most bearing on the writing *process*.

Writing the poem as reparation

Adrian Stokes and Hanna Segal both highlight the ways in which reparation, the urge to repair phantasized or actual damage for which one holds oneself responsible, may lie at the heart of creative endeavour. In the work of art, a whole version may be offered of the precious object—originally the good breast—which has been destroyed or lost, the object being not magically restored, but made real again symbolically. A poem by the American poet, James Merrill, makes this explicit.

The Broken Bowl

To say it once held daisies and bluebells
   Ignores, if nothing else,
Much diehard brilliance where, crashed to the floor,
The wide bowl lies that seemed to cup the sun,
Its green leaves wilted, its loyal blaze undone,
All spilt, its glass integrity no more.
   From piece to shattered piece
A fledgling rainbow struggles for release.

Did also the heart shatter when it slipped?
   Shards flash, becoming script,
Imperfection's opal signature
Whose rays in disarray hallucinate
At dusk so glittering a network that
The plight of reason, ever shakier,
   Is broadcast through the room
Which rocks in sympathy, a pendulum.

No lucid, self-containing artifice
  At last, but fire, ice,
A world in jeopardy. What lets the bowl
Nonetheless triumph by inconsequence
And wrestle harmony from dissonance
And with the fragments build another, whole,
  Inside us, which we feel
Can never break, or grow less bountiful?

Love does that. Spectral through the fallen dark,
  Eye-beam and ingle-spark
Refract our ruin into this new space,
Timeless and concentric, a spotlight
To whose elate arena we allot
Love's facets reassembling face by face,
  Love's warbler among leaves,
Love's monuments, or tombstones, on our lives.
[Merrill, 1996, p. 8]

I want to draw attention to the way Merrill fully takes on the depressive pain of the bowl never again being able to be the perfectly beautiful object it was; the way the breaking of it does violence for a moment to the whole sense of the world as a harmonious place. We are not told who broke the bowl, or how, or why—and in that way we can imagine ourselves implicated. Yet "love" can build it, whole again, inside us, and a bowl restored symbolically like this is durable in a way the original could never be—because it is the product of the kind of dwelling in the truth of loss which is inherent in healthy mourning. It is, in a sense, earned. The poem both describes, and is, a reparative act, an act of integration. The process of moving through shock and loss to some mode of recovery is not just described in the poem. The poem embodies that process. The word "tombstones" in the last line is a worry, though. It seems to convey an eleventh-hour loss of conviction that the poem can, after all, reconstruct the bowl—since a tombstone can be seen as merely a marker rather than a symbol.

What does Merrill mean by "love"? It is perhaps a surprising word to use, with such seriousness, of a glass bowl, even one so beautiful. His use of this word is an indication that more than a shattered artefact is at stake here. The bowl is an internalized good object—a "bountiful" object that "seemed to cup the sun" (the son).

Freud, (1914) in his essay *On Narcissism*, quotes the poet Heine—part of a poem in which God is imagined as saying this:

> Illness was no doubt the final cause
> Of the whole urge to create.
> By creating, I could recover;
> By creating, I became healthy.

In early nineteenth-century German usage, the word, "gesund", translated as "healthy" here and clearly related to the English word "sound", would have incorporated meanings of both physical and psychological well-being. Freud quotes this passage in support of a point which, at first sight looks rather different—namely that "we must begin to *love* in order not to fall ill, and we are bound to fall ill if ... we are unable to love" (my italics). Freud, and Merrill, seem to be seeing love as central to creativity—one definition of love, perhaps, being a devoted attention to a person or object (which might include the work of art itself)—the wish for it to be as fully itself as possible.

It has been said that we are constituted by what we do about loss, and reparation is one possible response to loss which a poem might carry. Another possibility is to build a bridge, to forge some sort of connection with the lost object. In a poem that attempts this, there may be an analogy between the time it takes to move through the poem and the time needed to reach the loved object—buttressed by a stubborn belief that the poem can be strong enough to sustain the writer, and the reader, through that journey.

Writing the poem as containment

In Kleinian terms, what precedes developmentally the capacity to acknowledge damage and the impulse to repair it is the experience of containment. The infant seeks to get rid of unbearable feelings (what seem like mangled and fractured bits of the world lodged inside him) and projects them—across an implied space which has to be great enough, but not too great—into the mother who, in normally satisfactory circumstances, is better equipped to handle them. The mother receives these projections, bears them, is able to process them, and returns them to the infant in a manageable form through the way she speaks to him, and the way she touches him. In this way, feelings that threatened to engulf the infant are transformed and made tolerable, and the infant, additionally, can learn from the experience that such feelings *can* be held and thought about. In time, he can internalize the good containing object—the object that could "cup the son"—and make it his own.

Yeats wrote: "Out of the struggle with others, one makes rhetoric; out of the struggle with oneself, one makes poetry". And it is perhaps not too fanciful to suggest that the poem can, to some extent, be for us, in our struggle, something like the original containing object/mother; can be a place where chaotic and disturbing experience can be held and given some sort of shape. I would guess that for most poets most of the time, the process of making a poem is an uncomfortable one. The poem does not usually arrive fully formed, impelled by inspiration. Rather, fragments litter the page, which has its own sweet regularities. Lines are written and discarded, in the attempt to find language adequate to the vision that one is trying to real-ize; language that will comprehend enough, in both senses of the word. One searches for language in which complexity of experience is not sacrificed to mere coherence.

Poets tend to talk rather scornfully about the notion of "writing as therapy", and what they are scorning is the idea that merely putting emotion down on paper, merely externalizing it, makes a poem. It doesn't, of course, because what the language of an achieved poem does is to transform experience, not merely provide a verbal equivalent of it. It isn't that something happens and then we write a poem about it. The *making* of the poem is an inherent part of the experience—just as much "life itself" as life itself. Form and content are not two neatly distinct entities. The form—the language—is, in part, the content.

Nevertheless, part of the pleasure (when it is a pleasure!) of making a poem—as of reading it—can be the kind of release attendant on finding a form for what was formless, something coherent which now exists at some distance from oneself, out in the world, as well as inside one's head.

If the poem is some sort of container, then how are we to think about what may be contained? A successful poem—by which I mean one that will resonate in the minds of strangers—cannot only be concerned with the unique personal experience of the poet. It will connect, in one way or another, with those elements that are common to all humanity through time and space. And in between personal experience on the one hand, and universal experience on the other, there is the experience of being a part of a society located at a *particular* time and place, even if being a part of it means being profoundly at odds with it. In very many societies it is, and has been, the role of the poet to "speak to the times", whether to bear witness, or to represent the times to people too immersed in them to be able to see clearly how things are. In such circumstances, the act of writing the poem is an act of giving a place to shared experience which otherwise might even be such as to negate the humanity of those who live through it. Anna Akhmatova (quoted in Forché, 1993, p. 101) writes about standing day after day for seventeen months in the line outside the prison in Leningrad, where her son was held. She says, "One day, someone in the crowd identified me. Standing behind me was a woman, with lips blue from the cold who had, of course, never heard me called by name before. Now she started out of the torpor common to us all and asked me in a whisper (everyone whispered there): 'Can you describe this?' And I said, 'I can.'"

Akhmatova's long poem, "Requiem", which does much more than describe, was the outcome and, as the above anecdote makes clear, she was writing out of a sense of shared catastrophe, a shared vocabulary of meaning. The painter Paul Klee (1948), writing earlier and from a very different place, comments on the way the contemporary artist lacks this sense of being able to draw upon a reserve of common meanings. To the extent that he or she reflects in his or her work a vision of social disconnectedness more stark than the public is willing to recognize, Klee says, they will reject the work as ugly, obscure, or meaningless. In relation to the idea of art as having a containing function, Klee's perspective may have a bearing on the question of why contemporary art, music, or poetry seem to be perceived as offering fewer satisfactions, more meagre consolations, as having less alchemical power, than those arts once did.

Writing the poem in "Potential Space"

Thinking about the poem as reparation or as containment seems to me only part of the story. In either case, one is thinking of the making of the poem as a secondary activity, as deriving its energy from the wish to solve a problem located in prior psychic processes or configurations. But, fruitful though these concepts are, I find them insufficient as accounts of the creative act, since neither tells us much about the process itself. When I write a particular poem, I may be able to recognize, especially in retrospect, that the impulse to write it was a wish to heal in some way, to bridge a gulf, or to give coherence to something. But the urge to make a poem, as distinct from recording my thoughts and feelings in some other form, seems to be about something else too, something distinct from, and more than, the need to work something out.

In looking at that "making" process, I think we are looking at a primary activity that is, an activity which is entirely about itself; which starts with an urge to create something, to shape materials— words, in the poet's case—in new ways "for the first time ever".

The quotation in the title of this chapter comes from D. W. Winnicott's essay "The location of cultural experience" (Winnicott, 1971). He writes,

> The place where cultural experience is located is in the potential space between the individual and the environment (originally the object [that is, the maternal figure]). ... Cultural experience begins with creative living first manifested in play. [pp. 100–101]

The baby, reaching the point of being able to distinguish between self and not-self, self and mother, finds an object that partakes of both these qualities—a cuddly toy, perhaps, or a piece of cloth—and in seizing hold of it is making use of a symbol for the first time. This is what Winnicott calls the transitional object. For this development to occur, the environment has to be favourable, or "good enough". The space in which play can happen is one in which, initially, the baby is alone in the presence of mother. The space must be trustworthy—psychologically small enough to feel safe, large enough to allow him to be oblivious of mother's presence. She must not take over the play herself.

Play is intensely pleasurable. "Everything physical", Winnicott says, "is imaginatively elaborated, is invested with a first-time-ever quality" (ibid., p. 101). The infant is both discovering and creating the world for the first time. The play "is neither a matter of inner psychic reality nor a matter of external reality" (ibid., p. 96) but both.

"... The potential space becomes filled with the products of the baby's own creative imagination" (*ibid.*, p. 102), products which are both and neither subjective nor objective. "The baby creates the object but the object was there waiting to be created ..." (*ibid.*, p. 12). In omnipotently creating and discovering the world in play, the baby creates and discovers himself. A carefully graduated exposure to the frustrations inherent in taking on the objective world will enable the baby to modify omnipotence in favour of a more realistic sense of what is possible. But Winnicott stresses that a satisfactory original experience of playing in potential space lays the foundation for creative living in the widest sense, throughout life—and, of course, for art. It is a profound paradox that the baby feels most wholly him or herself when the matter of what is self and what is not-self is least in question. The same is true for the artist.

What is at issue here can feel, as it did for Van Gogh, like a matter of life and death (see Balint, 1993). The artist may feel that only by making art can he exist at all. To imagine a void in which there are no objects is far more terrifying even than a state in which one is surrounded by damaged ones. As Michael Parsons (2000) says, "art which has this at stake is not about repairing damage, but about bringing something into existence and sustaining it in being".

In Winnicott's description of the infant's intense absorption in play, there is perhaps a connection with the state of mind that Keats called "negative capability", and which certain religions talk about—a state of receptiveness to immediate experience "without any irritable reaching after fact and reason".

Coming to write poetry, after years as an academic, did have something of a "first time ever" quality. Compared to the kind of academic writing I had done up to then, full of dutiful gestures towards people who had explored the territory first, writing a poem was, as my dream conveys, like discovering a room with new objects in it, which I could explore and rearrange as I liked (no footnotes!). Lacking a formal background in the study of literature, I could, for a while at least, be a sort of innocent. The objects—words—were, of course, ones I had been using all my life, but in this new context they felt newly coloured and textured; they had a new gravity. In the dream, access to the space where creative activity can take place is gained by first attending to, and then ignoring, the maternal figures. The tapestry has both a me and a not-me quality—

it is both who I am, and the means whereby I will make something new. As an art form, poetry is particularly aptly characterized as having this me/not-me quality since we are, as human beings, profoundly constituted by language in a way we are not by paint or stone or sound; we are language, and at the same time it exists independently of us.

The notion of the Muse, particularly when she does not take the form of a real person, owes something to the idea of the original mother who provided the facilitating environment. The poet is alone in her presence—ideally, she is there, but not breathing down the poet's neck, not prescribing the particular form the poem will take. The Muse is a benevolent and silent figure, and her presence gives the poet assurance that there will be a poem—that a poem is possible—even though it does not exist yet. She represents a sort of permission. She also, in the way she is often imagined, represents the paradox insisted upon by Winnicott: she is both an inner figure and is experienced as other. And the poem is thought to come both from the inspiration she provides and from the poet him or herself.

The transitional object, that first important symbolic object for the infant, as Winnicott makes clear, represents, most crucially, a process of discovery, making, and self-making about which the infant, of course, does not have to be self-conscious or accountable. For the poet too, as for any artist, the process and the object being made remain inextricably bound up. The art object embodies the process which gave rise to it. Many poets describe the way in which the poem, at best, can take them by surprise. To develop a point made earlier—it is not that the poet has "something to say" and proceeds to say it as felicitously as possible. It is more that the process of dwelling in the experience with one's pen or word processor to hand leads to the emergence of something which, at best, has about it a quality of "that's it"—a sort of surprised recognition. In the attempt to find expression for the often inexpressible, language has to be made to work harder—more vividly, surprisingly, obliquely—than in any other context. When this succeeds, something can become apparent as a result of the language having been created for it—as if the language and the experience it describes have found each other in the world of the poem.

The poet Donald Davie distinguishes between a view which regards words as consequences of things (Aquinas) and one which regards things, "in the last analysis, as the consequence of the words that name them". In potential space, this distinction can be suspended; both are true. Indeed, rather than thinking of words as a mode of access to experience, one can think of them as (also) being experience itself. Dylan Thomas (quoted in Oremland, 1997) described what for him amounted to an object relationship with language: "I had fallen in love with words ... what the words stood for, symbolized or meant was of very secondary importance. What mattered was the sound of them ..." I think many poets will identify with this—will have strong likes and dislikes of particular words that seem to have attributes of form, colour, weight, musicality, and so on quite distinct from their meaning.

The poet, unlike the infant, has to sustain his or her own facilitating environment, to protect the creative enterprise by holding off not so much "ghosts in the nursery" as what one might call "demons in the study", who arrive from all corners of the internal and external worlds with discouragement in mind. I say internal and external, but most of the time no real person comes into the room and stops us writing a poem; in one way or another the demons are usually internal saboteurs (see Fairbairn, 1952). They speak in many voices. They may have the crushing authority of the great tradition, the parental saboteur who says "I'm bigger than you". They may be voiced as sibling rivals who seem to have decided already what game is going to be played, and who seem to know something you don't. And, of course, they are more loved than you are! For a woman, the voice may be that of the established male poet who does not take women's work seriously. For the poet whose mother tongue is other than English, the voice may question his or her right to use the language, and his or her capacity to inhabit it in a sufficiently authoritative way. Then there are the voices originating in reality, but elaborated unhelpfully in fantasy. In my case, there are reviews which make it clear that what is often seen in my work is a small, well-mannered, quiet persona, which doesn't correspond at all to my poetic self-image—something altogether more loud, sharp, and forthright!

These persecutors, with their "malevolent part-object scripts" (Kavaler Adler, 1993), make quasi-territorial claims. They threaten to invade the space in which creative work may be done, and to take it over. When they are allowed to cast an eye over work in progress, the result can be "premature evaluation", with concomitant deflation and disappointment. Of course, the sabotaging voices don't often announce themselves as clearly as this suggests, and sometimes they may be hard to distinguish. More often, in my experience, they remain in the background, as part of the range of factors that make it just plain hard to write a poem!

But if the poem is to have the best chance of success (in its own terms) then it is important that a provisional omnipotence, a belief in one's capacity to generate a living poem, be sustained for long enough. There has to be a sort of ruthless assertiveness—not aggression exactly, but a commitment to doing whatever it takes. And what it takes may include killing off the ancestors as, in my dream, effectively I do, in order to clear space for oneself.

We need to understand the part played by destruction, thought about not as some prior event for which reparation needs to be made, but as *inherent* in the creative process itself. For, whether one thinks about the workings of the natural world, or about human endeavour, creation and destruction are inseparable. The same Hindu deity represents both. There is, first, the overarching fact that we can not attempt anything without destroying the possibility of something else. That may be a trivial point, but it can be experienced profoundly in the grain of the choices the poet has constantly to make. Every mark made on the paper has consequences for what the poem will become, and will not become. You must "murder your darlings", said Yeats, meaning that the poet has to be prepared to destroy those parts of the emerging poem to which he or she may be most attached, if they are seen in the end not to serve the poem. One has to be able to distinguish between the undermining voices of the internal saboteurs and the critical faculty which is an absolutely necessary part of creating anything worthwhile. And one has to have a sense of *when* is the right time to mobilize critical judgement—*when* (to use the analogy of sculpture) the essential poem must be recovered from the mass of "spurious and unwanted matter" (Mandelstam, 1975, p. 225) within which it is hidden.

When I look at the accumulated drafts of a finished poem, what strikes me is how much has been treated as rubbish. Only a fraction of the total words written becomes the eventual poem. The rest is crossed out, eliminated. At some point, it becomes clear that, out of the mess of fragments and scribbles, a poem will emerge. The destruction has been necessary to the survival of the original idea, to its making the transition from inside to outside, from an initial impulse to a finished poem. This process can feel as though it somewhat corresponds to what Winnicott describes as the infant's relation to the transitional object—one can treat the object (the poem) as rubbish, push it around, test its durability, neglect it for a while—and it survives.

The poem may start out as a feeling of desire, a wish to make something, or to move somewhere. It may start as a buzz inside the head, as Mandelstam described, or as a voice heard in the distance, where the tone is audible but the words cannot yet be made out. It may start with an image or an idea, or a word which seems to demand that a context be found for it. But, however it begins, the way it turns out in the end may very well fall short of the original conception of it, or ambition for it. In trying to find words for an experience, the experience has perhaps eluded us. Or we have perhaps destroyed the poem inadvertently.

In trying to understand why that should be the case, we can learn. It may be that we can identify the precise place where failure of nerve, or loss of concentration, or opting for the safely familiar, or simply inability to find the right words turned the poem aside on to a path that led to its becoming a smaller thing than we had hoped. I recently interviewed the poet Anne Ridler, now nearly ninety, about her writing life. On the question of playing safe, she said she had learned from T. S. Eliot, for whom she worked at Faber, to try never to repeat herself—that is, never to opt for an effect because it had been successful before—but constantly to explore new territory. The failure one risks this way may be more interesting than a success.

If one thinks of a poem as a communication between a writer and a reader, then at what point does the reader come in? Most poets I have talked to about this imagine—perhaps towards the end of the writing process—a potential reader. Perhaps this is a particular real person, or group of people. Perhaps it is a fictional composite, or a recognizable figure in the inner world. We know that real readers vary enormously in their capacity or willingness to attend to what the poem is communicating, and imagining the repertoire of possible mis-readings, or blindnesses, is part of the writing process, though probably not in the early stages of a poem's formation. It is also, of course, true that the writer is not necessarily conscious of all the poem contains, and may later be surprised by what a perceptive reader sees in it.

People often ask about a poem "is it autobiographical?" and poets dread that question, partly because it is usually intrusive, a wish to know more than the poet is inclined to reveal, but partly, also, because it feels like an irrelevance—one wants the reader to enter the poem as a creative participant in an aesthetic experience. The truest answer must be, "Yes, it is autobiographical—and no, it isn't; it always is—and it never is completely"—though that is not likely to satisfy the person who asked the question!

I want to conclude by presenting two poems of mine which, it now seems to me, are concerned with the space in which something can be created. The first is called "Life in Tall Houses" and its theme is envy. The starting point in experience was walking on winter nights along streets in Islington, past those flat-fronted Georgian houses, with their beautiful lit interiors, like a series of stage sets on display to passers-by. It always seems to me that it is not mere chance that the curtains are left open—that, consciously or unconsciously, a response is being provoked in the outsiders. However, the eventual poem is not located in Islington, any more than it is autobiographical. The outsiders become some sort of revolutionaries who take over the houses, but find that the view from inside is not as they'd imagined it.

Life in Tall Houses

So many years of the tall, smart
happy family museums
insulting us by their indifference to blinds;

blazing rooms, boasting
amply laid tables, modish clutter,
children playing chamber music;

bait, perhaps.

Years of impregnable locks
until we came to imagine more intensely
those hugs, those conservatory flowers;

and the tall houses
cracked open like pomegranates
under the arithmetic of our desire;

a bit too easily.

The people sprang from their beds
with a curdled look, as though we
were what they'd always dreaded and needed.

The light inside the tall houses seems
misplaced, furniture paper-frail,
jasmine bent on dying.

We are left with a fistful of flies
and the thought of how the happy families
scattered into the city

singing, or something like it.
[Satyamurti, 1998, p. 115]

One can think of the interiors of the houses as maternal spaces
with other babies inside, abundantly provided for in every way. The
usurping of the space by the outsiders springs from confusion: too
concrete an equation between actual objects and what is conceived
of as a blessed existence. The assault is rooted in a state of mind in
which there is a paranoid split between the desirable life inside and the
life outside which, by implication, is wholly impoverished. Furthermore, the pleasure of being inside is imagined (by the excluded) as
being heightened by awareness of the impotent envy of the outsiders.

The break-in is an attempt to occupy a space where creative
things are known to happen—where plants grow, music is played,
meals are made, things are allowed to be in a luxuriantly jumbled
juxtaposition to each other. Once in, however, the speaker quickly
sees that creativity can't be acquired in this way. There is the
suggestion that eviction is not an unmitigated disaster for the
original residents. Perhaps they felt trapped in a seductively cosy
but stifling mode of existence. Now they are free to explore a wider
world, and they depart singing, carrying with them their creativity.
By depriving them, the invaders have released them.

The speaker, in noticing this, has shifted in his or her view from
seeing the residents as sadistically generating longing in the
outsider to recognizing them as having a more complex relation
to their own way of living. And to the extent that the speaker, too,
had been locked into an envious, voyeuristic, and ultimately sterile
position through his or her fixed identification with the inhabitants

of the houses, then the scattering of the families into the city might
represent a new start and a liberation for the speaker too. The
recognition that the creative, abundant life is not a thing, but is
rather a process, means that it can't be simply grabbed. But the
speaker is now in a position, through the mourning consequent
upon this realization, to begin to live creatively him or herself, to
use the space in his or her own way—beginning, perhaps, with the
utterance that constitutes the poem.

The second poem, with which I will end, is about the
paradoxical relationship between fact and imagination. Play in
potential space can happen when there is no need *prematurely* to
recognize a "reality" which is incontrovertibly other. Instead, in the
in-between space described by Winnicott, there is no distinction
between subjective and objective. That distinction can arise
naturally, in the course of activity that consists both of discovering
and creating the world. For the adult, the issue may present itself as
a choice between alternative opportunities—between literal knowing, on the one hand, and imagining on the other. The poem
addresses this via a fantasy of greater intimacy with another person,
and likens that kind of discovery to the voyages of the early
European explorers—men of action rather than artists—who
wanted to *know*, but whose knowledge erased the imaginary. The
poem grapples with the idea that the creative space where
everything is possible is inevitably compromised by entering *too
early* into the entirely real-ised. Of course, the encounter with the
real world is an essential part of being human. But the explorer who
arrives is no longer an explorer—until the next landfall, or the next
poem. At the point of arrival, or the point at which the poem is
finished, the me/not-me distinction becomes clear-cut. The new
continent, the new poem, exists for all the world to visit. The poem
is called "My Wilderness":

My Wilderness

Landlocked, imagining licence to discover
the entire reach of you, island by island,
I think of early travellers. It wasn't men

whose medium was ink, paint or stone
who risked life for the literal, but people
who couldn't find a vessel for their dreams.

They would have started with prosaic tasks,
hustling and preparation; slipping out
in fair weather, prudently provisioned;

knowing where they were at first, then sailing
over the world's edge—though sea is sea,
its dangerous temperament at least familiar.

Wouldn't their hearts have thundered in their ribs
at the colossal cragginess of land,
fantasy, massed at the horizon's swell,

now irredeemably external?
What had kept them constant until then
was all they could envision but not yet touch:

all the sharp particulars of awe,
shimmering landscapes, demons and grotesques
that made the formed and formless *Wonderful*.

Hadn't they hoped to be transformed, until
imaginaries of ecstasy and fear
shrank, with the first scrape of keel on sand?

But as they opened up the wilderness—
staked out, mapped, collected, sketched—perhaps,
despite such rich empirical delights,

they paused to think how much more animate
had been their dream-creatures, their Fortunate Isles;
and found they couldn't quite remember them.
[Satyamurti, 2000, p. 18]

References

Balint, E. (1993). *Before I was I: Psychoanalysis and the Imagination.*
London: Free Association Books.

Fairbairn, R. D. (1952). *Psychoanalytic Studies of the Personality.* London:
Routledge.

Forché, C. (Ed.) (1993). *Against Forgetting: Twentieth Century Poetry of
Witness.* New York: W. W. Norton.

Freud, S. (1914). *On Narcissism: An Introduction.* In: Penguin Freud
Library, vol. 11. London: Penguin Books.

Hesse, E. (Ed.) (1969). *New Approaches to Ezra Pound*. London: Faber and Faber.

Kavaler Adler, S. (1993). *The Compulsion to Create: A Psychoanalytic Study of Women Artists*. London: Routledge.

Klee, P. (1948). *Paul Klee on Modern Art*. London: Faber and Faber.

Mandelstam, N. (1975). *Hope Against Hope*. London: Penguin Books.

Merrill, J. (1996). *Selected Poems*. Manchester: Carcanet Press.

Oremland, J. (1997). *The Origins and Psychodynamics of Creativity*. Madison: International Universities Press.

Parsons, M. (2000). *The Dove that Returns, the Dove that Vanishes*. London: Routledge.

Philips, A. (2000). *Promises, Promises*. London: Faber.

Satyamurti, C. (1998). *Selected Poems*. Oxford: Oxford University Press.

Satyamurti, C. (2000). *Love and Variations*. Newcastle upon Tyne: Bloodaxe Books.

Winnicott, D. W. (1971). *Playing and Reality*. London: Tavistock Publications.

CHAPTER THREE

Wordless words: poetry and the symmetry of being

Michael Maltby

> *"A poem should be wordless*
> *As the flight of birds."*
>
> Archibald MacLeish, "Ars Poetica", 1926

Whether written on the page or spoken aloud, the words of a poem seem to be selected and arranged to lead a double life. They may represent their agreed meanings and enact the logic of language but at the same time conjure something completely different and less predictable. What emerges may not always be understood but can be both deeply felt and strangely meaningful. This sleight of signification seems to lie at the heart of the poet's craft. It has a quality of magic, which is easily lost if the choice of words is too obvious or if there is a hint of clumsiness in their play together. If the magic works we are led into a distinctive form of experience that the poem brings alive in us. This is something that we apprehend as much sensually as verbally and that moves us through the realm of words to somewhere beyond them.

To the practising poet or the lover of poetry the double life of words feeds an irresistible attraction to the possibilities inherent in the poetic use of language. Poetry, for them, has a vitality that makes it a rewarding and meaningful domain of artistic activity and experience. For others, however, much of poetry can seem remote and inaccessible. Even the most informed and sympathetic reader is likely to find some generally acclaimed poetry is without meaning or resonance for them. One of the most common responses to a poem's "difficulty" is to question its meaning. Unfortunately, any descriptive answers given, however insightful and well phrased, do not necessarily lead to the poem as a poem becoming truly meaningful to the reader. As many people have observed, one of the defining qualities of poetry is that it defies paraphrase or a complete rendering of its significance in any other form than through the poem itself. Analysis and interpretation may add to a poem's appreciation but do not constitute its heart. If poetry is meaningful its meaning seems to reside, at least in part, outside the boundaries of logical explanation.

If the language of poetry points beyond words and conveys something that cannot be grasped fully by logical thought it is not surprising to find that poetry also requires more than the reasoned use of language for its creation. While poetry has its own recognizable devices and forms it has been argued that it is: "... in the last resort, an abuse of conventional language". (King, 1975, p. 16). It requires an ability to break rules as well as to follow them. Interestingly, in the many books now available offering advice on the writing of poetry there are only very qualified claims about how much can actually be learnt from such instruction (e.g. Oliver, 1994). The central encouragement is to read a lot of poetry and practise a lot of writing; to just become deeply immersed in the business of poetry. The history and principles of prosody can be taught and motivation stimulated, but the emergence of satisfying poetry is definitely not guaranteed. In fact the writing of poetry seems to depend on a process that may be nurtured and enhanced but not directly engineered.

The close connection between poetic creation and the qualities of poetry itself is implied in the word poiesis: the act of making containing within it the form of the thing being made. This creative action has long been associated with something other than the rational power of the mind. Just as the good poem transcends reductive explanation, creativity seems to require something more than just applied reason. This has traditionally been personified in the guise of a Muse, an inspiring goddess that seeds poetic imagination. Psychoanalysis, of course, has provided its own distinctive insights into this domain of otherness, particularly through its intimate investigations of the unconscious.

The poetic unconscious

Psychoanalysis has approached the subject of artistic creativity from a number of perspectives and has made influential contributions, particularly regarding the motivation for creative work. Freud saw artistic creativity as comparable in many ways to neurotic symptom formation, in that it was a more socially acceptable means of achieving the disguised fulfilment of unacceptable wishes (e.g. Freud, 1908e). In contrast, those working within the Kleinian tradition have often focused on the way creative activity can serve a reparative function, by striving for the symbolic repair of the good object that has been damaged in phantasy. When such unconscious impulses shape creation their representation may be expected in the created work, thus opening a fruitful door for the analytic interpretation and amplification of these aspects of a work of art.

However, if we set aside the motivation to create, we find another more basic line of observation about the process of unconscious creativity and the form that it takes. It must be remembered that the unconscious is, by definition, not known to us. We can only know it in terms of its products. Of these the dream is perhaps the purest example. One of Freud's most remarkable achievements was to look behind the dream and to decipher the dream-work, the unconscious manufacturer of the dream. In doing so he elaborated his well known theory of wish-fulfilment, but he also described some features of the mental activity that leaves its trace in the way dreams are constructed. This he formulated as primary process, a form of cognition characterized by the properties of condensation, displacement, timelessness, no-negation, and the replacement of external with internal reality (Freud, 1915e). Without these qualities our dreams would not be as they are.

The similarities between the distinctive properties of dreams and the properties found in poetry have been widely recognized. These parallels were explicitly drawn and utilized by Ella Freeman Sharpe in her work on dream interpretation (Sharpe, 1949). Sharpe argued that dreams and poetry could both trace their origins to unconscious experience of some sort, particularly of a felt or bodily kind. The dream functions to communicate this experience but in a manner that can only reveal what is unknown to consciousness in terms of what is or can be known. She takes as her approach to this what she sees as the accepted characteristics of poetic diction. Her justification for proceeding in this way is made explicit in the following statement:

> The laws of poetic diction, evolved by the critics of great poetry and the laws of dream formation as discovered by Freud, spring from the same unconscious sources and have many mechanisms in common. [Sharpe, 1949, p. 19]

From this point Sharpe goes on to show how the characteristic features of poetic diction such as the use of simile, metaphor, and metonymy are reflected in the nature of dreams and can be used as an aid to their interpretation. In so doing she particularly emphasizes the importance of the sound of language and its unconscious phonetic significance. She suggests this is closely tied to early developmental experiences, especially bodily states, and the way that language is acquired through the primary experience of speech as sound.

The parallels Sharpe draws are largely in the service of understanding the nature of dreams through comparison with the figures of speech and forms of imagery that have been identified in poetry. The underlying assumption is that both dreams and poetry take the form they do because they derive from, and reflect in their construction, a common form of unconscious mental activity. For the literary critic Lionel Trilling, adopting this analytic perspective brought with it profound implications. As he pointedly observed, it was a way of thinking "... which makes poetry indigenous to the very constitution of the mind" (Trilling, 1950, p. 49).

The linkage between the structure of language and the unconscious has subsequently been developed in a radical and far-reaching way in the work of Jacques Lacan (1977). Although our experience of dreaming is largely visual, Lacan did not see this as a purely pictorial mode of representation but as a kind of text or form of writing. This is structured by the unconscious according to its purposes, which for Lacan were pre-eminently concerned with processes of persuasion, or, put in linguistic terms, with rhetoric. The function of rhetorical language is to persuade or influence rather than convey accurate information or reveal true intentions. Rhetoric makes use of many of the same forms and figures of speech as poetry but predominantly in other contexts of discourse such as advertising and political debate where the aim is to get a desired outcome. However, for Lacan, everyday speech is also saturated by it in a way that is often completely unconscious.

Lacan's equation of language and the unconscious is built up from the equivalence that can be drawn, on the one hand, between condensation and metaphor—where one thing can stand for a number of others; and on the other, displacement and metonymy—where representation can move from one thing to another, usually by association. In effect he sees metaphor and metonymy as direct functions of the unconscious and privileges these linguistic terms over those coined by Freud. Indeed, we might note in passing the metaphorical nature of the terms "condensation" and "displacement", both of which seek to illuminate mental activity in terms of a known physical process. One of the merits of Lacan's emphasis is that it is closer to the account we actually give of our dreams, which is almost always in the form of a verbal description. It also brings us nearer to the process of listening to the action of language that is required in the analytic context. This is something that Thomas Ogden has recently paralleled with the quality of listening invited by poetry through what he describes, in words borrowed from Seamus Heaney, as "the music of what happens". (Ogden, 2001, p. 77).

Building on a Lacanian framework, Julia Kristeva (1984) has constructed her own distinctive model of the development of language as a signifying process. This moves from what she refers to as a "semiotic" pre-oedipal phase, to the "symbolic" post-oedipal order of acquired language. She has endeavoured to redress Lacan's predominant emphasis on verbal language by considering the pre-verbal stages of development where the child babbles and follows rhythms and patterns of sound in response to its maternal and bodily environment. In this unstable multi-sensory state of being infants have no fixed identity. Rather they are in a state of constant movement and fluid interchange with the world around them in a manner that accords with Freud's primary process. The acquisition of language and its rules is associated with the imposition of an order, associated with the father, which is a necessary pre-condition for achieving a relatively stable and separate identity. While this symbolic order arises from the semiotic, its coherence is threatened by any subsequent eruption of the semiotic. This results in the necessity for a kind of blanket repression of the semiotic level of experience. However, the semiotic may return in a number of subversive forms, such as Kristeva's trinity of madness, holiness, and poetry. Kristeva (1992) is explicit in stating that it is the experience of the semiotic emerging in and through language that produces poetry. Features such as metaphor, metonymy and musicality arise as a creative disruption of the limiting and differentiating experience of language and serve to open up this more extensive and vividly felt area of being.

In many ways Kristeva's observations about poetry take us back to those of Sharpe concerning the sound of language and the importance of very early forms of sense experience. Both are reflections of the increasing interest psychoanalysis has taken in these initial phases of development following the seminal work of Melanie Klein. Kristeva sees the semiotic as being significant in all forms of creativity and refers to the semiotic "chora", a space or receptacle formed by the infant's link with the mother's body. This has many features in common with Winnicott's ideas about the holding environment and the necessity for the emergence of a "potential space" for the realization of creative experience. This, too, has its origins in the mental and physical space between mother and infant and provides a context for potentially creative transitions in the way objects, including words, are experienced and used.

What Sharpe, Lacan, and Kristeva have in common is their establishment and elaboration of a clear link between the nature of poetry and the existence of a distinctive form of unconscious mental activity, which they each see as underlying it. This is a form of activity that is in marked contrast to the conventional thinking of consciousness and which owes its initial formulation to Freud's description of the primary process. They all represent this activity as fundamentally opposed to our normal patterns of thought and language use but as frequently pressing to intrude into it. This opposition, following Freud, is largely considered in terms of an active repressive process that sets out to exclude material from consciousness so that a required order in consciousness may be established and preserved. For Lacan and Kristeva these repressive forces take on a cultural dimension, which opens up the very broad scope of their wider theorizing.   .

Although this model has much to commend it and may help illuminate some of the painful personal struggles that can be involved in writing poetry, it privileges the process of exclusion over what could be termed the constructive difficulties that are inherent to the process of creative work. In the case of poetry this includes the challenges of working in the particular medium of language to realize a satisfying artistic product in the form of a poem; a poem being, quite literally, a "made thing" (Drury, 1995). This is a process that, as we have seen, appears heavily dependent on access to largely unconscious processes and sensibilities. However, in utilizing these the poet does not seem to be exclusively dominated by a struggle to overcome repression but is actually seeking to make something by drawing on as full and inclusive access to their emotional experience as possible—a depth of experience that is intimate to their being but which is inherently difficult to put into the form of words. Some of the profound satisfaction of creative work probably follows from the extent to which this basic constructive task feels as if it has been achieved.

Within the clinical theory of psychoanalysis the critical notions of repression and defence have been of central importance to the examination of the unconscious. The repressed unconscious exists because its contents are actively excluded from conscious awareness. Although there is a pressure to satisfy repressed desires or wishes this can only be achieved in a disguised form because of the need to maintain repression. Dreams and other manifestations of unconscious activity take the form they do partly from the need to maintain this exclusion. Seen in this light, artistic work is a "sublimation" of wishes or drives and the created form serves to obtain gratification or expression while still maintaining a level of disguise. Sublimation is, however, a developmental achievement because it is a far more adaptive compromise than neurosis or symptom formation.

Although the repressed unconscious is at the heart of clinical theory, many analysts have been interested in those aspects of unconscious creativity that are not shaped solely by its operation. Among these is Marion Milner. For example, she notes the following observation made on her work by Pontalis:

> ... he then said that I had considered the dream neither as a message or text to be deciphered nor as a compromise between repressed desires and ego defence mechanisms, but as a witness of a state of being; in fact as an attempt at symbolization rather than as a symbolic language to be decoded .... [Milner, 1975, p. 275]

This observation points to a process that seeks representation or symbolization for its own sake; a process which may seek to give conscious thought or external form to what is known or experienced but at an unconscious level of being. Milner points to one source of her own thinking about this in the writing of Anton Ehrenzweig (1967) who, in her words:

> ... came to the conclusion that the inarticulate structure of what he calls the "depth" mind is totally ungraspable by the "surface" mind, not because of repression of offensive content but because of its structure; and that, because of its peculiar structure it can achieve tasks of integration that are quite beyond the capacity of the conscious surface mind. [Milner, 1975, p. 276]

Ehrenzweig and Milner were both interested in art, particularly visual art, and clearly saw in it something more than a creative but disguised expression of the repressed unconscious. Rather, they saw it as an attempt to give form to a level of experience that is otherwise ungraspable by the conscious mind; the barrier to awareness existing not so much in its content as in its very nature. Milner argued that we needed a fuller understanding of the differences between the "two kinds of thinking" that distinguished these areas of the mind. This was a difference that, in her own experience, existed between the "... kind of thinking that makes an absolute separation of subject from object, me from not me, seer from seen, and the kind that does not" (Milner, 1957, p. 160). She pointed out that we know a lot about the logic and laws of reasoning of the former but less about the capacity for fusing or, from a rational point of view, con-fusing these distinctions, in the kind of thinking that underpins the formation of art.

Following Freud, the analyst who has undoubtedly devoted the most attention to formulating the logical form of unconscious processes is Ignacio Matte-Blanco (1975, 1988). In the remainder of this chapter I will focus on some of the key aspects of his work and examine what additional light this might be able to throw on the nature and writing of poetry.

The logical unconscious

To talk of the unconscious as logical appears contradictory. The common perception is that the unconscious is irrational and shaped by essentially emotional forces. What must be remembered is that anything we say about the unconscious is necessarily spoken from the point of view of the conscious mind and thus in terms of the logic associated with it. From this perspective the unconscious does not seem to be shaped by principles that are reasonable, they simply do not conform to the accepted conventions of logical thought. On the other hand, if there was no logic or order to unconscious processes it would be hard to see how any pattern at all would be visible in them. The necessary conclusion seems to be that the unconscious operates according to a form of logic that is distinctly its own. This is where Matte-Blanco starts from in his painstaking investigation into the form that this logic takes and the way that it can be represented and understood.

The problem is, how are we to understand a logic that is different from the logic that we normally use to understand things? This is where Matte-Blanco, in a manner reminiscent of Bion and the later Lacan, turns to a symbolic language other than words—the language of mathematics. Unfortunately, this aspect of his work can make it quite intimidating and inaccessible to the non-mathematically inclined. It can help to hold in mind that mathematics is essentially concerned with the identification of patterns that are originally observed from the world of experience. The abstraction of this pattern into a mathematical concept (like numbers or shapes) can lead to an investigation of the principles or axioms that operate to govern this. Through manipulation these may lead in turn to new findings and logical proofs that are independent of any observed phenomena and that usually rely on an increasingly abstract form of notation. Interestingly, many mathematicians find these proofs aesthetically pleasing and even when they appear counter to common sense they often lead back to tangible applications and unexpected discoveries in the "real" world.

The observations Matte-Blanco derives from experience are those made by Freud about the five characteristics of primary process thinking. These, as mentioned previously, are the features of displacement, condensation, timelessness, no-negation, and the replacement of external with internal reality. These clearly do not correspond to the logic of conventional thinking which, from the time of Aristotle, has insisted on propositions that are either true or false and recognizes the separation of events in time and space. What we have to keep in mind is that this is a form of logic that is abstracted from the way we normally think and therefore seems natural or "logical". However, it does not represent the only system of logic that is possible. For example, some of the paradoxical discoveries of quantum mechanics seem to be "illogical" from this point of view.

Matte-Blanco's approach was to try to abstract some kind of logic from the observed properties of unconscious thinking. What he hit upon was the concept of "symmetric logic". Following a detailed step-by-step argument he attempted to show that this could account for all the properties observed by Freud and thus provide a new perspective for thinking about the nature of the unconscious and its activity. It would be impossible to provide an adequate exposition of Matte-Blanco's argument here, but an excellent introduction is provided by Rayner (1995) and some interesting possible developments by Bomford (1998). What I will endeavour to draw out are some of the general features that seem relevant to the processes involved in both conscious and unconscious creativity.

The nature of symmetric logic is developed by Matte-Blanco from a consideration of the symmetrizations sometimes seen in conventional thinking, and a property of mathematical set theory, which means a member of a class can sometimes be identical to the class to which it belongs. A logical symmetrization occurs when the relationships between two elements can be reversed. For example, John is the brother of Peter is equivalent to saying Peter is the brother of John. However, it is normally more common to find asymmetric relationships such as: John is the brother of Mary. This does not imply its reverse because Mary is the *sister* of John. Similarly, in classing things in sets we find some sets where the elements may be loosely treated as identical to the set—for example, the set of "apples" consists of apples—and, in contrast, sets where this identity evidently does not hold, such as the set of "things in my kitchen", which may contain apples but also bananas, a toaster, and assorted cutlery. Although this is a contrived linguistic illustration it gives some impression of the relations that can hold when sets are examined mathematically.

In a system of pure symmetric thinking these symmetrizations of relationship, and of identity between the elements and the whole of a set, become the rule. In effect, a principle of identification operates that tends to make things equivalent to each other. In this state of mind one thing can stand for another, a part can become the whole and contradictions that would appear to normal thinking disappear. What is more, the dimensions of time and space also cease to have any significance, since if A follows B, B must follow A. As a result these differentiating continua collapse.

Matte-Blanco's contention is that this form of logic characterizes unconscious thinking and is what makes it appear so odd and irrational to normal reasoning. In fact, he goes further than this and suggests that it is the very nature of this form of thinking which makes it unconscious in the first place. This has nothing to do with what the unconscious contains but is structurally determined by the nature of consciousness. Our consciousness emerges and is constructed by processes of discrimination, particularly the identification of differences and, hence, relations between things in the external world. This becomes embedded in the very nature of language and our capacity for conscious thinking. Consciousness simply cannot contain too much symmetric thinking because it dissolves differences; for example, the difference between self and other, or a word and the thing that it signifies. As a result consciousness, as we generally know it, requires symmetric logic to keep firmly in the background.

This formulation offers an alternative to repression as a means of understanding the relationship between the activity of the conscious and unconscious mind. It also opens the door to an approach to the role of the unconscious in creativity that is not dependent on the construction of parallels with pathological processes. This would be congruent with Ehrenzweig's observation that:

> In contrast to illness, creative work succeeds in coordinating the results of unconscious undifferentiation and conscious differentiation and so *reveals* the hidden order of the unconscious. [Ehrenzweig, 1967, p. 4, my italics]

Now, it might be objected that Matte-Blanco's mathematically derived view of the unconscious feels too abstract and "logical" and that it fails to capture the intensity of emotional experience that psychoanalysis has located there and the strength of feeling that is reflected in artistic creativity such as poetry. However, this would be doing it a gross disservice. In fact, from this logical point of view the very distinctions we normally make between thinking and feeling are eroded and melt into something much nearer an experience of being. Feeling is thus rescued from its normal opposition to reason. It becomes instead one of the vital means by which we do have some knowledge of the operation of this level of mind. This is most clearly illustrated in intense and psychotic emotional states where the operation of a symmetric mode of thinking becomes almost self-evident as it overwhelms the power to discriminate according to rational principles. When you are in love it is "reasonable" to see the lover as perfectly lovable despite evidence to the contrary, in a paranoid state of mind it "makes sense" to feel fearful because so much is being located in the class of dangerous things.

Such examples of extreme feeling point to one of Matte-Blanco's most interesting ideas. He notes that one of the mathematical properties of sets where the elements are equivalent to the whole set is that the set must be infinite. For example, as I write this I have four books on my desk. Each book belongs to the finite set I might call "the books on my desk". Mathematically, none of the individual books can be treated as the same as the whole set "the books on my desk". However, each book can be treated as identical to the imaginary set of "all books", which is potentially infinite. This has a subtle emotional resonance, as I do sometimes find myself holding, examining, and looking at a book as if appreciating and savouring its quality of simply being a book. I cannot imagine any such experience for the quality of a book just being a book on my desk. In the case of extreme emotions this infinitization seems to be experienced far more concretely. Thus, when deeply in love all that is lovable can actually feel contained in one person or, for some, all dangerous ideas may seem located in one book. In effect, symmetrical thinking moves from the background of experience to a, usually temporary, domination of conscious awareness.

If symmetrical thinking dominates consciousness in a sustained way it can clearly be associated with what can become pathological states of mind. It would be a mistake, however, to conclude that it is somehow the fault of the symmetric form of thinking. The problem lies as much in the failure of consciousness to accommodate it. In other words, in the inability of consciousness to entertain this experience while also sustaining its capacity to discriminate adequately according to conventional reason. It is interesting to speculate whether herein resides both the similarity and difference observed between madness and mystical experience, and a possible reason why some poetry can feel as if it is walking a thin line between them. If the doors of perception were cleansed it might indeed be possible, according to symmetric logic, to see the world as infinite. However, without the power of discrimination we might not be able to see the world at all.

In discussing symmetric logic and the concept of the unconscious, Matte-Blanco makes it clear that he sees unconsciousness and symmetric thinking as just two attributes of what is essentially a different mode of being from the asymmetric form of experience that we are usually conscious of. He describes this deeper level of being as the symmetrical mode but indicates firmly that: "All our descriptions of symmetrical being are inaccurate because symmetrical being is indescribable in an accurate way and is ineffable" (Matte-Blanco, 1975, p. 101).

Developmentally, Matte-Blanco sees the symmetric mode as the fundamental mode of being and as the base from which asymmetric discrimination arises. However, in its operation symmetric thinking is always united in some degree with an element of asymmetric thinking and vice versa. Neither a totally symmetrical nor a totally asymmetrical pattern of thought seems cognitively sustainable. In the former everything would merge into a complete identity. We might imagine this as nothingness, literally a no-separate-thing-ness. In the latter everything would be split through an unlimited differentiation, which would lead to a strangely similar state of formlessness. This gives birth to what he describes as bi-logic, the intermixture of symmetric and asymmetric modes of thought. Bi-logic can take a wide variety of forms and structures according to the precise combination and use made of the different modes of thinking. It varies from forms that are largely based on symmetric logic and are thus most deeply unconscious, and forms that are largely asymmetric and therefore characteristic of conscious thinking. Bi-logic shifts the focus from the differences between the two modes of thought towards a focus on their dialectical interplay in all forms of knowing, both conscious and unconscious.

Bi-logic and poetry

Following a process of mathematically-based abstraction, Matte-Blanco leads us to the conception of different bi-logical forms or structures. This idea can then in turn be applied to the examination of concrete products of mental activity, such as different forms of speech and writing. It seems probable that any form of recognition or pattern making, including symbolization itself, owes its origins to a symmetric mode of thought that enables one thing to be identified with another. While the structure of language is largely asymmetric and built on discrimination, its development and use seem highly dependent on symmetric forms of thinking. The more language use is focused on factual communication and prepositional reasoning the more asymmetric it tends to become. When it is used to convey feeling, experience or value, it exhibits more symmetric features. As we have seen, in extreme emotional states the symmetric mode may even come to dominate both discourse and perception of the world.

Although poetry is extremely varied in the forms it takes it is possible to approach it in a generalized way from a bi-logical point of view. Indeed, Matte-Blanco suggests, in passing, that art and especially poetry corresponds to a particular bi-logical structure, which he labels as "Simassi" (Matte-Blanco, 1988, p. 68). This stands for the simultaneous use of asymmetric and symmetric thinking. Now, we know poetry is associated with the conveying of feeling and experience so we would expect it to contain a high level of symmetrization. However, if this were to predominate it may result in a form of irrational emoting rather than the highly disciplined form of expression found in poetry, famously characterized by Wordsworth as emotion recollected in tranquillity. In order to contain a high level of symmetrization without allowing it to overwhelm our sense of reason, it may be necessary to find a way of simultaneously increasing some asymmetric features of language use, and also to find a way of combining these two elements together in a satisfactory way.

At this stage it may be helpful to exchange Matte-Blanco's logically derived terms for expressions that may be easier to grasp in the context of poetry. The symmetric mode in particular cannot be reduced to any one form of words, so this seems a reasonable step to take. My suggestion is that we can consider poetry in terms of its exhibition of, on the one hand, "patterns of identity", which correspond to symmetric thinking, and, on the other hand to the construction of "means of differentiation", which is an essential feature of asymmetric thinking. In applying these two dimensions it is useful to remember that the identities that lie behind symmetric thinking are not merely verbal but arise from a pre-verbal background of sense experience. So, identities can be established in terms of sound, image, or patterns of movement. Identities established at that level can, in turn, be differentiated in terms below a level of verbal statement. For example, the rhythm of a poem like Auden's "Night Mail" has a very clear pattern of identity with the actual rhythm and sound of a steam train on a track. When the tempo of the rhythm alters the identity remains but we have a differentiated sense of the train speeding up or slowing down without any need to use these words.

One of the most widely noted qualities of poems is their condensed use of language. This, taken together with the preceding argument, suggests a refined proposal for the way we might consider the characteristics of poetry from a bi-logical point of view. The proposal is that, compared with ordinary language, poetry typically makes use of an increased density of both "patterns of identity" and "means of differentiation" in a constructed combination that enables them to operate simultaneously. This, of course, is an extremely general thesis and not an attempt to reductively explain poetry. It may, however, provide a means of linking the nature of poetry with a more extensive view of the capacity for knowing and being that can arise through the interrelation of the conscious and unconscious mind. Before considering further the process that may underpin such creative activity, it is worth stopping to see whether some of the forms and features that are commonly found in poetry can be correlated with the bi-logical framework that is proposed.

It is useful to start by considering the fact that, when written down, a poem exists as a differentiated object in its own right. It usually stands out from the page in a much more obvious way than normal prose and this contributes to its distinct identity as a poem. We are already alerted to approach it in a particular way, as poetry, and thus to distinguish it from other forms of writing. This creates a differentiating boundary to the contents of the poem much in the same way as a frame separates a picture from the wall. All that is within is identified together as constituting the poem. However highly differentiated the contents may be, everything is required to belong to the poem for the poem to be effective. Editing can often involve the painful excision of wonderfully poetic lines or phrases that simply do not meet this requirement.

Poetry frequently makes use of forms of verse involving patterns of structural identity in areas such as rhythm, rhyme, and stanza length. This creates an identifiable form to these poems that ensures the contents are made identical in some respects, for example, through the continuity of metre or rhyming sounds, while being more clearly differentiated in terms of others; for example, through the effects of stress, selection of rhyme, or position in the formal sequence. An illustration of the latter would be the closing couplet of a Shakespearian sonnet. Regular verse forms also identify the poem as belonging to a class of poems against which its individual features will stand out more clearly. Even poetry that eschews a regular form is almost always written in lines. In fact, many people see the line as the single most defining property of poetry. The use of lines means the usual logic of sentences can be subtly disrupted. Words are differentiated according to their place on the line rather than just through the rules of grammar and syntax. At the same time each line serves to break up and differentiate the poem. The identity between lines is obvious when established metrically, but can also be established and varied through the use of line length and cadence. Most fundamentally lines share the property of simply being lines, which is, as far as bi-logic is concerned, essentially a pattern of identity or symmetry. Lines thus seem to provide a central means through which poems can be constructed to increase both identity and differentiation and to combine them in a satisfying way.

Figures of speech, such as metaphor, simile, and metonymy, have already been considered in relation to the work of Sharpe and Lacan. Metaphor is perhaps the purest example of a pattern of linguistic identity between one thing and another but all tropes seem to depend on some form of it for their operation. Simile, for example, may be viewed as an identity where a means of differentiation is inserted by use of the word "like". Poetry is, of course, rich in these figures and their associated imagery, but authors such as Lakoff & Johnson (1980) have also drawn attention to how much we rely on metaphorical language in everyday life. It has been noted that what distinguishes everyday use of metaphor and the form it takes in poetry is the degree to which the metaphors are specific rather than more generalized (Holland, 1999). The choice of words and use of metaphors in poetry is usually highly specific and often original. The concrete term is usually preferred over the abstract, unlike normal conversation that is usually conducted in terms of the familiar and general. The net effect of this is to make the language of poetry, including its use of figurative imagery, highly differentiated and particular. Identities are established, but in terms that are very specific and precisely chosen.

We could extend this kind of analysis further into the specific uses of sound, rhythm, and repetition, but the same essential observation recurs. There does indeed seem to be an increased density of patterns of identity and also of means of differentiation in poetry. What is more, these symmetric and asymmetric features are tightly intertwined in a way that must make their operation effectively simultaneous. Poetry seems to be characterized by a bi-logical form of high symmetry closely conjoined with high levels of asymmetry. It is as if the one allows or enables the increase of the other in a mutually supportive interplay. Although defined in purely logical terms through their opposition, symmetric and asymmetric modes seem to exist in poetry in a remarkable form of synergy.

Poiesis

The model of poetic creation implicit in the bi-logical view of poetry that has been outlined suggests that it reflects more than the activity of the repressed unconscious mind or simply the creative representation of the unconscious in a conscious form. Rather, the creative process would seem to require a complex coordination between both conscious and unconscious forms of thinking and feeling to create a new entity that moves beyond both. The poem comes to represent and generate experience in a way that would be inherently inconceivable without it, either consciously or unconsciously. It is a unique bi-logical structure and thus comes to embody what is in a sense a new form of being—its own.

The process of creative construction, or poiesis, is unlikely to yield to any facile formulation, but some elements of it may be discernible when approached from a bi-logical angle. As Ehrenzweig suggested, it is likely to involve a process of coordination because it requires the simultaneous operation of principles that, according to Matte-Blanco, exist in a fundamental antinomy. Matte-Blanco argued that for symmetric thinking to enter consciousness at all requires some form of translation or unfolding function. This meant that conscious thinking could only represent symmetric logic in a modified or indirect way. He suggested this could be visualized in terms of a mapping of points in a higher dimension of space to the corresponding points represented in a lower dimension. Thus, if you picture the corners of a triangle that has been cut out from a card they are clearly spread out; however, looked at endways they correspond to three points on a line. The reality of a two-dimensional space is always modified when it is represented in a one-dimensional form and thus loses some of its most important qualities. This is equivalent to saying that poetry cannot be paraphrased.

Moving in the opposite direction, if you take a one-dimensional form like a line and imagine bending it round until the ends touch, you have created a circle which, in fact, contains a two-dimensional space. Similarly, if you fold the line through ninety degrees at three equidistant points and join the ends, you enclose a two-dimensional space in the shape of a square. Through similar acts of folding you can move from a two-dimensional space to a three-dimensional one, which should be apparent if you imagine how a packet of cornflakes is formed from making a series of folds in a flat sheet of cardboard. From a mathematical point of view, this process can be carried on indefinitely. From a poetic point of view, we have an analogy for how high levels of symmetry may be enclosed in language by increased amounts of asymmetric differentiation. In poetry the symmetrical mode does not appear to be simply unfolded or translated into a conscious form of thinking. On the contrary, it seems more accurate to say that it emerges enfolded in language. We might imagine this as arising through the construction of numerous linguistic folds where the differentiated words, sounds, and images are bent back to meet in symmetrical patterns of identity.

In the practice of the poet's craft the processes of both folding and unfolding may take place repeatedly in the search for adequate means for ultimately embodying patterns of identity and difference that arise from experience. A bit like origami, it may take an extremely complex series of folds, creases, and tucks before any worthwhile poetic shape can be achieved. In the meantime quite a lot of paper is likely to end up in the basket.

This idea of repeatedly moving between an integrating and differentiating process in the process of writing poetry is similar to Christopher Bollas's ideas of how we make creative use of objects to elaborate psychic experiences and their potential for meaning. Bollas (1995) proposes that in creativity there is a largely unconscious process of repeatedly "cracking up" and re-combining experience. He argues that this is at the heart of the dream-work and the process of free association in psychoanalysis. Psychic experience or intensities gather or combine into the symbolic contents of dreams, which are cracked up by free association and are then re-combined into further emerging themes. He suggests this as the psychoanalytic equivalent of the process of artistic creativity, which he sees as working through alternating processes of fragmenting experience on the one hand and unifying experience on the other, but in the medium of the art form. The dream is thus once again visited as a paradigm of the creative, but in a way that is more reflective of this being an emergent bi-logical process.

Ending on infinity

Matte-Blanco's work recasts Freud's formulation of the unconscious mind and introduces a new dimension, that of infinity. The division conscious–unconscious is reframed into a distinction between two fundamental and apparently irreconcilable modes of being that he characterizes, in terms of logical cognition, as the symmetric and asymmetric modes. Paradoxically, however, these antithetical modes must co-exist and even cooperate together in both conscious and unconscious forms of mental life. Indeed, in artistic creativity, at least of a poetic kind, some form of reconciliation may even be what is sought.

The apparent impossibility of uniting opposing principles or modes of being, or of the poet using words wordlessly, can be compared to the huge difficulty we have in grasping the existence of infinity. Logical thought leads us to it because we can, for example, "see" that the largest number we can think of could always have one added to it. However, this does not enable us to imagine it. There seems to be no adequate means of representation. And yet for many people the contemplation of infinity does give rise to a very definite experience, for if infinity cannot be imagined then neither can a completely finite world. Blake, in "Auguries of Innocence" has immortalized a poetic response to this situation:

> To see infinity in a grain of sand,
> And heaven in a wild flower,
> Hold infinity in the palm of your hand,
> And eternity in an hour.

The key Blake offers is to see the infinite in the particular, to find one within the folds of the other. This is not a reductive process but a dialectical one. Through it we may glimpse one means by which the "concrete universal" (Wimsatt, 1947) could come to exist in poetry. In mathematical terms, an infinite set is made up of a potentially infinite number of elements; it is only when there is an infinite number of elements that any particular element can be treated as identical to the whole set. This means that the capacity for ever greater differentiation is directly associated with a state of identity or unity with a wider whole. As Matte-Blanco noted: "It can be said that it is in the infinite that both natures of man, the symmetrical and the asymmetrical, meet" (Matte-Blanco, 1975, p. 289).

What in conscious thought can only be conceived with difficulty may, at an unconscious level, be recognized through a form of felt experience. This constitutes a type of knowing that may only achieve realization through an act of imagination that can both unfold and enfold it in a particular created form. I have tried to show that this is one way in which we can approach and think about poetry. Archibald MacLeish (1926) has, as poets do, put one conclusion that emerges into words—words that are, in spite of their logic or maybe because of it, by no means meaningless.

> A poem should not mean
> But be.

References

Bollas, C. (1995). *Cracking Up*. London: Routledge.

Bomford, R. (1998). Mapping mental processes. A new approach to symmetric logic and the unconscious. *Journal of Melanie Klein and Object Relations, 16*: 35–46.

Drury, J. (1995). *The Poetry Dictionary*. Cincinnati: Story Press.

Ehrenzweig, A. (1967). *The Hidden Order of Art*. London: Wiedenfeld & Nicholson.

Freud, S. (1908e). Creative writers and day-dreaming. *S.E., 9*: 141–154. London: Hogarth.

Freud, S. (1915e). The unconscious. *S.E., 14*: 166–215. London: Hogarth.

Holland, N. N. (1999). Cognitive linguistics. *International Journal of Psychoanalysis, 80*, 357–363.

King, A. (1975). *The Unprosaic Imagination: Essays and Lectures on the Study of Literature*. Nedlands: University of Western Australia Press.

Kristeva, J. (1984)[1974]. *Revolution in Poetic Language*, M. Waller (Trans.). New York: Columbia University Press [reprinted in T. Moi (Ed.), *The Kristeva Reader*. New York: Columbia University Press, 1986].

Kristeva, J. (1992). A question of subjectivity—an interview. In: P. Rice & P. Waugh (Eds.), *Modern Literary Theory*, 2nd edn. London: Edward Arnold.

Lacan, J. (1977)[1966]. *Ecrits*, A. Sheridan (Trans.). London: Tavistock.

Lakoff, G., & Johnson, M. (1980). *Metaphors We Live By*. Chicago: University of Chicago Press.

MacLeish, A. (1926). "Ars Poetica", in *Collected Poems 1917–1982*. Boston: Houghton Mifflin, 1985.

Matte-Blanco, I. (1975). *The Unconscious as Infinite Sets: An Essay in Bi-logic.* London: Duckworth [revised edition, London: Karnac Books, 1998].

Matte-Blanco, I. (1988). *Thinking, Feeling, and Being.* London: Routledge.

Milner, M. (1957). *On Not Being Able to Paint* (2nd edn). London: Heinemann.

Milner, M. (1975). A discussion of Masud Khan's paper "In Search of the Dreaming Experience" [reprinted in M. Milner (Ed.), *The Suppressed Madness of Sane Men* (pp. 275–278). London: Routledge, 1987].

Ogden, T. H. (2001). *Conversations at the Frontiers of Dreaming.* London: Karnac.

Oliver, M. (1994). *A Poetry Handbook: A Prose Guide to Understanding and Writing Poetry.* New York: Harcourt Brace.

Rayner, E. (1995). *Unconscious Logic: An introduction to Matte-Blanco's Bi-logic and its Uses.* London: Routledge.

Sharpe, E. F. (1949). *Dream Analysis: A Practical Handbook for Psycho-Analysts.* London: Hogarth.

Trilling, L. (1950). *The Liberal Imagination.* New York: Viking.

Wimsatt, W. K. (1947). *The Concrete Universal*, PMLA LXII [reprinted in: *The Verbal Icon: Studies in the Meaning of Poetry* (pp. 69–83). Lexington: University of Kentucky Press, 1954].

CHAPTER FOUR

The poet and the superego: Klein, Blake and the Book of the Prophet Ezekiel

Priscilla Green

Introduction

Ezekiel has traditionally been thought of as a prophet, one who experienced his radical message as of crucial significance to the religious and political life of the community in which he lived, and whose writings had a transforming influence on Jewish society. In this paper, however, I wish to consider instead the ways in which the exile of part of the Jewish nation to Babylon in the 6th century BC provided Ezekiel with a metaphor for schizoid processes within the psyche. Ezekiel himself was among those sent to Babylon, and this bitter experience seems to have helped to clarify and structure his awareness of his inner world in a remarkably developed way. I also intend to focus on the intra-psychic processes symbolized by his visions and prophecies, those internal experiences which determined the poetic content of his work; experiences which inspired great poets many centuries after he lived and can still evoke a profound response today.

On first reading Ezekiel, I was struck by the way in which the text oscillated between great poetry and the sort of violent and primitive outpourings often associated with madness. I thought it was possible that these extreme contrasts might be intrinsic to the integrative process the prophet seemed to be describing, and in thinking about how this process might be structured, I found Kleinian accounts of the superego illuminating. Post-Kleinian explorations of symbol formation have also helped me to understand something of what it might be that Ezekiel meant by prophecy, in its internal sense, and what kind of processes he was setting in train, both in his own mind and, ultimately, in the minds of his readers, by this activity.

Ezekiel's few psychoanalytic commentators have described him as psychotic and have been interested in his writings primarily as evidence of this pathology (Arlow, 1951; Kris, 1939; Strachey, 1930). The experience of reading Ezekiel tends to confirm, initially at least, this interpretation of the prophet. Much of the text consists of storming tirades, full of self-righteousness and savagery. The reader may well feel revulsion, confusion, and a recurring conviction of the writer's insanity, but Ezekiel also contains passages of such beauty and profundity that they have influenced many poets, including Dante and Shakespeare. Blake, in particular, regarded Ezekiel both as a mentor and as a source of imagery. In the last of his own prophetic books, *Jerusalem* (1820), he describes an integrative process which has many points of similarity to Ezekiel's, and which offers insights into Ezekiel's ancient and obscure text.

While working concurrently on the texts of Ezekiel and of Blake's *Jerusalem*, my experience of reading Ezekiel altered, and I began to find traces of a mind whose insane outpourings seemed to be the result of a deliberate creative act: a mind capable of great clarity and self-abnegation. I also began to confront limitations: those imposed on my understanding of the prophet's mind and his purposes by my own level of psychic development.

Symbolic action and the poet's task

"Now lie on your left side [said God], and I will lay Israel's iniquity on you; you shall bear their iniquity for as many days as you lie on that side ... lie down a second time on your right side, and bear Judah's iniquity ... You are to eat your bread baked like barley cakes [i.e: in contact with the hot ashes], using human dung as fuel, and

you must bake it where people can see you." Then the Lord said,
"This is the kind of bread, unclean bread, that the Israelites will eat in
the foreign lands into which I shall drive them". [Ezekiel 4: 4–13]

Blake seems to have considered true poetry to be almost
synonymous with prophecy and in considering Ezekiel's "symbolic
actions" he had this to say.

I then asked Ezekiel why he eat dung and lay so long on his right
and left side? He answered, the desire of raising other men into a
perception of the infinite ... is he honest who resists his genius or
his conscience only for the sake of present ease or gratification?
[Blake, 1790: 1.13]

Blake's exceptional awareness of his own intra-psychic processes
enabled him to comprehend the nature of Ezekiel's enterprise in
ways that are not readily available to most of us, and in this passage
he sets out both his own, and what he perceives to be Ezekiel's deep
convictions about the psycho-dynamic nature of the poetic task. By
eating dung and lying first on his right side and then on his left,
Blake meant, and understood Ezekiel to have meant, the poet's way
of acknowledging, living through and taking back into the
integrated part of the psyche extremes of early rage and sadism
and the split and partial states of mind that stem from them. Blake
felt that both poets experienced this form of psychic activity as
something which created new levels of awareness in the mind.

In this passage, Blake also asserts his belief that a true poet does
not, merely, "for the sake of present ease or gratification", evade the
humiliating, disgusting or cripplingly restrictive aspects of this
process, or his duty to communicate them truthfully to others. This
is so, even though it requires him to feel to the full what it is to be an
evil man, and to write debased forms of poetry in order to reach, by
giving expression to, parts of his psyche he has yet to modify or
integrate. As Ezekiel puts it when he castigates the false prophet in
himself: "... you misused your wisdom to increase your dignity"
(Ezekiel, 28: 17).

Should not the shepherd care for the sheep? You consume the milk,
wear the wool, and slaughter the fat beasts, but you do not feed the
sheep. You have not ... bandaged the hurt, recovered the straggler,
or searched for the lost ... [Ezekiel, 34: 2–4]

This reintegrative process is evidenced by the varying quality of Ezekiel's verse: at times primitive, bombastic, vituperative, dictatorial, bloodthirsty, legalistic, or pedantic as the poet enters into and voices the various ways in which parts of his psyche express themselves, but also recurrently "depressive" in content as new levels of integration are achieved (Klein, 1935).

For both Ezekiel and Blake, there is an inescapable and paradoxical connection between the level of psychic development which enables men to perceive the infinite, and the incorporation of the most disgusting and discarded parts of the psyche; a connection between the ability to make full imaginative contact with, and give expression to, the partial, the split-off and the one-sided, and a true experience of the self. In describing this reintegrative poetic task, Ezekiel says:

> As a shepherd goes in search of his sheep when his flock is dispersed all around him, so I will go in search of my sheep and rescue them, no matter where they were scattered in dark and cloudy days. [Ezekiel, 34: 12]

In the frontispiece to *Jerusalem*, Blake illustrates a similar psychic process. He depicts the poet as a night-watchman, stepping through a doorway into the dark regions of his spirit, lantern in hand. In Kleinian terms, he is choosing to experience split-off parts of his psyche in order to reintegrate them.

This way of interpreting the Book of Ezekiel is, of course, both restricted and potentially restricting. It is also highly speculative. The text seems to deal, in places, with very early states of mind, and it expresses these states, and their interactions with more mature parts of the psyche, through the use of highly complex symbols. These seem to contain many levels of awareness, from the most primitive or debased to the most sublime. The work of interpretation is further complicated by the fact that the text, which dates from the 6th century BC (Eichrodt, 1970), is corrupt and probably only gives us an approximation of the prophet's writing. The book we now have appears to have been collated, not always coherently, from various sources (Von Rad, 1965). Despite these difficulties, a strong identity speaks through the text, which clearly had other purposes in creating the Book of Ezekiel besides those suggested in this chapter.

Poetry and verbal thought

Ezekiel's poetic enterprise has some similarities to Bion's psycho-analytic approach to the treatment of psychotic and schizophrenic patients. Bion (1955) discusses:

> ... the difficulties that attend communication between the schizoid patient and the analyst. For the most part the discussion centres on the rudimentary stages of what, for want of a better term, I have called verbal thought. But, before that stage is reached in analysis, much work has to be done ... [Bion, 1955: 223–224]

Schizoid patients may inhabit parts of the self for which there are no words, and which have no access to words. The words have to be provided by their analysts via their interpretations. At this pre-verbal level, the patient cannot communicate through speech, and, as Bion (1955) goes on to say "... the only evidence on which an interpretation can be based is that which is afforded by the counter-transference".

By empathizing imaginatively with, and receiving pre-verbal communications from, split-off parts of his own mind, Ezekiel perhaps can be said to be using a form of counter-transference, and employing it for much the same integrative purposes as Bion. However, the whole interaction between, as it were, analyst and patient, is taking place within Ezekiel's own psyche. The fact that God, in the text, communicates with Ezekiel in part through visions is in itself suggestive of non-verbal thought processes: an image-making capacity of the mind which does not depend on words to convey meaning and can consequently express pre-verbal parts of the psyche.

There are several places in the text where Ezekiel describes himself as struck dumb through contact with his visions, i.e., through a fully-experienced acceptance of pre-verbal states of being. In one instance where this has happened, God then tells Ezekiel:

> "Soon fugitives will come and tell you their news by word of mouth. [By being transmitted through the prophet and thus given verbal form, the experience of the exiled parts of the psyche can become the experience of the integrated part of the self.] At once you will recover the power of speech and speak with the fugitives; [the reintegrated parts can now be modified as a result of contact

with the whole part of the self] you will no longer be dumb." [There will be no more need for you to share their pre-verbal state.] [Ezekiel, 24: 26–27]

By naming phenomena, by uttering them, Ezekiel gives them psychic substance and admits them to psychic reality. In Ezekiel's time it seems that the words of a prophet did not only express his awareness of the world, both internal and external, they were also held to perform the creative function of bringing that world into being (Von Rad, 1965). This compares interestingly with Bion's account of the connection between verbal thought and the functions of the ego in connecting the psyche with reality. It is through verbal thought, according to Bion, that the ego acknowledges and gives form to its awareness of the world and to the pain that stems from that awareness (Bion, 1955).

Visions of the superego

The Book of Ezekiel describes an integrative process: the giving of words to part of the psyche split off in the earliest pre-verbal phase of infancy. In order to bring about this integration, the poet must, of necessity, confront the agency responsible for the original schism: the early superego, agent of splitting and disintegration (Klein, 1933). This confrontation is at the heart of the Book of Ezekiel and it is first symbolized (among other very different psychic experiences) in the vision of God with which the text opens. Aspects of this vision may represent the infantile ego's realization of some presence within the psyche that is other than the self and more powerful than the self: the dawning of the superego.

... The heavens were opened and I saw a vision of God ... the word of the Lord came to Ezekiel ... the hand of the Lord came upon him. I saw a storm wind coming from the north ... [Ezekiel, 1: 1–4]

The vision of the cherubim, which precedes the vision of the Godhead itself, seems to symbolize, in part, the multi-faceted nature of the superego, its potential for transforming both its own nature and that of the psyche it inhabits:

In the fire was the semblance of four living creatures in human form. . . . Their faces were like this: all four had the face of a man and the face of a lion on the right, on the left the face of an ox and the face of an eagle. Their wings were spread; each living creature had one pair touching its neighbours', while one pair covered its body. They moved straight forward in whatever direction the spirit would go; they never swerved in their course. The appearance of the creatures was as if fire from burning coals or torches were darting to and fro among them; the fire was radiant, and out of the fire came lightning. [Ezekiel, 1: 5–13]

The association of these creatures with very early states of awareness is suggested by the breast imagery of the passage which follows:

As I looked at the living creatures, I saw wheels on the ground, one beside each of the four. . . . in form and working they were like a wheel inside a wheel . . . All four had hubs and each hub had a projection which had the power of sight, and the rims of the wheels were full of eyes all round. [Ezekiel, 1: 15–18]

The equation of breasts and eyes is familiar from psychoanalytic accounts of infantile phantasy, as is the state of projective identification suggested by the last part of the description (Klein, 1952): ". . . when the creatures rose from the ground, the wheels rose together with them, for the spirit of the creatures was in the wheels" (Ezekiel, 1: 21).

The wheels which accompany the cherubim may also symbolize the integrative principle itself, the infant's experience of the good breast taken in whole, around which the psyche organizes itself (Klein, 1957). The poet's awareness of and contact with this internal integrative breast experience is a vital aspect of his ability to endure and survive his journey through death-filled and split-off parts of his psyche. In the frontispiece to *Jerusalem*, Blake depicts the poet's lantern in the shape of a breast, from which rays of light radiate.

The vision of the cherubim also recreates, both in the passage above and in the version that appears in Ezekiel 10, early states of ecstatic awareness, the reservoir of psychic capacity from which the poet will draw to nourish his mature work of integration: the "young-ey'd cherubins" which Shakespeare (1600) describes, with dazzling compression, in *The Merchant of Venice* (V, 1: 62). This is the sort of sublime infantile experience described by Likierman (1989,

p. 139) as inspiring "awe for a 'good' that is greater than the self, as opposed to the omnipotent 'ideal' which magnifies the self". Likierman goes on to comment that:

> the infantile splitting of the object is not only defensive, but also has the positive function of exposing the infant to a "good" which is unmodified by opposite elements, and whose boundless, "inexhaustible" aspect becomes a measure of its infinite value. [Likierman, 1989: 139–140]

Ultimately, also, the vision of the cherubim suggests the state of modified omnipotence and heightened awareness which the poet hopes to achieve as a result of the integrative process he has in prospect (my interpretation in brackets).

> Under the wings of the cherubim there appeared what seemed a human hand. [In contrast to the "hand of the Lord" at the start of the vision] ... Their whole bodies, their backs and hands and wings, as well as the wheels, were full of eyes ... [Ezekiel, 10: 8–12]

Dante (1321), at the culmination of the Purgatorio, as he is about to attain Paradise, describes similar creatures guarding Beatrice's chariot,

> As star follows on star in the serene
> Of heaven's height, there came on at their backs
> Four beasts and these wore wreaths of living green.
> Each had three pairs of wings and every pair
> Was full of eyes ...
> But read Ezekiel where he sets forth
> How they appeared to him in a great storm
> Of wind and cloud and fire out of the North:
> And such as he recounts, such I did see.
> [Dante, 1321, *Purgatorio*, 29: 91–103]

In the last scene of Shakespeare's *Merchant of Venice* (1600) the association between the ecstatic awareness of the infant at the breast and the heights of developed psychic experience is exquisitely suggested in a passage which, like Dante's, contains a reference to Ezekiel's cherubim,

> ... look how the floor of heaven
> Is thick inlaid with patens of bright gold.

> There's not the smallest orb which thou behold'st
> But in his motion like an angel sings
> Still quiring to the young-ey'd cherubins:
> Such harmony is in immortal souls ...
> [*Merchant of Venice*, V, 1: 58–63]

The central paradox of the Book of Ezekiel, that the most developed psychic states result from contact with, and full inclusion of, some of the earliest, is symbolized by the multi-faceted nature of the cherubim, their four-fold faces in which the human and the animal touch each other. This continuing contact between human and animal conveys the wholeness of the integrative endeavour, its multi-dimensional quality. This is in contrast to the linear model of development in which earlier phases are grown out of and left behind. A psyche structured in such a way cannot draw on its infantile experience of the infinite either to nourish or to transcend itself. The threat posed by the primitive superego to the multi-dimensional way of experiencing the psyche, and the association of that superego with the words by which the self is structured are both conveyed by lines in Henry Vaughan's poem "The Retreat" (1650).

> Before I taught my tongue to wound
> My conscience with a sinful sound
> Or had the black art to dispense
> A several sin to every sense
> But felt through all this fleshly dress
> Bright shoots of everlastingness.
> [Vaughan, 1650, "The Retreat": 15–20]

The acquisition of words in infancy shapes the psyche in conformity to a set of values and a system of definitions imposed from without, and it is this early shaping process which it is the poet's task to re-enact and modify in order to adjust the frontiers of the psyche and expand its horizons. The visionary nature of much of Ezekiel's most psychodynamic experience suggests that his non-verbal thought processes enabled him not only to communicate with pre-verbal parts of his mind, but also to apprehend ways of being which were potentially verbal but for which the words had not yet been developed by the culture he lived in. His vision may also have allowed him to experience psychic realities that are always beyond the capacity of words to contain; experiences that transcend the verbal. Dante links the pre-verbal and that which is beyond words in the preface to his description of God at the end of the *Paradiso*.

> Now in my recollection of the rest
> I have less power to speak than any infant
> wetting its tongue yet at its mother's breast
> [Dante, 1321, *Paradiso*, 33: 106–108]

Ezekiel's prophetic call

The cherubim are the precursors of the vision of God, and it is during this vision that Ezekiel receives his prophetic calling. The vision may in part symbolize the irruption of a new idea of the potential content of the self into the poet's psyche, an experience that is, initially at least, non-verbal, and is inaugurated by the maturest aspect of the superego (the aspect of the cherubim that has the face of a man). The mature superego is aware of its need to redeem those parts of the infantile psyche which were split off by its own primitive aspect, if it is to develop further. It proposes to send the poet as its agent into those parts of the psyche that are under the dominion of the primitive superego, to reintegrate them.

The poet can be sent on this mission because of his peculiar receptivity to both mature and primitive aspects of the superego, as well as to the integrative principle within the psyche.

> [God said] "Open your mouth and eat what I give you." Then I saw a hand stretched out to me, holding a scroll. He unrolled it before me, and it was written all over on both sides with dirges and laments and words of woe. [Ezekiel, 2: 9–10]

> Then he said to me, "Man, eat what is in front of you, eat this scroll; then go and speak to the Israelites". So I opened my mouth and he gave me the scroll to eat. Then he said, "Man, swallow this scroll I give you, and fill yourself full". So I ate it, and it tasted as sweet as honey. [Ezekiel, 3: 1–3]

In this account of Ezekiel's call, God (symbolizing the mature superego at this point in the narrative) instructs Ezekiel to introject and thus vividly experience (perhaps also, at a more mature level, to contain) both the paranoid–schizoid superego and the parts of the psyche it has split off (symbolized respectively by God and the Israelites). He is to do this from within the depressive position (the dirges, laments, and words of woe which the split-off parts call forth and are thus symbolized by) in order to reintegrate the split-off parts with the more mature aspects of the psyche (a process symbolized by the sweet taste of the scroll). The prophet will then be "filled full", i.e., he will be fully integrated and no longer lacking the split-off parts of his psyche.

It is not enough for the poet, the integrative agency, to make contact with these split-off parts of the self: they must first have been acknowledged as death-filled and mourned over, as this passage suggests, if they are not to overwhelm and pollute the psyche as a whole. It is the mourning that makes it safe for the poetic symbol-making capacity to cross the defensive splits between good and bad in order to redeem the bad. By eating the scroll, Ezekiel may also be accepting a symbolic reversal of his maturity: participating in an oral–sadistic destruction of the depressive position (depicted as a scroll on which words of woe are written, underlining its verbal nature) to enable him to re-enter split off areas of his mind.

Modifying the primitive superego

Immediately following the account of his calling, Ezekiel, as instructed, enters into the state of mind of the primitive superego and begins to express this aspect of the Godhead. God's sudden descent into barbarism is a shocking experience for the reader, coming, as it does, so soon after the sublimities of the God of the visions:

> Outside is the sword, inside are pestilence and famine ... If any escape and take to the mountains, like moaning doves, there will I slay them, each for his iniquity, while their hands hang limp and their knees run with urine. [Ezekiel, 7: 15–17]

Passages of oral–sadistic savagery recur throughout the text:

> I will fling you on land, dashing you down on the bare ground. I will let all the birds of the air settle upon you and all the wild beasts

gorge themselves on your flesh. Your flesh I will lay on the mountains, and fill the valleys with the worms that feed on it. I will drench the land with your discharge, drench it with your blood to the very mountain-tops, and the watercourses shall be full of you. When I put out your light I will veil the sky and blacken its stars ...
[Ezekiel, 32: 4–7]

But throughout the text also, Ezekiel draws our attention to changes in the developing superego, by the use of the recurring phrase, "you shall know that I am the Lord". At this early stage in the prophet's contact with God, the superego is death-filled and death-dealing: "with the slain falling about you, you shall know that I am the Lord" (Ezekiel, 6: 7). It also experiences its function solely as that of splitting off and projecting the unacceptable parts of the self:

I will follow them with drawn sword. Then they shall know that I am the Lord, when I disperse them among the nations and scatter them through many lands. [Ezekiel, 12: 14–15]

In the terrible states of mind into which Ezekiel has been sent by the mature superego, he is to experience, powerless and alone, God at his most ruthless and destructive:

... kill without pity [said God]; spare no one. ... Defile the temple ... and fill the courts with dead bodies; then go out into the city and kill." While they did their work, I was left alone; and I threw myself upon my face, crying out, "O Lord God, must thou destroy all the Israelites who are left ...? [Ezekiel, 9: 5–8]

This God is savagely retributive:

I, the Lord, have spoken; the time is coming, I will act. I will not refrain nor pity nor relent; I will judge you for your conduct and for all that you have done. This is the very word of the Lord God. [Ezekiel, 24: 14]

But by the choice of words in which he expresses God's purpose, Ezekiel is able to begin the work of metamorphosis. To say, "I will not refrain nor pity nor relent" is to suggest the possibility of their opposites:

When I set armies in motion against a land, its people choose one of themselves to be a watchman ... he sees the enemy approaching

and blows his trumpet to warn the people . . . Man, I have appointed
you a watchman for the Israelites. You will take messages from me
and carry my warnings to them. [Ezekiel, 33: 1–7]

In this interesting passage, God seems aware that the Israelites
need defending against him, and that this is what Ezekiel has been
doing, though he still needs to experience this in terms of his own
omnipotence. The watchman metaphor links Ezekiel's activities
with the eyes of the cherubim, and may suggest that the primitive
superego has a growing awareness of the purposes of its mature
counterpart. Significantly also, God now sees himself as in
communication with the Israelites (the split-off parts of the psyche),
using the prophet as intermediary. His retributive and projective
function is gradually being modified by the prophetic process:

Man, say to the Israelites, You complain, "We are burdened by our
sins and offences; we are pining away because of them; we despair
of life". So tell them: As I live, says the Lord God, I have no desire
for the death of the wicked. I would rather that a wicked man
should mend his ways and live. Give up your evil ways, give them
up; O Israelites, why should you die? [Ezekiel, 33: 10–11]

In this passage a new association between the primitive superego
and the life instinct is underlined by repeated references to life:

. . . I pitied them too much to destroy them and did not make an end
of them in the wilderness. [Ezekiel, 20: 17]

. . . I swore to them with uplifted hand that I would disperse them
among the nations and scatter them abroad . . . I did more; I
imposed on them statutes that were not good statutes, and laws by
which they could not win life. [Ezekiel, 20: 23–25]

Here, God is becoming able to acknowledge his disintegrative and
death-dealing aspects to some extent, and even to feel compunction
for them. Ezekiel holds this new development in a delicate interplay
with the psyche's continuing need for a disciplining superego to
provide some sense of conscience and right living.

As I live, says the Lord God, I will reign over you with a strong
hand, with arm outstretched and wrath outpoured. I will bring you
out from the peoples and gather you from the lands over which you

> have been scattered by my strong hand ... there will I state my case against you. ... I will pass you under the rod and bring you within the bond of the covenant. [Ezekiel, 20: 33–37]

This last sentence depicts God as a modified superego, in which the balance has shifted from death to life, and a measure of discipline can co-exist with integrating tendencies. In this passage, Ezekiel acknowledges God's case against the Israelites, but this can now be acted on within an integrative context. God can now recognize Ezekiel's role as a link between the superego and the split-off parts of the psyche:

> The word of the Lord came to me: Man, they are your brothers, your brothers and your kinsmen, this whole people of Israel, to whom the men who now live in Jerusalem have said, 'Keep your distance from the Lord ...'. Say therefore, These are the words of the Lord God: I will gather them from among the nations and assemble them from the countries over which I have scattered them, and I will give them the soil of Israel. ... I will give them a different heart and put a new spirit into them; I will take the heart of stone out of their bodies and give them a heart of flesh. ... They will become my people, and I will become their God. [Ezekiel, 11: 14–21]

In the second half of this passage, God demonstrates that he can now identify with the transforming and life-giving nature of the integrative principle.

In a later passage, there is a moving description of the role of this transformed superego and its relation to the poetic part of the psyche:

> Then I will set over them one shepherd to take care of them, my servant David [the poet king]; he shall care for them and become their shepherd, I, the Lord, will become their God, and my servant David shall be a prince among them ... I will rid the land of wild beasts, and men shall live in peace of mind on the open pastures and sleep in the woods. I will settle them in the neighbourhood of my hill and send them rain in due season, blessed rain. ... They shall know that I am the Lord when I break the bars of their yokes, and rescue them from those that have enslaved them. ... They shall know that I, the Lord their God, am with them, and that they are my people Israel, says the Lord God. You are my flock ... the flock I feed, and I am your God. [Ezekiel, 34: 23–31]

In the concluding line, God becomes fully identified with the poet shepherd.

The reintegration of split off parts of the self

The hand of the Lord came upon me, and he carried me out by his spirit and put me down in a plain full of bones. He made me go to and fro across them until I had been round them all; they covered the plain, countless numbers of them, and they were very dry. He said to me, "Man, can these bones live again?" I answered, "Only thou knowest that, Lord God." He said to me, "Prophesy over these bones ...". [Ezekiel, 37: 1–4]

In this famous interchange, the countless dry bones, symbolizing parts of the self that are infinitely split and death-filled, are to be encompassed by the poet as a preliminary to their ultimate containment. He is to experience their great dryness, which suggests their distance from the depressive aspects of the self and the degree to which their emotional content has been denied. Having confronted the poet with the bones and found that he has survived them, God acknowledges, by his question, Ezekiel's insight: "Man, can these bones live again?". The poet's subtle answer, "Only thou knowest that, Lord God", could be understood as disclaiming insight, suggesting that he prefers to respect the superego's omniscience a little longer. The answer also gives due acknowledgment to the fact that, just as God was responsible for the original splitting, so it is ultimately within his power to prevent or promote the work of reintegration. Ezekiel's reply also contains something of the poet's humility when he is confronted with the transcendent aspects of the mature superego, whose qualities are foreshadowed in the nature of God's question.

God's response is to initiate the reintegration of the bones by instructing Ezekiel to prophesy over them. God's instruction implies both a recognition of the role of the superego as gatekeeper, its power over the boundaries of the self, and also a ceding of its omnipotence, an acknowledgement that, in this crucial initial stage, it is Ezekiel who must do the prophesying and not God.

There follows a remarkable account of the process of reintegration itself.

He said to me, "Prophesy over these bones and say to them, O, dry bones, hear the word of the Lord. This is the word of the Lord God to these bones: I will put breath into you and you shall live ... and you shall know that I am the Lord." I began to prophesy as he had bidden me, and as I prophesied there was a rustling sound and the bones fitted themselves together. As I looked, sinews appeared on them, flesh covered them, and they were overlaid with skin, but there was no breath in them. Then he said to me, "Prophesy to the wind, prophesy, man, and say to it, These are the words of the Lord God: Come, O wind, come from every quarter and breathe into these slain, that they may come to life." I began to prophesy as he had bidden me: breath came into them; they came to life and rose to their feet, a mighty host. He said to me, "Man, these bones are the whole people of Israel. They say, 'Our bones are dry, our thread of life is snapped, our web is severed from the loom'. Prophesy, therefore and say to them, These are the words of the Lord God: O my people, I will open your graves and bring you up from them, and restore you to the land of Israel ...". [Ezekiel, 37: 4–13]

By prophesying on behalf of the bones, the poet enables the process of reintegration to begin. The bones fit themselves together: they acquire a linking capacity (the sinews) emotional substance (the flesh) and containing and defining boundaries (the skin) (Bick, 1968). They are thus made ready for the life instinct (the wind) to rush into them, reanimating them and uniting them with the part of the self already held together by the life instinct. The wind may also represent a reversal of the original splitting process; a stream of beta elements, infinitely split and projected (Bion, 1965) rushing together to form a coherent entity again. Having been prophesied on, the bones are now able to use words themselves, to acknowledge and communicate their former predicament, and the superego has become their spokesman rather than their gaoler. "Man, these bones are the whole people of Israel. They say, 'Our bones are dry, our thread of life is snapped, our web is severed from the loom'" (Ezekiel, 37: 11).

The power of prophecy has transformed the split-off parts from dry bones to "the whole people of Israel" in a reunifying process which harnesses the original splitting agency to promote the work of integration. God is not only allowing the bones to live; he is identified with the integrative process.

You shall know that I am the Lord when I open your graves and
bring you up from them, O my people. Then I will put my spirit into
you and you shall live ... [Ezekiel, 37: 13–14]

The destruction of Jerusalem and catastrophic change

So these are the words of the Lord God: In my rage I will unleash a
stormy wind; rain will come in torrents in my anger, hailstones hard
as rock in my fury, until all is destroyed. I will demolish the
building which you have daubed with whitewash and level it to the
ground, so that its foundations are laid bare. It shall fall, and you
shall be destroyed within it; thus you shall know that I am the Lord.
[Ezekiel, 13: 13–14]

One of the central concerns of the Book of Ezekiel is the
destruction of Jerusalem. It is both threatened and described
recurrently throughout the text, until the last eight chapters, which
describe the new holy city, Jehovah-Shammah, that is to replace it. In
the passage quoted above, the building daubed with whitewash is
synonymous with Jerusalem and both symbolize the coherent part of
the psyche at the start of the reintegrative process: it, too, needs to
change if development is to take place. Jerusalem is defined by a
boundary which depends on self-righteousness (the whitewash) and
the splitting and projection of aspects of the self which are unflattering
to the self-image. The wind, the rain, and the hailstones symbolize
parts of Jerusalem itself, infinitely split and projected, returning in a
storm of retaliatory reintrojections (Klein, 1946). The superego's
aggression, formerly channelled into splitting processes, is now
directed at the psychic defences which stand in the way of integration
and development. The destruction of Jerusalem is one of Ezekiel's
metaphors for catastrophic change: the seemingly disastrous
collapse of the existing order which can be the necessary precursor
to its reconstruction at a higher level of development (Bion, 1967).

The transformed superego and the integrated self

In his culminating series of visions, Ezekiel describes the design of a
new holy city, the architecture of a new internal world, and his

account begins with a depiction of the superego standing at the gate of the city, with tape measure and measuring rod in hand, preparing to mark out the dimensions of the new Jerusalem.

> In a vision God brought me to the land of Israel and set me on a very high mountain, where I saw what seemed the buildings of a city facing me. He led me towards it, and I saw a man like a figure of bronze holding a cord of linen thread and a measuring-rod, and standing at the gate. "Man" he said to me, "look closely and listen carefully; mark well all that I show you, for this is why you have been brought here. Tell the Israelites all that you see". [Ezekiel, 40: 2–4]

In this passage, the transformed superego stands at the gate, the point of contact between inner and outer worlds, to give structure to the psyche and define its boundaries according to its acknowledged and pre-existent nature (the measuring) rather than by excluding parts of the self that are unacceptable to the omnipotent self-image. That this city is the result of integrative activity rather than a regressive retreat to an idealized paranoid–schizoid state is suggested by the instructions that Ezekiel is given: "Mark well all that I show you, for this is why you have been brought here. Tell the Israelites all that you see" (Ezekiel, 40: 4).

The new city is not a place where Ezekiel is to stay: he has been brought there so that he can return to the Israelites with an awareness of the psyche's potential for integration; to enable him to integrate them in new ways and at deeper levels. This is suggestive of the oscillation between the paranoid–schizoid and depressive positions in creative personalities (Bion, 1963). At this stage in the creative process, the poet is no longer required to mourn or introject unacceptable parts of the psyche. Instead, he is to "look closely and listen carefully", accepting the guidance of his internal objects. As Blake puts it, "I am but the Secretary—the Authors are in Eternity" (Blake, 1803a).

> Round the outside of the temple ran a wall. ... He measured the thickness and the height of the wall; each was one rod. He came to a gate which faced eastwards, went up its steps and measured the threshold of the gateway; its depth was one rod. [Ezekiel, 40: 5–8]

Ezekiel's lengthy and painstaking description of the superego's measuring activity enacts the transition from its primitive role as a splitting agency to its new function of discrimination: setting limits, defining boundaries, and structuring the spaces of the internal world. In the following passage, Ezekiel makes clear the link between this measuring and the process of integration: the way in which the measuring replaces the splitting. As the superego measures, so it ceases to split, and the poet experiences the rising waters of integration:

> When the man went out eastwards he had a line in his hand. He measured a thousand cubits and made me walk through the water; it came up to my ankles. He measured another thousand and made me walk through the water; it came up to my knees. He measured another thousand and made me walk through the water; it was up to my waist. Another thousand, and it was a torrent I could not cross, for the water had risen and was now deep enough to swim in. ... [Ezekiel, 47: 3–5]

The city that the superego is measuring is also a temple. Within its containing wall there are four gates, places, perhaps, where introjections can be regulated. One of these gates, the "gate which faced eastwards" is a place of ingress for the infinite and the transcendent.

> He led me to the gate, the gate facing eastwards, and I beheld the glory of the God of Israel coming from the east. His voice was like the sound of a mighty torrent, and the earth shone with his glory. The form that I saw was the same as that which I had seen when he came to destroy the city, and as that which I had seen by the river Kebar, and I fell on my face. The glory of the Lord came up to the temple towards the gate which faced eastwards. A spirit lifted me up and brought me into the inner court, and the glory of the Lord filled the temple. Then I heard one speaking to me from the temple, and the man was standing at my side. He said, Man, do you see the place of my throne, the place where I set my feet, where I will dwell among the Israelites for ever? [Ezekiel, 43: 1–7]

In this vision, Ezekiel senses something of the ultimate nature of the superego: a nature which contains both a mature capacity for transcendence and a full acknowledgement of the primitive aspects of the psyche on which that capacity depends: "The form that I saw was the same as that which I had seen when he came to destroy the city ..." (Ezekiel, 43: 3).

Ezekiel's description of the superego makes the connection between the waters of integration and the giving of words to split-off parts of the psyche, "His voice was like the sound of a mighty torrent". It also identifies the God of Israel whose glory fills the temple with the man standing at Ezekiel's side (an identification Blake refers to as the "Divine Human"), in contrast to God in his primitive aspect, full of projected infantile omnipotence and dependent on splitting to preserve his idealized goodness.

> God Appears and God is Light
> To those poor souls who dwell in Night,
> But does a Human Form Display
> To those who Dwell in Realms of day
> [Blake, 1803b]

> He brought me back to the gate of the temple, and I saw a spring of water issuing from under the terrace of the temple towards the east; for the temple faced east. ... He said to me, "This water flows out to the region lying east, and down to the Arabah; at last it will reach that sea whose waters are foul, and they will be sweetened. When any one of the living creatures that swarm upon the earth comes where the torrent flows, it shall draw life from it. The fish shall be innumerable; for these waters come here so that the others may be sweetened, and where the torrent flows everything shall live".
> [Ezekiel, 47: 1–10]

The springs of integration, that are able to sweeten even the Dead Sea, issue from beneath the eastern side of the temple, suggesting that the good breast (the original integrative principle, provider of springs of milk) and the primitive superego (the God of Israel) no longer function as hostile principles in separate regions of the psyche, but can interact creatively within a coherent whole. "The perimeter of the city shall be eighteen thousand cubits, and the city's name for ever after shall be Jehovah-shammah" [That is, "The Lord is there".] (Ezekiel, 48: 35).

The integrative principle has itself been transformed by contact with all aspects of the superego. It is no longer experienced in a split way, as the idealized provider of milk to nourish and hold together the coherent part of the psyche (Klein, 1946). The waters of the spring beneath the eastern side of the city flow through a creative internal space which is acknowledged to contain mother's babies and father's penis. "The fish shall be innumerable". The waters are developmental, not regressive in nature: "These waters come here so that the others may be sweetened, and where the torrent flows everything shall live" (Ezekiel, 47: 10). Blake describes similar waters in the last book of Jerusalem:

> And every Man stood Fourfold; each Four Faces had ...
> And the dim Chaos brightend beneath, above, around!
>   Eyed as the Peacock
> According to the Human Nerves of Sensation, the Four Rivers
>   of the Water of Life.
> [Blake, 1820, 98: 12–15]

In this passage, Blake creates a new symbol by combining Ezekiel's description of the water of life (Ezekiel, 47: 1–10) with his account of the cherubim, "their whole bodies, their backs and hands and wings, as well as the wheels, were full of eyes" (Ezekiel, 10: 12). Blake's fourfold rivers of insight, "eyed as the peacock", symbolize the heights of integrative awareness resulting from the coming together of the good breast and the developed superego. These are the "crystal springs whose taste illuminates" described by Marlowe's Tamburlaine, whose waters, tempered by experience, "like tried silver run through Paradise" (Marlowe, 1590, 2, II, IV: 20).

Conclusion

When the Book of Ezekiel is considered both in the light of subsequent poetic experience and from the standpoint of Kleinian psychoanalytic theory, it becomes possible to understand its repellent and psychotic aspects as part of an integrative process. The act of reading Ezekiel enables us to experience something of the terrors and wonders of this process within our own minds. His book may, in part, have lasted down the centuries because it speaks to the schizoid elements in most of us, and charts a route through madness into a profounder sanity.

References

Arlow, J. (1951). The consecration of the prophet. *Psychoanalytic Quarterly*, 20: 374–397.

Bick, E. (1968). The experience of the skin in early object relations. *International Journal of Psycho-analysis, 49*: 484–486.

Bion, W. (1955). Language and the schizophrenic. In: M. Klein, P. Heimann & R. Money-Kyrle (Eds.), *New Directions in Psychoanalysis* (pp. 220–239). London: Tavistock.

Bion, W. (1963). *Elements of Psychoanalysis*. London: Heinemann.

Bion, W. (1965). *Second Thoughts*. London: Heinemann.

Bion, W. (1967). Catastrophic change. Unpublished paper.

Blake, W. [1785]. Introduction to "The Bard". Cited in Raine, K. (1970) *William Blake*. London: Thames and Hudson.

Blake, W. (1975) [1790]. *The Marriage of Heaven and Hell*, G. Keynes (Ed.). London: Trianon Press.

Blake, W. (1803a). Letter to T. Butts 6 July. Cited in Gilchrist, A. *Life of William Blake*. London: Dent, 1942.

Blake, W. (1971) [1803b]. Auguries of innocence. In: W. Stevenson (Ed.), *Complete Poems*. London: Longman.

Blake, W. (1820). *Jerusalem*. In: M. Paley (Ed.). London: Blake Tmst/Tate Gallery, 1993.

Dante, A. (1321). *The Divine Comedy*, J. Ciardi (Trans.). New York: Mentor, 1964.

Eichrodt, W. (1970). *Ezekiel*. London: SCM Press.

Klein, M. (1975) [1933]. The early development of conscience in the child. In: *Love, Guilt and Reparation* (pp. 248–257). London: Hogarth.

Klein, M. (1935). A contribution to the psychogenesis of manic-depressive states. *International Journal of Psycho-Analysis, 16*: 145–174.

Klein, M. (1946). Notes on some schizoid mechanisms. *International Journal of Psycho-Analysis, 27*: 99–110.

Klein, M. (1952). Some theoretical conclusions regarding the emotional life of the infant. In: M. Klein, P. Heimann, S. Isaacs & J. Riviere (Eds), *Developments in Psychoanalysis* (pp. 198–236). London: Hogarth.

Klein, M. (1957). *Envy and Gratitude*. London: Tavistock.

Kris, E. (1939). On inspiration. *International Journal of Psycho-Analysis, 20*: 377–389.

Likierman, M. (1989). Clinical significance of aesthetic experience. *International Review of Psychoanalysis, 16*: 133–150.

Marlowe, C. (1590). *Tamburlaine the Great, Part 2*.

New English Bible, The (1970). The Book of the Prophet Ezekiel, pp. 1005–1068. Oxford: Oxford University Press.

Shakespeare, W. (1690). *The Merchant of Venice*.

Strachey, J. (1930). Some unconscious factors in reading. *International Journal of Psycho-Analysis, 11*: 322–331.

Vaughan, H. (1650). The retreat. In: A. Rudrum (Ed.), *Henry Vaughan: The Complete Poems*. London: Penguin.

Von Rad, J. (1965). *Old Testament Theology*. Edinburgh: Oliver and Boyd.

CHAPTER FIVE

"Time will come and take my love away": love and loss in three of Shakespeare's sonnets

Kate Barrows

T he lasting strength of love lies in its capacity to endure
separation and loss. From the infant's ability to tolerate the
absence of the mother to the adult's capacity to bear being
left by, or losing, a partner, child, or parent, love and separation are
intrinsically linked. None has shown us this connection more
memorably than Shakespeare in his sonnets. These poems evoke
some of the deepest emotions that are aroused by the absence of the
loved person, and demonstrate how our experiences of loss and
separation inform our perceptions of the world and of nature,
history, and humanity.

In the following pages I hope to show not only how psychoanalytic thinking informs my appreciation of these sonnets, but also
how the sonnets themselves have enriched my work. An essential
part of the analyst's contribution in the clinical setting is his or her
associations to the patient's material, and while these are not usually
explicitly shared, they nonetheless inform his or her response to the
patient. Inevitably, some of these associations are cultural. For
instance, a poem or a musical theme that has been evoked by the
patient's communications will come to mind and, if thoughtfully
considered along with the other information available in the session,

it can help to clarify and deepen the experience and assist in the process of understanding what the patient brings.

I will be looking at some parallels between three of Shakespeare's sonnets and some developments that took place during the course of an analysis, where difficulties in being able to love and let go were paramount. My understanding of the sonnets, as of my patient, has been profoundly influenced by the writings of Freud and Klein, and I shall start with a brief introduction to some central concepts that are relevant to my theme.

In "Mourning and melancholia", Freud (1917) described some of the vicissitudes of dealing with loss. He suggested that unconscious aggression towards the object can lead to it being internalized in a damaged form, rather than being relinquished: "Thus the shadow of the object fell upon the ego" (p. 249). This emphasis on the fate of the object within the ego paved the way for Klein's work on mourning, which she saw as a cornerstone of human development. She viewed the ability to accept the absence of the person on whom we depend as fundamental to the capacity to establish a separate identity and a mind of one's own, and she suggested that this begins with the infant's relationship to the breast and mother. She described how phantasied attacks upon the absent person or their functions can lead to a ruined internal world, and how love, remorse, and compassion can be crucial in terms of putting this damage to rights and restoring a state of inner harmony and acceptance of reality. Love for the other, as she describes it, entails having the courage to face up to the effects of ambivalence about their independent existence. The idea of the centrality of the conflict between love and hatred was explored by both Freud and Klein more fully than I can do justice to here, and has led to many important developments in psychoanalytic thought.

However, the ideas outlined above also bring us to the territory of Shakespeare's sonnets, to his expression of the turmoil entailed in letting his loved one go and the fear of being destroyed by the experience. He demonstrates with consummate skill how his feelings of love, anger, and loss colour his view of the world around him, and how the world itself then comes to represent the conflict in his mind between his wish to possess and his recognition of the need to relinquish the object of his love. Shakespeare uses the sonnet form in a new way, breaking the conventions of the poetry of praise and the representation of idealized love, instead making the sonnet a vehicle for more ambivalent and intensely personal emotions (see Fineman, 1986). The freshness and immediacy of these sonnets bears witness to the ubiquity of the emotions which they express.

The first sonnets that I would like to consider form a pair, numbers 64 and 65. In these two poems loss and the effects of time are experienced as tragedies.

Sonnet 64

When I have seen by time's fell hand defaced
The rich proud cost of outworn buried age,
When sometime lofty towers I see down razed,
And brass eternal slave to mortal rage,
When I have seen the hungry ocean gain
Advantage on the kingdom of the shore,
And the firm soil win of the watery main,
Increasing store with loss, and loss with store,
When I have seen such interchange of state,
Or state itself confounded to decay,
Ruin hath taught me thus to ruminate,
That time will come and take my love away.
   This thought is as a death, which cannot choose
   But weep to have that which it fears to lose.

Shakespeare's imagery in this sonnet invokes many layers of meaning, from the all-inclusive "state itself" (with "state" implying "matter" as well as states and kingdoms) to the intimacy of the relationship with the beloved. He sees the "fell hand" of Time as furiously defacing and destroying man's inheritance from past generations, recognizing that the despoilment of what we have received from our parents and ancestors—"outworn buried age"— can undermine our own sense of security or permanence. Shakespeare wrote within the historical context of the recent desecration of the monasteries by Henry VIII, as well as the ever-present possibility of war. The imagery suggests both cultural and military endeavours as well as personal and intimate emotions. The sexual symbolism of the "lofty towers down razed" and the "rage" (an Elizabethan term for lust as well as anger) implies anger at the sexuality of the parental generation. So it is as though Time, or the poet, rails against the cultural and sexual productivity of our forebears. Perhaps the "fell hand" is also that of the writer, whose creation of something new despoils the old, familiar conventions.

In addition to this, Shakespeare was expressing the fear that violent passions—rage, hunger, desire—can destroy both the object of love and the capacity for love. The anthropomorphism of Time renders it terrifying, for while we are helpless in the face of it, it also seems a part of us. Its hand, its hunger, its destructiveness are equated with humanity's, so that reflecting on the effects of time is bound up with reflecting upon our own destructiveness.

The lines, "When I have seen the hungry ocean gain / Advantage on the kingdom of the shore", combine human imagery—hunger—with nature on a vast scale and the notion of a kingdom to be devoured. The military metaphor suggests an endless enmity which might take its force from the generational rivalry of the opening lines. In the second quatrain the battle is equal and is symbolized with a syntactical symmetry—"increasing store with loss and loss with store"—but in the last quatrain we are taken to another level, "state itself confounded to decay". By this time, with the rumination over ruination, the feeling is of internal as well as external destruction and loss. This movement from seeing things externally—"When I have seen"—to ruminating on them and feeling them internally draws the reader into proximity to the poet as the language comes closer to home. By the end of the poem the reader feels the possibility of internal devastation, through the loss of the loved person and of his own capacity to love. He also fears death and abandonment. The feared inability to survive the loss of the object is due to the state of inner catastrophe with which the reader now identifies: the resources that might have sustained him have been undermined and eroded; in particular the solace of nature or of cultural achievements. He comes to feel that the world outside as described in the sonnet also represents the inner world, that there is no possibility of drawing a saving boundary between the two. The ambiguity of "my love" derives from this movement inwards, so that the loss that is feared is both that of the absent person and of the poet's (and the reader's) capacity to love.

The relationship between the way in which we see the world and our inner states of mind is of course the subject of psychoanalysis as well as poetry; perhaps the common element is a containing context for the expression of vital human experiences. While psychoanalysis is not always poetic, nevertheless a central feature is the search for words to express the emotions and the workings of the mind. I shall go on to describe a patient who brought Shakespeare's lines strikingly to my thoughts, and whose expression of her experience of love and loss developed in a way that seems to me to parallel the developments in these sonnets. The first session that I shall describe contains elements similar to those in Sonnet 64.

Clinical material

Mrs Z came to analysis suffering from panic attacks and had defined herself for many years as a hard person who prided herself on her detachment and negativity. This negativity soon extended towards her analyst and to analysis *per se*, and it became gradually clear that she was attacking anything or anyone on whom she might depend. When she did become dependent on people she would become extremely possessive and distraught about being left. She went to great lengths to avoid feeling dependent on me. As soon as she made some gains in the analysis, they would be undone, as though it was unbearable to be aware of taking in anything valuable. She attacked her parents, friendships, and culture at large, and found herself, therefore, unable to pursue anything with interest or enthusiasm. She felt that there was no point in anything. However, during a few years of analysis her symptoms improved, and she became generally happier and more resourceful. As she became aware that she was undermining her own inner resources as well as what the world and analysis had to offer her, the atmosphere gradually softened.

Session

Mrs Z had come to the session distraught because a family friend was dying of leukaemia. She described this friend as a good and caring man, who had grown up in poverty but had made the most of his opportunities and had a real and generous commitment to change. She also liked his wife, who was lively and optimistic despite her challenging work with deprived women. When I pointed out how much she liked and respected this man and his wife she agreed, and said that it didn't seem fair for someone like him to die. She went on to talk about not having suffered any immediate losses in her life, and how she felt that she wouldn't be able to bear it if she did.

She then gradually returned to her more usual way of talking, shifting the topic to people who die from self-destruction, from alcoholism. As she talked, her voice became monotonous and repetitive, like that of an alcoholic, and she was scornful. I suggested that she seemed to be killing off her capacity for respect and liking of someone's good qualities but that perhaps she had been feeling that, like her friend and his wife, I was committed to change and managed to remain optimistic, even when working with her feelings of deprivation. She seemed afraid to risk holding on to her appreciative feelings and the fear of a loss that she might not be able to bear. She agreed that this did happen, and that she wanted to be able to do her analysis all by herself. She said that she didn't want to need me, because she would then want the analysis to go on forever and she might not be able to live without it.

After this session, the final couplet of Sonnet 64 came to my mind: "This thought is as a death which cannot choose / But weep, to have that which it fears to lose". It was poignantly clear how much a fear of loss underlay Mrs Z's general negativity. The loss that she feared seemed partly due to a history involving early separations and she was also afraid that her negativity could damage people or drive them away.

The content of this session had much in common with Sonnet 64. There was initial recognition of people and values that Mrs Z respected and felt drawn towards, and of the fact that her friends had made the most of their lives. The man who had grown up in poverty had managed to use his background to develop personal qualities of integrity and commitment that she appreciated: these were the riches which he took from his past. She was, unusually for her, able to see the importance of personal qualities and the background from which they emerged—"outworn buried age". However, in her monotonous talk of alcoholism there was a feeling of "state itself confounded to decay": some insight achieved, only to be worn away with maudlin ruminations. My pointing out that the patient was eroding the very qualities which she valued led to her becoming aware of the fear that so much of her destructive behaviour defended against: if she allowed herself to value what she was given, she felt that she would not be able to live without it. At this point her difficulty in maintaining positive feelings during absence was such that she felt that she would be utterly bereft by loss. However, she did gradually become more able to maintain positive feelings during separations, and to cope with losses. An account of a later session will illustrate some of these developments, but for now I would like to return to Shakespeare, and the development of the themes of love and loss, life and death, in Sonnet 65.

Sonnet 65

Since brass, nor stone, nor earth, nor boundless sea,
But sad mortality o'ersways their power,
How with this rage shall beauty hold a plea,
Whose action is no stronger than a flower?
O how shall summer's honey breath hold out
Against the wrackful siege of batt'ring days,
When rocks impregnable are not so stout,
Nor gates of steel so strong but time decays?
O fearful meditation; where, alack,
Shall time's best jewel from time's chest lie hid?
Or what strong hand can hold his swift foot back?
Or who his spoil or beauty can forbid?
   O none, unless this miracle have might
   That in black ink my love may still shine bright.

Sonnet 64 ends with a sudden revelation of the fear of intolerable loss. This seems to lead, in Sonnet 65, to an awareness of feelings of a different order from the brass, stone, rocks, and endless sea which refer back to the previous sonnet. In Sonnet 65 the qualities which have found their way to the poet's awareness include the fleeting if luxuriant beauty of "summer's honey breath", and the poignant fragility of the flower. We imagine beauty, intimacy, vitality, and inspiration. The fact that these images are transient also suggests a benign aspect of time: some of our most precious experiences only occur in the context of the passing of time. Their value is intrinsically linked to their place in time.

However, the poetry gathers momentum as the fear of time as

the relentless pursuer builds up through a crescendo of panic. Opposing images—the flower and summer's honey breath in contrast to "the wrackful siege of battering days"—convey the desperate imbalance of implacable destruction and transient beauty. There is a hint of rape and pillage, and the impregnable rocks subject to decay suggest that there is nowhere on earth, nowhere in the mind, which can escape the forces of decay and destruction. Instead of a pregnancy, the potential birth of a new thought or feeling, there is devastation, which in this sonnet can only be overcome by a somewhat brittle ending, the tension between "black" and "bright" still unresolved, only to be saved by a "miracle". Mahood, however, suggests that the apparently transient qualities under siege do in fact have a different kind of strength.

> There is a sense in which both flowers and summer are stronger than rocks, because they are endlessly renewed while rocks are continually eroded away; and with this in mind, we can read both lines three to four and lines five to eight as exclamations, rather than as rhetorical questions compelling a negative answer. [1957, p. 105]

The legal metaphor of beauty's plea and action has a power—the power of thought and argument—that belies the flower's evident frailty. As Mahood points out, this begins to prepare us for the final couplet, which invokes the enduring quality of poetry.

Nevertheless, the tensions in the poem seem to remain unresolved. There is great power conveyed in the monosyllables of the final line, but there may also be a sense of desperation or of defiance in the face of the fact that in "black ink", after all, it may not be fully possible to recapture the illuminated brightness of a love which has been so relentlessly under siege. The black ink and the bright shine of love seem brittle and lacking in depth, compared to the diversity and passionate intensity of the rest of the sonnet.

There is a fine balance in these two sonnets between opposing qualities: hard and vulnerable, black and bright, fleeting and timeless, and implicitly between the poet's (and hence the reader's) capacity to love and his fury towards the absent object. This ambivalence is expressed in several ways, for instance in the ruminations of Sonnet 64 and in the ambiguous "Time's chest" in Sonnet 65. This has the meaning of "coffer" or "jewel casket" as well as of "coffin" (see Booth, 1977, p. 247) and as such "it raises the question of whether the poem figures as revivifying space, a birth chamber perhaps, from which new treasures can come out to seek the light; or whether the poem is a mausoleum, a consoling space where we can come to visit the tomb of love" (Punter, personal communication). What is revealed in these ambiguities and oscillations is that the new is fragile, that it may not survive the further onslaughts of internal and external worlds.

Issues of harshness and vulnerability, ambivalence and loss, were fundamental in the analysis of the patient whom I described earlier. In a session a few months after the one already discussed, Mrs Z developed the theme of how to manage separations without losing her appreciation of the important people in her life and the treasured contents of her own mind. This session reminded me of the themes and of some of the imagery in Sonnet 65.

Session

Mrs Z started by telling me that she was thinking about her daughter, who was going abroad and was anxious about the journey, travelling on her own. She described in some detail the long journey and the anxiety about managing it. She talked about how her daughter wasn't used to carrying her own equipment—it was hard to know how she would manage.

I said that Mrs Z, like her daughter, wasn't used to thinking in terms of the equipment that she needed to be able to take inside herself, to enable herself to deal with separations. After some discussion about how she managed the gaps between the sessions (and between other things too) by trying not to be aware of them, she said that she was thinking about her jewellery box, she didn't know why. She described some of the things in it in detail, for instance a brooch given to her by a grandmother she had been fond of, a souvenir from the days when she and her husband were courting, other things which she treasured because of the people who had given them to her, and the little plastic name-bracelets which her son and daughter had worn in hospital when they were born. She had thought of giving these to her son and daughter, but decided not to as they wouldn't look after them. She said in a harsh voice that they would find them in amongst her clutter after she died. Then her voice softened again as she said that it was hard to remember that her children had once been so little!

This account was moving and the cherished contents of the box were described in a way that brought them to life, as well as the individual personalities who had given them to her. I said that these were also her memories of the people she was fond of and the things that they had given her. I wondered whether she found it hard to remember how small she had felt when she started her analysis, and to treasure what it had given her, to think in terms of that also being what she wanted to look after inside herself.

She said that she felt that she did want to, though she didn't often allow herself to think about it. She also thought, painfully, of some ear-rings which she had been given by a former partner who had deserted her, and remembered that he had actually given her the jewellery box. That made her feel like chucking it out, but she wouldn't because by now it was part of her.

I suggested that she seemed to be feeling that she could keep something good even despite her painful memories and anger and despite the fact that even now she didn't like being left to manage on her own. After a silence, she said that she found it hard to talk of the good things that have survived. She usually kept those feelings hidden.

Discussion

The similarity between Mrs Z's jewellery box and "time's chest" is striking. Its contents are cherished for their human connections. In so far as it is possible, they capture in their individuality the ephemeral, represented in Shakespeare's sonnet by the flower and "summer's honey breath". Yet in the angry reference to her children going through her box after her death, it becomes for a moment a coffin, whose treasures will not have the same life for her inheritors as they do for her—her personal memories. But she recovers her good feelings through remembering her children as babies, and thinking about how much they have developed, even if they still have difficulties in looking after things. In containing her anger, she seems also to be demonstrating her own development from the extremely fragile and small person that she had been at the start of her analysis, at the mercy of enormous anger and panic that she was unable to control. Now she could experience anger without necessarily being thrown off balance and could continue to think and to value the contents of her mind. She could begin to be aware of her own difficulties in looking after what she has taken in, without destroying her own attempts with scorn.

Mrs Z's tendency to keep her appreciative feelings hidden also puts me in mind of Shakespeare's question: "where, alack / Shall time's best jewel from time's chest lie hid?" However she now seemed to be moving beyond the desperation that she had been prone to feel and which is a driving force in Sonnets 64 and 65. She was no longer hiding the treasured contents of her mind, but was sharing them and how much they meant to her. They no longer seemed to be under such threat. She was able to contemplate their meaning to her in a perceptive and thoughtful way, and to think of them with tenderness.

This leads me to the last sonnet that I would like to consider, where the poet's relationship to love and death is less anguished, and he seems to approach death with relative equanimity. We might speculate upon whether it took time and some of the intervening sonnets for him to work through the feelings which seem unresolved or almost unbearable in the two earlier sonnets discussed above. (Though there is notorious disagreement as to the order of the sonnets, it seems undisputed that 73 was written some time later than 64 and 65, which occur as a pair.) However, there is not time here to trace the evolution of Shakespeare's ideas through the possible intervening sonnets, so I shall focus on Sonnet 73.

Sonnet 73

That time of year thou mayst in me behold,
When yellow leaves, or none, or few, do hang
Upon those boughs which shake against the cold,
Bare ruined choirs, where late the sweet birds sang.
In me thou seest the twilight of such day
As after sunset fadeth in the west,
Which by and by black night doth take away,
Death's second self, that seals up all in rest.
In me thou seest the glowing of such fire,
That on the ashes of his youth doth lie
As the death-bed whereon it must expire,
Consumed with that which it was nourished by.
  This thou perceiv'st, which makes thy love more strong,
  To love that well which thou must leave ere long.

The mood here is one of acceptance. While there is pain and loss, there is also beauty and a sense of growth, of love which can grow "more strong" through acceptance of separation and death. The reader is invited to think about the poet, and to see that the external scenes described represent his state of mind. So the reader is in the position of *thinking about* the poet rather than being unwittingly drawn in to identify with him. This tells us that the writer can let his reader, as well as his loved one, go; and that we must let him go— quite another state of mind from the feelings of unbearable loss and desperation in Sonnets 64 and 65.

The invitation "thou mayst in me behold" immediately strikes a different note from the sadness of "When I have seen" (64), and the scene is one of fullness and beauty as well as of depletion and ruin. The verb "mayst" suggests that the poet can bear to be seen, and that he can bear to see himself, and "behold" brings an element of joy and wonder which belies the apparent bleakness of the description. The evocation of winter suggests a natural season of life rather than the violent tragedy of the two sonnets discussed above. While there is an immeasurable sadness in the notion of bare ruined choirs there is also beauty in the memory of "where late the sweet birds sang".

The imagery in this quatrain is ambiguous and evocative, the branches of the trees suggesting arms, the choirs suggesting pews, perhaps in ruined monasteries. The atmosphere is thoughtful, rather than tragic or panic-stricken, open to future development rather than condemned to closure. The reference to the ruination of the monasteries suggests sadness and regret, in contrast to the "mortal rage" of Sonnet 64. We are seeing the past in a different way. The poet, writing as if an old man, accepts his death with relative equanimity, despite the third quatrain and the implications of being a fire "consumed with that which it was nourished by". Though the passions of youth still consume him, he seems to be relinquishing them and their object, and accepting his stage of life and his state of mind. This self-awareness is linked to the writer's ability to use his insight, and hence to invoke the same capacity in his reader: the reader is told: "This thou perceiv'st, which makes thy love more strong". It is not just the impending leave-taking which makes the reader's love more strong, but the fact of being able to be perceptive: this increases the capacity to love, as well as perhaps making the loved person ("thy love") feel stronger.

In this sonnet, the emphasis of "love" is on the reader's capacity to love, with the object of love as the secondary meaning. In Sonnet 64 the emphasis was on the external "time will come and take my love away", with the internal, the capacity to love, as the implied secondary meaning. Shakespeare has moved to a state of inner perceptiveness and acceptance of his feelings and the passing of time that enable him, and the reader, to love and let go. Sonnet 73 contains some elements of the earlier sonnets, though in a more reflective form. The starkness of the "black ink", for instance, has been replaced by a softer version of darkness: "which by and by black night doth take away". Both the urgency of time and the terror of death and loss have given way to acceptance, but the embers of earlier passions and their attendant fears are still glowing.

"Thou mayst in me behold" leads me back to Mrs Z allowing me to contemplate the contents of her jewellery box, the part of her mind where she kept her treasures and her good memories. This reviewing of the mementos of the past is akin to Shakespeare's images which recall the past—the "bare ruined choirs" and the memory of the birds singing, for instance. Treasures in the mind and in the memory offer consolation for the loss or absence of cherished objects or people and make it more possible to let go. There is also tenderness towards the loved person, who is being prepared for the poet's death. This capacity for concern is an aspect of love which leads to keeping memories or good feelings alive rather than killing them off with rage, or feeling destroyed by loss.

In Shakespeare's day, the likelihood was that death (through illness) could come at any time, and comparatively early in life, so the question of being prepared for it must have been ever present. Perhaps, though, there is also an element in this sonnet of withdrawal: it may be easier to separate through contemplating death than through having to live and let live. In our day and our society, however, we may be more likely to try to ignore the inevitabilities of age and death. This was the case with Mrs Z.

For a long time in her analysis she avoided thoughts of ageing or death, declaring that she could not face the thought of getting old, of dying, or of anyone close to her dying. She lied about her age and tried to ignore her own birthdays. As she came to accept her own ambivalent feelings and fears of loss rather than repudiating them or feeling that they necessarily ruined everything, she also became more able to accept feelings about death and ageing. An aunt who was close to her died and she was surprised to find that she survived feeling upset about the loss, and that being able to mourn actually strengthened her awareness of her positive feelings.

Session

Before an analytic holiday, Mrs Z said that she was not used to being without her aunt's regular phone calls. I wondered whether she felt that the coming holiday, without the regular sessions, was like a death and she replied that she had forgotten when I was coming back—it seemed so long that it was like forever. I suggested that this was due to her killing me off for going away, and killing off her knowledge of my return. A little later on, Mrs Z said that she was thinking about being hard, and about how it ran in her family: her mother hated her grandmother for being harsh, her mother was harsh herself and so was Mrs Z, though each one slightly less so. She wondered how many generations it took for something like that to change, how much was due to genes, how much to the way we are brought up.

I wondered whether Mrs Z might also be thinking about how much analysis would be needed to change such a pattern, and she agreed that she was. I went on to say that she might be afraid of being aware of her positive feelings, of not being harsh, and that the harshness served as a protection.

She said that she was still afraid of rejection and loss. She said, very unusually for her, that she would miss her analysis during the holiday. She then added half-jokingly that her husband says that she is the most negative person he's ever met. From the way in which she spoke it sounded as though her husband had said this in an affectionate and understanding kind of way. I pointed out that this couldn't be all that there was to it, and wondered if she hoped that I could see past her negativity and accept her positive feelings.

Mrs Z replied that feeling cared for made her afraid of loss, and that she didn't want to end here, thinking of loss. I wondered whether thinking of what she would be missing felt like loss or death, as if she wouldn't be able to keep it alive inside her during my absence.

She then noticed the noise of people up above and said that it sounded as though there were elephants upstairs. She remembered being in her room in the night as a child and noises sounding very loud, particularly the noise of her parents talking together. I wondered aloud whether the noises she heard might have been not just of her parents talking but also of their intercourse, and she replied that she could not actually remember, but it felt as though that was what it was about. After a silence she said reflectively that she felt that her parents' relationship was so exclusive that there wasn't a lot of room for her and her sisters.

I suggested that she might be feeling now as though the holiday felt like my being part of an exclusive couple, with no room for her feelings, either her positive feelings or her feelings of anger or rejection. She was afraid of not being remembered. Mrs Z ended by saying thoughtfully that she could see that if she could bear to miss her analysis, she would be able to keep it in her mind.

Discussion

In this session the patient is able to perceive her own feelings, and be aware of how she can still make herself hard (like rocks, brass, or stone) to protect herself against loss or the effects of her negative feelings. But she is also aware of feeling different, of the prospect of missing her analysis and wanting to be able to keep it in her mind. Her perceptiveness about herself, as well as about her parents, makes it more possible for her to leave before the analytic break and to begin to think about leaving her analysis. Her perceptiveness about the analyst may have expressed itself in her thoughts about the noise of elephants—she may well have felt that the analyst was making too much "noise" about the impending holiday and forcing it upon her attention when she would rather not be aware of the break. She made the connection between missing the analysis and being able to retain it in her mind, and her having this insight at the end of the session felt somewhat like the couplet at the end of a sonnet, a breakthrough which leads forward into the unknown. "This thou perceiv'st, which makes thy love more strong / To love that well which thou must leave ere long".

The final couplet in a sonnet can represent a moment of new

understanding, a sudden opening on to an unexpected landscape. These landscapes are as various as the sonnets and the poets who wrote them. There can be similar moments in psychoanalysis, perhaps as varied as patients and their analysts. Mrs Z's realizations at the end of two of the sessions that I have described opened new possibilities of emotional experience. The fact that these realizations remind me of the final couplets of two of Shakespeare's sonnets is not just because of the content that they have in common. The similarity also lies in the quality of revelation—the emergence of the previously unknown. These final moments of understanding emerge out of the emotional work of the sonnet or of the session and suggest that arising from an ending there can also be a future.

In the final couplets of the three sonnets considered above, there is a sad vista: "... weeps to have that which it fears to lose"; there is a hoped-for miracle of consolation in the enduring quality of poetry that can "... still shine bright"; and there is an ending that implies resolution—"... which makes thy love more strong / To love that well which thou must leave ere long".

It would be misleading to imply that in poetry, psychoanalysis, or the rest of life there is some higher state of permanent acceptance of loss. The earlier sonnets, with their violent desperation and fear of loss, speak to us as powerfully as Sonnet 73, but in different ways. They express states of mind that we revisit when we fear or suffer loss and experience anew the emotions which it arouses. The development between the sonnets is similar to the evolution of feelings in an analysis—the earlier feelings are still there to be re-evoked, though insight and experience may lead to them having less power to destroy the capacity to love and the object of that love within the mind.

Acknowledgement

I am grateful to David Punter, Professor of English Literature at Bristol University, for some illuminating discussions about these sonnets.

References

Booth, S. (1977). *Shakespeare's Sonnets*. New Haven and London: Yale University Press.

Fineman, J. (1986). *Shakespeare's Perjured Eye*. London: University of California Press.

Freud, S. (1917). Mourning and melancholia. *S.E.*, *14*. London: The Hogarth Press and The Institute of Psycho-Analysis.

Klein, M. (1940). Mourning and its relation to manic-depressive states. In: *Love, Guilt and Reparation and Other Works, 1921–1945* (pp. 344–369). London: The Hogarth Press and The Institute of Psycho-Analysis.

Mahood, M. M. (1957). The sonnets. In: *Shakespeare's Wordplay* (p. 105). London: Methuen.

CHAPTER SIX

The preacher, the poet, and the psychoanalyst

Ronald Britton

T he preacher, the poet, and the psychoanalyst are all concerned with mental or spiritual reality, that is with psychic reality, which I regard as the individual's conscious and unconscious beliefs. However, the preacher, poet, and psychoanalyst can be distinguished from one another by their different approaches to belief. The preacher expounds what he considers it necessary to believe; the poet seeks to discover and communicate his own beliefs; and the psychoanalyst aims to discover and explore the beliefs of his patients. In practice, the psychoanalyst might be tempted to become the preacher, trying to convert his patient, or to be the poet, exploring his own psychic reality by attributing it to his patient. But when doing either of these things he has forfeited his role of analyst.

Milton and Blake, the two poets with whom I am concerned in this chapter, were both given to preaching. I am going to suggest that they both urged one belief system when they were preaching and revealed another when functioning poetically. The religious belief systems that they preached were different, but both were the counterpart to what, in modern psychoanalytic terms, we call defensive organizations, built on counter-belief systems; that is, belief systems erected to counter an already existing underlying belief of a catastrophic kind. I suggest that Milton, as a preacher, produced a theological counterpart to Rosenfeld's (1971) description of destructive narcissism, but as a poet he revealed his fear of a theological nightmare that resembles the inner world of the melancholic. Blake as preacher puts forward a belief system that resembles Winnicott's description of the True/False self-organization (1965) and as a preacher he advocates a return to primary, libidinal narcissism as salvation. However, as a poet he conveys a fear of the void, with the world fragmented and the self annihilated such as we meet in the analyses of borderline personalities. What I am suggesting is that the pathological organizations (Steiner, 1987) of these narcissistic disorders are defences against catastrophic states of mind and, analogically, that Milton and Blake's counter-belief systems as preachers are defences against the psychic reality they reveal as poets.

I am making three assumptions. One is that poetry at its best provides a special route to psychic reality; another, that thanks to psychoanalysis we can treat theological statements as meta-psychological descriptions; and a third is that religious belief is not restricted to formal religions, but is a type of believing. I am also suggesting that a good poem is a better guide to psychic truth than a good sermon: but only to poetic truth. What do we mean by that?

Louis MacNeice wrote

> Poetry gains body from beliefs [but] not necessarily because they are the right beliefs. It is not the absolute, or objective, validity of a belief that vindicates the poetry; it is a gross over-simplification to maintain that a right belief makes a poem good and a wrong belief makes a poem bad. [MacNeice, 1941, p. 6]

My own answer to the question of how a misguided belief can be the basis of a great poem, would be to make a distinction between a true representation and the representation of the truth. Both Milton and Blake's poetic accounts are true, vivid, and insightful description of various mental states, even though the beliefs informing these states may be misguided.

With this in mind I want to look at Milton's *Paradise Lost* as a study of his mental state and at Blake's extraordinary determination to change Milton's mind posthumously by writing an alternative poetic account in which Milton figures as a character. It is as if Blake wanted to cure Milton of being Milton.

Milton was not only a great poet; he was a considerable essayist and pamphleteer, particularly in matters of religious doctrine. Yet he turned to poetry to attempt what was of most importance to him, to "justify the ways of God to men" (Elledge, 1975, p. 9). Given the circumstances of his own life, at the time of writing *Paradise Lost*, Milton's belief that God ordained all things and also that he was a personal, loving, merciful God gave him a lot to explain.

Milton was blind from the age of forty-four, he had lost two wives in childbirth and his only son died as a one-year-old; Cromwell, his political leader, was dead, his beloved republican administration defeated and the monarchy restored; some of his friends were executed and he only just escaped the same fate. His three adolescent daughters resented him and were a grave trouble to him and he to them. In the words he gave to the blind Samson of his "Samson Agonistes" we can see his state of mind:

> Now blind, disheartened, shamed, dishonord, quelled,
> To what can I be useful? Wherein serve
> My nation, and the work from heaven imposed!
> But to sit idle on the household hearth,
> A burdenous drone, to visitants a gaze,
> Or pitied object?
> [Campbell, 1990, p. 525]

In this state he wrote "Paradise Lost". He began with an invocation of the poetic muse and a prayer to the Creative Spirit whom he equates with the very God whose ways he aims to justify. His poem, he says, "pursues / Things unattempted yet in prose or rhyme" (Elledge, 1975, p. 8). As the poet Milton appeals to his God for inspiration, so that as an advocate he might defend him as his client. This makes us, his readers, the jury. It also goes to the heart of the problem as a plea from Milton to God to give him the means with which he can defend him. In *De doctrina* Milton had written

There are some who, in their zeal to oppose this doctrine [predestination], do not hesitate even to assert that God himself is the cause and origin of evil. Such men, if they are not to be looked upon as misguided rather than mischievous, should be ranked among the most abandoned of all blasphemers. An attempt to refute them would be nothing more than an argument to prove that God was not the evil spirit. [*ibid.*, p. 613–614]

So he scorns to do this in prose but in *Paradise Lost* he turns to poetry to accomplish this, trusting that it will give him direct access to the divine parent whom he so desperately wants to defend from these accusations;

> what in me is dark
> Illumine, what is low raise and support;
> That to the highth of this great argument
> I may assert Eternal Providence,
> And justify the ways of God to men.
> [*ibid.*, p. 9]

Milton wished to fortify his belief that his God loved him and that God's omnipotence was unqualified and unimpaired. To do this he needed to account for his suffering at the hands of God and for the presence of evil in God's world. In his *De Doctrina Christiana*, written in Latin as two pamphlets, he functions as a preacher promulgating his beliefs and he seems quite satisfied by his explanations. Having dismissed atheism as self-evidently foolish, he is left with the alternative belief that

> either God or some supreme evil power of unknown name presides over the affairs of men. But it is intolerable and incredible that evil should be stronger than good and should prove the true supreme power. Therefore God exists. [*ibid.*, p. 402]

As to what God is like, he simply states

> It is safest for us to form an image of God in our minds which corresponds to his representation and description of himself in the sacred writings ... he could never say anything about himself which was lower or meaner than his real nature. [*ibid.*, p. 402–403]

Milton firmly declared that his beliefs about God's actions were entirely based on the bible and on the bible alone. This meant he had to justify God's curses, such as those found in the book of Ezekiel, on the men and women he had created:

> In the place where you were created, in the land of your origin, I will judge you. And I will pour out my indignation upon you; I will

blow upon you with the fire of my wrath; and I will deliver you into
the hands of brutal men, skilful to destroy. You shall be fuel for the
fire; your blood shall be in the midst of the land; you shall be no
more remembered; for I the Lord have spoken. [*Holy Bible*, Ezekiel,
21: 28]

In psychoanalysis this is a familiar internal god; it is the
superego of those unfortunate enough to suffer from melancholia.
As Freud first described it:

> If we turn to melancholia [first], we find that the excessively strong
> superego ... rages against the ego with merciless violence, as if it
> had taken possession of the whole of the sadism available in the
> person concerned. Following our view of sadism, we should say
> that the destructive component had entrenched itself in the
> superego and turned against the ego. What is now holding sway
> in the superego is, as it were, a pure culture of the death instinct.
> [Freud, 1923, *S.E.* XIX, p. 53]

Freud also said "To the ego, living means the same as being loved—
being loved by the superego ..." (*ibid.*, p. 58). Translated into
theological language this reads as "not to be loved by God is the
same as death".

Some years ago I wrote a paper on the analyses of patients who
had a seriously disturbed parent. I described in that paper the
evolution of an unassimilated internal object opposed and hostile to
these patients' normal ego functions. I called it an *Alien Object*. If this
internal enemy took position as the superego it acquired moral force
and supernatural power. This often resulted in terrible indictments
of worthlessness and death threats in the form of hypochondriacal
convictions of fatal illness. This would be the equivalent of the
theological nightmare that Milton attempted to dismiss.

> ... either God or some supreme evil power of unknown name
> presides over the affairs of men. But it is intolerable and incredible
> that evil should be stronger than good and should prove the true
> supreme power. Therefore God exists. [Elledge, 1975, p. 402]

If this internal object could be dethroned, though it remains a
disturbing presence, it loses its moral power. It is preferable to
believe in the Devil than to think of oneself as created by a cruel and
hostile God. From the latter there is no escape and indeed one

cannot even want to escape, for there is nowhere to go to be saved. Such is, I think, the psychological force of the superego.

Freud commented "The Devil would be the best way out as an excuse for God" (1930, p. 120). Faced with the need to firmly establish belief in a just and loving God, Milton turned from prose to poetry. In order to exonerate God he changed the plot and made Satan a more central character than God. What changes the theological and psychological picture in *Paradise Lost* is the central presence in the poem of Satan. Psychoanalytically, it changes the internal world described from that of melancholia to that which was described by Herbert Rosenfeld as *destructive narcissism* (Rosenfeld, 1970). The initial innocence of the subject self and the restoration of the superego, or internal god, as the source of goodness is accomplished by the creation of another character; a destructive, evil interloper who seduces the ego from its natural propensity to worship and obey the superego. Our ancestral parents were supposedly prompted and seduced by Satan, who personifies envy and pride, and worships only himself. In psychoanalytic terms, belief in the goodness of the internal parent/god of the superego is restored by the proposition that a destructive, narcissistic aspect of the personality exists that leads the naïve self into betraying his or her relationship to the source of nothing but goodness.

To take first the clinical formulation of Rosenfeld of destructive narcissism:

> In some narcissistic patients the destructive narcissistic parts of the self are linked to a psychotic structure or organization which is split off from the rest of the personality ... the whole structure is committed to narcissistic self-sufficiency and is strictly directed against any object relatedness ... When narcissistic patients of this type begin to make some progress and to form some dependent relationship to the analysis, severe negative therapeutic reactions occur as the narcissistic psychotic part of the self exerts its power and superiority over the analyst, standing for reality, by trying to lure the dependent self into a psychotic omnipotent dream state which results in the patient losing his sense of reality and his capacity for thinking. [Rosenfeld, 1987, p. 112]

In Milton's *Paradise Lost* we find Satan, personifying destructive narcissism, excluded from God's heaven, and determined to see his exile as a triumphant entry into his own diabolical narcissistic kingdom:

... Farewell happy fields ...
Infernal world ...
Receive thy new possessor; one who brings
A mind not to be changed by place or time.
The mind is its own place, and in itself
Can make a heaven of hell, a hell of heaven ...
Here we may reign secure, and in my choice
To reign is worth ambition though in hell:
Better to reign in hell, than serve in heaven.
[Elledge, 1975, p. 16]

Starting with his own version of Christian theology and his own reading of the bible, Milton elaborated an imaginative account of the fall in *Paradise Lost*. This has had such an impact that it is misguidedly taken by many people to be the one in the book of Genesis. He accounts for the suffering and death of mankind as punishment for our ancestors' sin of disobedience and for the existence of evil in the world by the presence of Satan, the fallen angel whose pride and envy led to defiance of God. He suggests that God's loving character is made manifest by his readiness to offer his divine son as a human sacrifice to be mocked, vilified, tortured, and unjustly executed. If we were to remove Satan from Milton's poetic account we would be left with humanity banished, unloved, and undergoing indefinite punishment by God on grounds of ancestral disobedience. The tyrannical, cruel, and vengeful nature of Milton's God, in *Paradise Lost* has been commented on by a number of authors, notably William Empson (Elledge, 1975, pp. 605–618). (He thought that Milton really had in mind that God would abdicate in favour of his son who was "Both God and Man". This, as Empson put it, "is what makes the whole picture of him just tolerable" (*ibid.*, p. 610).) As I suggested, this baleful picture of the occupant of the seat of divine judgement is not unfamiliar if we translate it into our own psychoanalytic terms. Substituting the term superego for God we would have a perfect picture of the internal world of the melancholic.

However, as a poet, in giving us this account Milton cannot resist giving us the history, adventures, and soul searching of Satan. As a poet he inadvertently leads us to understand and identify with Satan as human while as a preacher he is seeking to demonstrate to us that he is evil personified. In *Paradise Lost* Satan is not an abstract power but someone who suffers intense envy and jealousy and is trapped in eternal reprobation by his pride. In Book IV of *Paradise Lost* Milton surprisingly presents us with Satan as someone capable of feeling conflict and guilt. He had been destined to be the personification of pride and envy, and wholly evil; in psycho-analytic terms a part object, an object in which part is whole; a character manifesting only one quality. Instead Satan becomes a whole person experiencing conflict, remorse, and dread: not an object but a subject. And Milton in this passage anticipates what Melanie Klein was to call the depressive position.

In Book IV of *Paradise Lost*, after his journey from Hell Satan arrives on a mountain top from where, looking south, he can see Eden. His purpose is to revenge himself on God by tempting the primal couple to betray their creator. Milton reminds the reader of Satan's future identity as the dragon of the Apocalypse who will do battle with God for the soul of mankind. At the moment of his arrival on Niphates, fuelled by his rage, he is hell-bent on revenge and insulated by his indignation from doubt, dread, or pity; he is not simply in a rage, he is outraged. His hurt pride reassures him that his pre-existing belief in the supremacy of his position need not be questioned, telling him that he is wronged, usurped, and unnaturally deprived. While he continues to believe this he is protected not only from reproach but also from envy. However, at the moment of giving birth to his vengeful project something happens to him; that which,

> Boils in his tumultuous breast ...
> like a devilish engine back recoils
> Upon himself. [Elledge, 1975, pp. 8–86]

Satan recoils upon himself; in psychoanalytic language he ceases to project and finds that hell is within himself and is not his unjustly imposed prison. Suddenly,

> horror and doubt distract
> His troubled thoughts, and from the bottom stir
> The hell within him, for within him hell
> He brings, and round about him, nor from hell
> One step no more than from himself can fly
> By change of place: now conscience wakes despair

That slumbered, wakes the bitter memory
Of what he was, what is, and what must be
Worse; of worse deeds worse sufferings must ensue ...
I fell ...
Warring in heav'n against heav'n's matchless King:
... he deserved no such return
From me ...
[*ibid.*]

Milton also, like his character Satan, has "back recoiled" upon
himself in the sense that he has looked inwards into his own human
nature to find an explanation for Satan's continuing destructiveness.
He does so in the vicissitudes and complexities of a depressive
position compounded by despair and unbearable envy, and the
"debt immense of endless gratitude". He makes Satan human, and
in this short passage makes clear why this particular human cannot
remain in the depressive position and is left with a choice between
melancholia or the role of the destructive narcissist.

Me miserable! which way should I fly
Infinite wrath, and infinite despair?
Which way I fly is hell: myself am hell;
And in the lowest deep a lower deep
Still threat'ning to devour me opens wide,
To which the hell I suffer seems a heav'n.
O then at last relent: is there no place
Left for repentance, none for pardon left?
None left but by submission; and that word
Disdain forbids me, and my dread of shame ...
But say I could repent and could obtain
By act of grace my former state; how soon
Would hight recall high thoughts, how soon unsay
What feigned submission swore; ease would recant
Vows made in pain, as violent and void.
For never can true reconcilement grow
Where wounds of deadly hate have pierced so deep
Which would but lead me to a worse relapse,
And heavier fall.
[*ibid.*]

Satan cannot bear the thought that if he repents and is forgiven he
will once again be provoked by envy into a rebellious attack, and
once again have to repent. He cannot imagine that he will be able to

contain his feelings and integrate them with his acknowledged admiration and gratitude. So he re-dedicates himself to the active pursuit of destruction which promises triumph over the goodness which he believes he cannot sustain:

> So farewell hope: and with hope farewell fear,
> farewell remorse: all good to me is lost;
> Evil be thou my good ...
> [*ibid.*, p. 88]

Even now Satan seems to need further and final provocation before committing himself to the destruction of mankind's future happiness. Milton provides it by having Satan witness the primal scene, that is, Adam and Eve making love:

> ... aside the devil turned
> For envy, yet with jealous leer malign
> eyed them askance, and to himself thus plained.
> "Sight hateful, sight tormenting! Thus these two
> Imparadised in one another's arms
> The happier Eden, shall enjoy their fill
> Of bliss on bliss, while I to hell am thrust,
> Where neither joy nor love, but fierce desire,
> Among our other torments not the least,
> Still unfulfilled with pain of longing pines".

This finally confirms him in his conviction that he is better off as the self-appointed ruler of destruction in hell than suffering the pangs of envy in the beauteous world:

In a few lines Satan restores his pride by scornfully imagining the unsuspecting couple's downfall and once his pride is re-established he is free from the torments of envious and jealous feeling:

> "... Live while ye may,
> Yet happy pair; enjoy, till I return,
> Short pleasures, for long woes are to succeed."
> So saying, his proud step he scornful turned
> [*ibid.*, pp. 99–100]

Pride is the fuel of his destructive narcissism and protects him from the "infinite despair" of his melancholia.

So I suggest Milton as a preacher seeks to justify the ways of God to men by interposing Satan, as the evil angel, between them. He offers us destructive narcissism, evil personified, as a defence against the despair of melancholia. However, as a poet he presents us with something different: an analysis of Satan as a tragic man. In the prose of his *On Christian Doctrine* Milton promulgates a somewhat fierce Protestant faith; in *Paradise Lost* he shows himself to be a great humanist poet of English verse.

Blake

William Blake was probably the first to suggest that Milton, his literary hero, was not really on the side of God but of Satan when writing *Paradise Lost*. Blake based this claim on the quality of the verse: he regarded the passages concerning Satan as sublime and those concerning the Angels and Heaven as mundane.

Note. The reason Milton wrote in fetters when he wrote of Angels & God, and at liberty when of Devils and Hell, is because he was a true Poet and of the Devil's party without knowing it. [Blake, 1825–1827, p. 6]

More than a century after Milton wrote *Paradise Lost* Blake set about trying to reverse it in his illustrated book *The Marriage of Heaven and Hell*. This can be most clearly seen by looking at the engraving later entitled "The Good and Evil Angels". At first sight it appears that a good angel, white and fair, is protectively clasping an infant (representing mankind) to keep it from a bad angel, of dark coloration, who is pictured rising from the flames, where he is chained, to reach for the child. This would appear to illustrate the essence of Milton's account of the fall in *Paradise Lost*, with Satan trying to get his clutches on infant Adam who is in the protective arms of a good Angel. Blake's own explanation of his picture, however, is exactly the reverse. He says the ostensibly "good" white angel is a representation of diabolical, organized religion stealing infant mankind from the sources of energy within himself, represented by the dark angel (*ibid.*, p. 4).

According to Milton, Man's loss of Paradise was due to disobedience but according to Blake it was a consequence of obedience.

For Milton, the fall results from the defiance of the reality and morality created by a just God. But for Blake, Man's fallen state is a consequence of his acceptance of the spurious reality of his senses and his compliance with the tyrannical morality of a false god.

Not satisfied with his correction of Milton's allegiances in *Paradise Lost* he makes him the central character in his own epic, the "Prophetic Verses" entitled *Milton Book the First* and *Milton Book the Second*. He subtitled it, in case we did not get the point, "To justify the ways of God to Men". Blake addresses us in this poem at the outset as the narrator, whom he called "the Bard", an Ancient British version of an Old Testament Prophet who says:

> I am Inspired! I know it is Truth! For I Sing
> According to the inspiration of the Poetic Genius.
> [Keynes, 1959, p. 495]

The phrase "Poetic Genius" comes from Blake's tract *All Religions are One* in which he wrote "all religions & as all similars, have one source. The true Man is the source, he being the Poetic genius" (*ibid.*, p. 98). In other words, Blake as a preacher tells us that the only source of truth is poetic genius. If we take my suggestion that poetic revelation is psychic reality we can paraphrase Blake as saying that psychic reality is *the only reality*.

The first book of *Milton* has a preface in which Blake makes clear that he is going to rescue mythic truth from misguided allegiance to Greek and Roman literature. As he puts it: "The stolen and perverted writings of Homer & Ovid, of Plato & Cicero which all men ought to contemn". Even his literary heroes Shakespeare and Milton were infected by "the general malady". The two books are meant to replace Greek mythology with Blake's own. The hero is Milton, who is Ulysses, Prometheus, Hercules, and Jason all in one. Blake's other mythic characters include such as Albion, Los, Urizen, Orc, Enitharmon, etc., who are familiar from his other prophetic books. It parallels *Paradise Lost* with Blake's own version of the fall and Satan's journey through hell to earth. This time, however, Satan is an aspect of Milton: his false selfhood which relies on biblical authority, reason, and memory and not on inspiration. Satan is Milton's false obedient self who bows to institutional religion. "I" says Milton, "in my Selfhood am that Satan: I am that Evil One! / He is my Spectre" (*ibid.*).

Blake's saga tells us of Milton casting off his spectral (false) self, and then meeting it again in the form of Urizen. Urizen is Milton's own reasoning power, whom he defeats in a wrestling contest on his way to earth. Milton then comes to earth in London by entering Blake's left foot. Blake, now full of Milton, accepts death pending resurrection and sees the coming of the Apocalypse.

Blake said more than once "I must create a system or be enslaved by another Man's / I will not reason & compare: my business is to create". In his "Prophetic Verses" and *The Everlasting Gospel* he sets out to do that. Most of this prophetic verse is written in the preaching mode but it contains passages where the poet can be heard speaking through the preacher, revealing the state of mind that is prompting the urgent polemic. The character Milton's big speech is one such passage; he begins saying:

> "There is a Negation, & there is a Contrary:
> The Negation must be destroy'd to redeem the Contraries.
> The Negation is the Spectre, the Reasoning Power in Man,
> This is a False body, an incrustation over my Immortal
> Spirit, a Selfhood which must be put off & annihilated always."
> [*ibid.*, p. 533]

Blake distinguishes between beliefs that are Contraries, and Negation. Contraries in Blake's Beulah (as in Freud's "System Ucs") can co-exist without contradiction, whereas Negation refutes a belief by demonstration of its invalidity, in other words by reality testing. In *The Marriage of Heaven and Hell* Blake states that "Anything that can be believed is true". *Contraries*, therefore, are welcome, but the enemy is *Negation*.

> The Negation is the Spectre, the reasoning Power in Man ...
> I come in Self-annihilation & the grandeur of Inspiration!
> To cast off rational Demonstration by Faith in the Saviour,
> To cast off the rotten rags of Memory by Inspiration,
> To cast off Bacon, Locke, & Newton from Albion's covering,
> To take off his filthy garments, & clothe him with Imagination!
> To cast aside from Poetry all that is not Inspiration ...
> To cast off the idiot Questioner who is always questioning ...
> Who publishes doubt & calls it knowledge; whose Science is despair,
> Whose pretence to knowledge is Envy: whose whole Science is
> To destroy the wisdom of ages to gratify ravenous Envy.
> [*ibid.*]

In this passage he reveals his fearful belief that objectivity will destroy subjectivity, that the reality testing of belief, which he calls negation, will annihilate the true self. The psychic reality of the individual can be destroyed by any other reality opposed to it. The snag with this system is that there is not only material reality to contend with, there is another reality external to the self, namely that of the psychic reality of other people. These fears resemble those found in some patients in analysis, often referred to as "borderline", whom I would also describe as "thin-skinned narcissistic patients" (Rosenfeld, 1987, p. 274). In such patients the attempted integration of subjective being and objective thinking is believed to cause a psychic catastrophe. As it is an aim of psychoanalysis to integrate subjective experience and objective understanding, the very process of analysis is felt to be a threat to this group of patients. Until analysis has produced some modification, objectivity is believed to be the death of subjectivity. In the analysis this amounts to the psychic reality of the analyst being regarded as incompatible with the psychic reality of the patient: unless it is the same, the mind of the other will be the death to the self. Blake had a solution to this; it was called Beulah, a place that corresponds to what John Steiner called "psychic retreats" (Steiner, 1993).

> There is a place where Contrarieties are equally True;
> This place is called Beulah. It is a pleasant lovely Shadow
> Where no dispute can come ...
> Beulah is evermore Created around Eternity, appearing
> To the inhabitants of Eden around them on all sides.
> But Beulah to its inhabitants appears within each district
> As the beloved infant in his mother's bosom round incircle
> With arms of love & pity & sweet compassion.
> [Keynes, 1959, p. 518]

In 1895 Freud drew attention to a state of mind which he described as the "blindness of the seeing eye" in which "one knows and does not know a thing at the same time" (Freud, 1893–1895, p. 117). Later he was to use the noun *Verleugnung* to describe this phenomenon, which Strachey translated as *disavowal* (Freud, 1924b, 1927b, 1938). He wrote of it as a "half measure" in which "the disavowal is always supplemented by an acknowledgement; two contrary and independent attitudes arise and result in ... a splitting of the ego" (1938, p. 204). I suggested in *Belief and Imagination* (Britton, 1998) that there is a syndrome in which disavowal is not partial but all pervasive: what Helene Deutsch had called the "As-If" personality (1942). In this pathological organization *disavowal* is placed at the centre of the individual's mental life and characterizes his whole relationship to the world. When it operates there is no outcome and therefore no consequences. No firm belief is established that cannot immediately be reversed. *Either and* rather than *either or* is the mode and inconsequentiality is the result. One could characterize the whole organization as sustaining inconsequence by suspending belief. As in Blake, Negation does not exist and Contraries co-exist. As he wrote in *The Everlasting Gospel*:

> The Vision of Christ that thou dost see
> Is my Vision's Greatest Enemy
> Thine has a great hook nose like thine
> Mine has a snub nose like to mine.
> Both read the Bible day & night,
> But thou readst black where I read white
> [Keynes, 1959, p. 748]

For Blake, Beulah was a realm of mild moony lustre, and soft sexual delusions, and "a place where Contraries are equally True". It relieved mankind of those two important distinctions that condemn us to live in a fallen world: the differences of *gender* and of *generation*. Judging from his unpublished explicit erotic drawings and his textual references to *male–females* and *female–males*, hermaphroditism prevailed in Beulah. The fallen world of material reality he called "Generation"; he also called it "Experience".

Blake unashamedly propounds as the route to salvation what in psychoanalysis has been called infantile megalomania. In this state, he claims, we are what we imagine we are and our imagination is our share of the divine. In our infantile innocence, he argues, we unselfconsciously believe this and when redeemed will do so again. This state of mind he celebrated in his *Songs of Innocence*. The other part of that collection, *Songs of Experience*, is an altogether different matter. In these he brilliantly captures the cruelty of human nature and the horrors of Regency London.

> In every cry of every Man,
> In every Infant's cry of fear,
> In every voice, in every ban,
> The mind-forg'd manacles I hear.
> How the Chimney sweeper's cry
> Every black'ning Church appals;
> And the hapless Soldier's sigh
> Runs in blood down Palace walls.
> [ibid., 1959, p. 216]

In Blake's view experience does not teach, it corrupts, with its deprivation, pain, and provocation and compels innocent egocentricity into giving a place to envy, jealousy, and covetousness.

> What is the price of experience? do men buy it for a song
> Or wisdom for a dance in the street? No, it is bought with the price
> Of all that a man hath; his wife, his children.
> Wisdom is sold in the desolate market where none come to buy,
> And in the withered field where the farmer plows for bread in vain.
> [ibid., p. 290]

And yet Blake the poet will out even when Blake the preacher is about his business. The *Songs of Innocence* have charmed generations of poetry readers but for me they only come into their own in juxtaposition with the *Songs of Experience*, first *Innocence*; from "The Divine Image":

> For Mercy has a human heart
> Pity, a human face:
> And Love, the human form divine,
> And Peace, the human dress.
> [ibid., p. 117]

Now *Experience*, entitled "A Divine Image":

> Cruelty has a Human Heart
> And Jealousy a Human Face;
> Terror, the Human Form Divine
> And Secrecy, the Human Dress.
> [ibid., p. 221]

For me the two taken together induce a sense of sadness and reflection rather than the bliss or catastrophe described in the

Prophetic verses. The mood is one that we often characterize as that of the normal depressive position as opposed to the despair of the melancholic depressive position described in *Paradise Lost*. For Blake, however, judging from his verse, there was an obstacle to his finding a place to his liking in the world of generation, where love is complicated by its separate sexes and generations, its envy, jealousy, and painful losses. There is a hint of it in a poem he never published:

> What to others a trifle appears
> Fills me full of smiles and tears
> [Blake, unpublished]

And in a letter to a friend:

> O why was I born with a different face?
> Why was I not born like the rest of my race?
> When I look each one starts when I speak, I offend;
> Then I'm silent & passive & lose every Friend.
> Then my verse I dishonour, My pictures despise,
> My person degrade & my temper chastise;
> And the pen is my terror, the pencil my shame;
> All my Talents I bury, and dead is my Fame.
> I am either too low or too highly prizd;
> When Elate I am Envy'd, When Meek I'm despise'd".
> [Johnson & Grant, 1979, p. 461]

Summary

Blake, looking at the justification of God to Men in Milton's *Paradise Lost*, decides this will not do and, on poetic grounds, decides this is a defensive organization. I concur with this on psychoanalytic grounds and identify the pathological, defensive organization with that described by Herbert Rosenfeld as "destructive narcissism". But when Blake reverses this he reproduces another recognizable defensive organization, that of the True/False self model described by Winnicott. As preachers, both Milton and Blake have given us verse form precursors of what, in twentieth-century psychoanalysis, were described as pathological organizations. Milton produces Satan to exonerate God, a bad self alongside an ideal self to protect him from believing in a cruel superego. Blake abolishes God the father, the superego, and substitutes the divine self, the idealized ego.

As poets they give us the possibility of seeing something of the states of mind that these were organized to keep at bay. In Milton's case it was a defence against melancholia; in his terms the fear of living in a world created and ruled over by a cruel, hostile, god; in my terms the fear of an ego destructive superego. In Blake's case it was a defence against the fear of psychic annihilation and falling forever into what he called "the void outside existence", a place commonly referred to these days as a psychic black hole.

However, both, as poets, also present us with alternative possibilities that as preachers they appear to have rejected. Milton gives us Satan capable of feeling guilt and remorse, briefly contemplating swallowing his pride. Blake gives us a world in his *Songs of Experience* that is a sadder and grimmer place than in *The Songs of Innocence*, and less blissful than Beulah but with the great advantage of being as real as it sounds.

References

Blake, W. (1825–1827). *The Marriage of Heaven and Hell* [reprinted in facsimile. London & Toronto: J. M. Dent & Sons, 1927].

Britton, R. (1995). Psychic reality and unconscious belief. *International Journal of Psycho-Analysis, 76*: 1.

Campbell, G. (1990). *John Milton Complete English Poems, Of Education, Aeropagitica*. London: J. M. Dent.

Elledge, S. (1975). *John Milton Paradise Lost* (2nd edn). New York: W. W. Norton.

Freud, S. (1923). The ego and the id. *S.E., 19.*

Freud, S. (1930). Civilization and its discontents. *S.E., 21.*

Holy Bible (1952). Revised Standard Version. London: Collins.

Johnson, M. L., & Grant, J. E. (Eds) (1979). *Blake's Poetry and Designs* . New York & London: W. W. Norton.

Keynes, G. (Ed.) (1959). *Blake Complete Writings*. Oxford: Oxford University Press.

Klein, M. (1946). Notes on some schizoid mechanisms. *Int. J. Psycho-Anal., 27*(III).

MacNeice, L. (1941). *The Poetry of W. B. Yeats*. Oxford: Oxford University Press.

Rosenfeld, H. (1971). A clinical approach to the psychoanalytic theory of the life and death instincts; an investigation into the aggressive aspects of narcissism. *Int. J. Psycho-Anal.*, 52: 169–178.

Steiner J. (1987). The interplay between pathological organizations and the paranoid–schizoid and depressive positions. *International Journal of Psycho-Analysis*, 68: 69–80.

Steiner, J. (1993). *Psychic Retreats*. London: Routledge.

Winnicott, D. W. (1965). Ego distortion in terms of true and false self. In: *The Maturational Processes and the Facilitating Environment* (pp. 140–152). London: Hogarth.

CHAPTER SEVEN

Ghosts in the landscape: Thomas Hardy and the poetry of "shapes that reveries limn"

Graham Shulman

I hold that the mission of poetry is to record impressions, not convictions.

F. E. Hardy, 1962, *The Life of Thomas Hardy*

that enkindling ardency from whose maturer glows
The world's amendment flows

T. Hardy, "A Commonplace Day", in Wright (1978)

"questionings" in the exploration of reality

T. Hardy, 1922, "Apology" from *Late Lyrics and Earlier*

Introduction: the visible signs of mental and emotional life

T homas Hardy wrote poetry throughout his life, but—apart from four poems—began publishing it only after the last of his novels, when he was nearly sixty, and wrote much of it later still. This late effusion of poetic publication and creativity can be seen as figured in the poem "The Darkling Thrush", in the "full-hearted evensong" of Hardy's celebrated "aged thrush ... / In blast-beruffled plume" (Wright, 1978). In this classic Hardyan poem of point and counterpoint, two contrasting visions related to two states of mind—desolation, depression, and loss of creativity in the first half, and self-expression, hope, and creative inspiration in the second half—are beautifully balanced. It is just such a poetic dramatization and counterbalancing of contrasting or discordant states of mind that MacDowall (1928) identified as "the most instinctive trait of [Hardy's] poetry—the contrast and comprehension of opposites" (p. 112).

This feature of disparate or opposing elements is reflected in Hardy's original published collections of poems. Wright (1978) highlights how each of the original collections contained poems that were written at widely different times in Hardy's life, and that the poems also ranged widely in form, style, and subject. The effect of this was that each collection was, as Hardy observed, "a book of various character" (Wright, 1978, p. 446). Hardy was conscious of the possible impact of this on the reader and commented on this in his "Apology" from the collection entitled *Late Lyrics and Earlier*. Here Hardy referred to "the juxtaposition of unrelated, even discordant, effusions; poems perhaps years apart in the making, yet facing each other" (*ibid.*). Hardy goes on to say that "the difficulties of arranging the themes in a graduated kinship of moods would have been so great that irrelation was almost unavoidable with efforts so diverse" (*ibid.*, p. 447). This "irrelation" turns out to be a central theme and feature of the individual poems.

And yet, typically, Hardy's poems share a distinctive and highly personal quality of passionate intensity, profound resonance, and lyrical evocation. In his poetry people, living creatures, objects, and landscapes become the subject of intense contemplative or retrospective reverie. This kind of reverie, which is a hallmark of Hardy's poems, might be more accurately described as *poetic reverie*—a state of mind in which the object of contemplation becomes suffused with *associative and figurative meaning*. I see the prototype for this poetic reverie as having its roots in the intensity, "passionate potentiality", and transforming experience of aesthetic reciprocity (Meltzer & Harris Williams, 1988) between mother and infant. Aesthetic reciprocity is seen as the intense mutual impact of mother and baby on each other with regard to their reciprocal "apprehension of beauty", suffused with a sense of "awe and wonder"; it involves the perception of "interior qualities" experienced initially in terms of "mystery", but with the potentiality of becoming known and understood (intimacy). Harris Williams (1988) discusses how this lays the foundation for the "aesthetic response" to literature and art: she describes how in this state of aesthetic response the mind both holds, and is held by, the "dream" evoked by the literary or artistic "aesthetic object" (p. 179).

The role and workings of the imagination are integral to this process, and are either an implicit or explicit subject of Hardy's poems. It is not surprising that literary critics have repeatedly commented on the Wordsworthian quality of Hardy's poetry. Chandra (1999), for instance, stresses "the similarity between Wordsworth and Hardy in respect of the composition of their poems from remembered experience" (p. 19), while Harvey (1999) writes of Hardy's "Poetry of Transcendence" and refers to "the transfiguring power of the imagination" (p. 147) in his poetry; he argues that Hardy's moments of transcendence "register the achievement of meaning" (p. 148) and are "a celebration of meaning and value" (p. 149). Harvey sees the domain of Hardy's poetry as the dynamics of the generation of meaning, and suggests that "the intrinsic quality of the mind is the overt subject" (p. 149). Hardy (1922) himself saw in poetry "the visible signs of emotion and the mind" (Wright, 1978, p. 448), and literary critics in general agree that a key aspect of Hardy's poetry is the centrality of the imagination, and *the activity of the mind and emotions*. Thus, Hardy's poems are expressions of the internal dramas of reflection, introspection and contemplation as they are coloured by the imagination—they dramatize the dynamic workings of the mind, and the lights and shadows cast by emotion. In this respect Hardy's poetry shares a significant area of interest with psychoanalysis.

This is true at both a thematic and a formal level, in which space and time are so prominent in Hardy's poetic "exploration" of psychic reality and the mind. Space and time are fundamental features of literary and psychoanalytic formulations of the mind. Space and time are also primary defining elements of poetry, in terms of structure and rhythm. I think this is one reason why— because of its formal qualities—poetry is so closely bound up with conceptions of the mind. This is reflected, for instance, in Maiello's

(2000) suggestion that primitive infantile "song-and-dance" experiences of rhythmicity are fundamental to the development of the mind, as well as to self–other differentiation and creative representation, and that "these primary levels of experience are not lost, but continue to be expressed ... and ... re-emerge in poetry, music and the figurative arts" (pp. 77–78). Or again, in Segal's (1991a) observation that artistic *"form*, be it musical, visual, or verbal, can move us so deeply because it symbolically embodies an unconscious meaning" (italics added), and that in this way "art [including literature] ... symbolizes and evokes ... a certain kind of archaic emotion of a pre-verbal kind" (p. 81).

Another reason why poetry is so closely bound up with conceptions of the mind is poetry's characteristic *self-reflexive* interest in the imagination, which of course became a keynote of the Romantic poets. Barbara Hardy (2000) sees the "imagining of imagination" (p. 3) at the heart of Hardy's poetry (and fiction), as expressed in Hardy's preoccupation with "the ordering and invention of our reveries" (p. 2). She discusses how notions of "space", "interiority", "thresholds", and "limits" are fundamental to Hardy's poetic conception of the imagination, and explores Hardy's interest "in revealing how the creations of memory are acts of imagination" (p. 193). Barbara Hardy argues that Hardy's poetry is characterized by an emotional and intellectual recognition of the boundary between the internal—specifically, imaginative—and external worlds, a recognition that acknowledges "otherness" and the "other" as having "an independent existence outside the possessive imagination" (p. 209). In contrast to the historical and "naïve" reading of Hardy's writing as an example of the "pathetic fallacy" (the projection of internal states on to the world of nature, or identifying the natural world as an expression or reflection of internal states), Barbara Hardy sees Hardy's poetry as being concerned with "the fallaciousness of the pathetic fallacy" (p. 104). In psychoanalytic terms, I understand this as corresponding to Britton's (1998) idea of a state of recognition of "poetic space" as the locus of the imagination—that is, an acknowledgement of the psychic "other room" of phantasy as a place where "we know we are *imagining* something" (original italics) (p. 121).

Hardy's poetry is thus partly *about* the symbolic activity of the mind, and implies a knowing consciousness of the activity of subjective and imaginative perception or conception. It is in part about the ways in which the mind can invest personal and emotional meaning in the external world—which may make a particular impression on the mind as a result of a particular mood or state of mind—but the world is not mistaken or romantically construed as *containing* or embodying this kind of subjective meaning. Unlike the poetry of the Romantics, in Hardy's poetry the world—and in particular nature—is not seen solipsistically as a mirror of the mind–self or as a personification of the other–mother, and there is no illusory "congruence", or mystical "union", between the mind and nature.

Instead, there is an imaginative integration of subjective and objective realities, in which the discreteness of the two is acknowledged, and this is a specifically creative achievement. Brooks (1971) suggests that in Hardy's poetry the "complex of objective reality and subjective response add up to a poetic unity" (p. 205). Segal (1986, 1991b) has proposed that the "aesthetic experience" involves "a particular combination" of the "ugly" and the "beautiful" which contributes to a sense of "wholeness" (this can certainly be seen in Hardy's poetry), and which in turn she links with Klein's depressive position. I would add that aesthetic experience also involves the imaginative and artistic integration of subjective and objective realities, where the discreteness of the two is acknowledged. This is characteristic of Hardy's poems.

The past in the present: the intenser stare of the mind

Hardy has been described as "supremely the poet of memories" (King, 1925, p. 105). In Hardy's poetry the past in the present carries a variety of connotations, and I shall explore some of these in my discussion of particular poems. The continuing impact and influence of the past in the mind is a central tenet of psychoanalytic thinking. Hardy's poems are concerned with the ways in which past and present interact in the mind and act upon it. Past and present are at different times felt to *occupy* consciousness, cast a mutual light on each other, or create a dual perspective. The mind is felt both to organize, and be organized by, the impressions of past and present. This occurs through the active mediation of the imagination in conjunction with a receptiveness to subjective association. Past and present are felt to be inseparable in the mind, the one always implicit in and invoking the other. MacDowall (1931) nicely captured this when he suggested that it is "as though, with [Hardy], nearness and remoteness called up each other" (p. 123).

Hardy evokes a sense of the past which is not merely a store of memories to be recalled or re-created in detail, with accompanying emotion which held sway according to the mood or immediate situation that prevailed at the time; rather, the past is a living and changing part of the landscape of the mind, with its own voices, echoes and rhythms. Landscape—such a prominent feature of Hardy's poetry, as of his fiction—takes on a richly figurative meaning, representing the psychic "scene", "stage", or "screen" for the drama and play of the mind's projections. The past—sometimes remembered and sometimes imaginatively construed—is felt to haunt the mind, creating "ghosts in the landscape".

Furthermore, the past in Hardy's poetry is not constituted as part of a chain or sequence of psychic causality or narrative, but instead is poetically and imaginatively construed as a source and object of reverie and *emotional* meaning. Memory or recollection are shown to predominate at times in the mind—Brown (1954) observed that "the memory itself absorbs the consciousness" (p. 164) in Hardy's poetry, and referred to "the candid submission of the spirit to recollection, and its alteration of focus" (p. 167).

This "alteration of focus" can take different forms but invariably involves a process characterized in the poem "In Front of the Landscape". Here, memories of "scenes, miscalled of the bygone" are viewed under "the intenser / Stare of the mind" and "Show ... with fuller translation than rested upon them / As living kind". Hardy vividly portrays how this process can enrich the mind and lead to new meanings or perceptions but can also be a source of psychic strain or conflict—it is seen to generate internal tensions within the mind, as well as between the internal and external worlds.

The poem's opening wonderfully captures this experience of psychic strain in its laboured and irregular rhythm, its over-stretched syntax, its vocabulary of effort and its imagery of enfeebled sight:

> Plunging and labouring on in a tide of visions,
>> Dolorous and dear,

Forward I pushed my way as amid waste waters
　　Stretching around,
Through whose eddies there glimmered the customed landscape
　　Yonder and near

Blotted to feeble mist. And the coomb and the upland
　　Coppice-crowned,
Ancient chalk-pit, milestone, rills in the grass-flat
　　Stroked by the light,
Seemed but a ghost-like gauze, and no substantial
　　Meadow or mound.

The "visions" of past "scenes" are variously described in the poem as "infinite spectacles", "re-creations", "shining sights", "images ... shadowed and sad", "lost revisiting manifestations" and "ghosts": the effect is to make their source and status within the mind ambiguous and unsettling, as they are not reducible to a stable or unitary psychic entity or location. The mind's internal tensions are dramatized in the contrasting adjectival descriptions of the visions as "Dolorous and dear", "halo-bedecked" yet "Dreaded, suspect". On another level, the poem contrasts the mind's preoccupation *in* the past with "Things more coveted, reckoned the better worth calling / Sweet, sad, sublime", and the present "insistent" visions which "as the rhyme / Sung by the sea-swell, so in their pleading dumbness / Captured me these". These past preoccupations are felt as a source of isolation and exclusion from "those who had shared in the dramas" of life.

The ending of the poem introduces a further dimension of psychic tension, this time felt to be between the internal and the external worlds. The poem moves outwards in scope from a protracted state of troubling but rewarding introspection to a state of alienating self-consciousness in the last stanza. This latter state is related to the imagined "surmise" of "passing people" who wonder

　　... whose is this dull form that perambulates, seeing nought
　　　　Round him that looms
　　Whithersoever his footsteps turn in his farings,
　　　　Save a few tombs?

In this surmise of the surmise of others, there is an implicit possibility of "misprision"—the very affliction of the figures in his "visions"; in other words, the poem's ending enacts a repetition of alienation between self and others. This cyclical re-appearance and elaboration of the past in the present is reflected in the rhyme scheme, in which the unrhymed ending of the fourth line of each stanza is taken up as the rhyming sound for the following stanza's rhyme pattern.

Whereas in the poem "In Front of the Landscape" the ghosts in the landscape are equivocal in terms of their emotional and psychological impact and associations, in the poem "At Castle Boterel" the single "phantom figure" in the scene is a symbol of love, loss, lasting remembrance, and relinquishment, and the emotional tone is hence more affirmative and elegiac. This remarkable poem—written after the death of Hardy's first wife—powerfully captures the elemental quality of love and its impression on the mind, in a way that is strikingly reminiscent of the tone and atmosphere of Emily Brontë's *Wuthering Heights*. The poem charts a moment and a movement, both literal and metaphorical, in its reminiscence of a love-scene of youth revisited in the last years of life.

The literal movement is of downward falling rain and the forward-moving "waggonette" which "the drizzle bedrenches"; the waggonette is driven by a solitary figure in the scene who, approaching the "junction of lane and highway", turns to "look back at the fading byway". There he "sees" on its "slope, now glistening wet" an image of the past: "Myself and a girlish form benighted / In dry March weather". Here Hardy invokes a sense of *dissonance* arising from the working of the imagination by super-imposing a past scene "In dry March weather" on to the "glistening wet" scene of the present.

The metaphorical movement of the poem is, of course, that of inexorably forward-moving time, and of mourning and relinquishment in the later years of life: "I look back ... / For the very last time; for my sand is sinking". What enables this mourning and relinquishment is the internal elemental sense of value of an intimate experience remembered; this sense of value is perceived as a source of personal meaning and is based on the emotional knowledge of "Something that life will not be balked of / Without rude reason till hope is dead, / And feeling fled". The moment remembered, one of intimacy and privacy, is not revealed in the poem—"What we did ... and what we talked of / Matters not much"—and Barbara Hardy (2000) points out how the poem "turns on reticence and absence ... the speaker refuses to tell ... a refusal which makes the place sacred, possessed, enclosed and private" (p. 144). What the poem centrally declares, in the middle stanza, is the *personal* sense of the moment's quality:

> It filled but a minute. But was there ever
>   A time of such quality, since or before,
> In that hill's story? To one mind never,
>   Though it has been climbed, foot-swift, foot-sore,
>   By thousands more.

The sense of primal and elemental experience is imaginatively transformed in the image of the next stanza, in which the poet imagines that a part of the *landscape* records the original scene:

> Primaeval rocks form the road's steep border,
>   And much have they faced there, first and last,
> Of the transitory in earth's long order;
>   But what they record in colour and cast
>   Is—that we two passed.

The corporeal "Primaeval rocks"—a fixed and lasting feature of the landscape—are a metaphor for the permanent registering and recording of "transitory" yet *subjectively meaningful* events or experiences along the road of consciousness in the landscape of the mind. By the use of this metaphor, such passing events or experiences are imbued with archaic and primitive meaning, personal yet "substantive". Hence the following stanza:

> And to me, though Time's unflinching rigour,
>   In mindless rote, has ruled from sight
> The substance now, one phantom figure
>   Remains on the slope

This "phantom figure" is not an hallucination, nor is it merely a memory; it is also—uncannily—a " 'figure' of speech". Another of Hardy's poems with a parallel theme, "The Phantom Horse-woman", contains the line "A phantom of his own figuring", and the word "figure" is one of the most frequently recurring words in Hardy's poems, carrying the whole range of its literal and metaphorical connotations. In the poem "At Castle Boterel", I believe Hardy is engaged in an "exploration of reality" (Hardy,

1922) concerning psychic experience and the construction of subjective emotional meaning. The poem "At Castle Boterel" testifies to the *figurative construction of intimate, subjective recollected experience*, and the need to revisit the "locations" within the mind of such metaphorical constructions as part of the process of mourning and relinquishment.

A different kind of "haunting", together with a different kind of mourning and relinquishment, are involved in the poem "Logs on the Hearth", subtitled "A MEMORY OF A SISTER". In this extraordinarily evocative and moving poem, written after the death of one of his sisters, Hardy interweaves a series of descriptive and metaphorical images that dramatize the workings of memory and imagination in the process of mourning.

Logs on the Hearth

A MEMORY OF A SISTER

 The fire advances along the log
  Of the tree we felled
Which bloomed and bore striped apples by the peck
 Till its last hour of bearing knelled.

 The fork that first my hand would reach
  And then my foot
In climbings upward inch by inch, lies now
 Sawn, sapless, darkening with soot.

 Where the bark chars is where, one year,
  It was pruned, and bled—
Then overgrew the wound. But now, at last,
 Its growings all have stagnated.

 My fellow-climber rises dim
  From her chilly grave—
Just as she was, her foot near mine on the bending limb,
 Laughing, her young brown hand awave.

This deceptively simple poem achieves an emotional depth and resonance through a richly complex mix of associative, symbolic, and formal features. The poem expresses an acknowledgement of profound and unique loss and absence (of a dead sister), together with an intimation of guilt at destruction ("the tree we felled"), which are nevertheless complemented by a feeling of enduring love and psychic companionship sustained in memory and the mind's imaginative activity. The mind is felt to be able to continue to bear fruit (a memory, a poem) in a time of grief and loss, and the imaginative fruits of the mind in this time of grief are experienced—through association—as a source of emotional life, growth, and warmth.

The poem works through a series of interconnected parallels and contrasts, the patternings of which reflect the emotional links between the various feelings and states of mind experienced in the process of mourning. There is a central parallel in the poem between the death of the apple tree that has been "felled" and the death of the sister. The powerful sense of loss expressed in relation to the tree is conveyed through the phrases "last hour" and "bearing knelled", and in the funereal association of the fire with cremation; the finality of death is evoked in features such as the phrases "at last" and "growings all have stagnated", the halting rhythm of "lies now / Sawn, sapless", and the repeated sentence closure marked by the full-stop at the end of each stanza. The sense of death as a failure or stagnation of growth is reflected in the effect of the half-rhyme (like a "failed" rhyme) of the third stanza "bled" / "stagnated", where it is as if rhyme itself "stagnates". A striking sense of *absence* of the dead sister is conveyed through the absence of direct mention of her in the poem in the first three stanzas. There is a mournful, sombre, and almost regretful feeling, subtly conveyed, of having inflicted a mortal blow to the apple tree; perhaps this feeling, conveyed in relation to the felled tree, reflects the location of feelings of guilt as an *undercurrent* in the emotional life of the bereaved.

Throughout the poem there is a central contrast between horizontal and vertical, and movements in these directions ("advances along" as against "upwards" and "rises"). These directions and movements carry a network of emotional associations around life and death. The advancing movement of the fire "along" the log is on one level suggestive of the body being consumed by life ("fire") in the forward movement of time, while the log that "lies" carries overtones of the inertness of a prone corpse. The "climbings upward inch by inch" reflect the strivings of childhood aspiration as well as the gradualness of childhood *growth*, echoing the growth of the tree that "bloomed". The "fork" that had been part of the live apple tree and an aid to the shared childhood "climbings" of brother and sister ("my fellow climber"), now "lies" dead and dismembered ("sawn") in the hearth: thus the fork symbolizes both the bond between the brother and sister and their separation through the sister's death. The ambiguity of the word "lies" perhaps also carries the hint of a feeling that the now dead tree "belies" the youthful experience of life and the bond between the brother and sister.

However, the final stanza begins with the image of the "fellow-climber" who "rises dim / From her chilly grave", and the overriding impression of the poem is that of the lasting impression in the mind—forged by the early childhood bond between a brother and sister—which transcends the death of the sister and survives in the face of loss and grief, through the work of mourning. The image at the end of the poem of the sister who "rises"—with its associations of awakening, sunrise, and resurrection—conveys a sense of greater ease of movement in contrast to the effort and gradual progress involved in the earlier "climbings upwards inch by inch"; this perhaps reflects a state of greater freedom of spirit in the mind of the poet, the outcome of the struggle and gradual progress involved in the work of mourning.

The immediacy and poignancy of the final two lines of the poem speak to the intensity and intimacy of feeling, and the power of imaginative transformation of such feeling into poetic form. The extended and expansive third line of this final verse, combined with the fact that this last verse is the only one containing a double rhyme scheme ("dim" / "limb", "grave" / "awave"), creates a sense of plenitude and poetic fruition, balancing the earlier feeling of lost plenitude of the tree that "bore striped apples by the peck". The reference to the sister's "foot" and then "hand" echoes and mirrors the earlier reference to "my hand" and "my foot", conveying a continuity of connection between alive brother and dead sister, while an ongoing inner experience of emotional closeness is evoked in an image of physical contiguity—"her foot near mine". Finally, the vivid closing image of the sister "Laughing, her young brown hand awave" captures the haunting memory of a dead sister's youthful joy and liveliness, while the ambiguity of the "hand awave" allows the possibility of both a greeting and a farewell.

In the poem "Old Furniture", the past is imaginatively conceived in terms of the continuing presence in the mind of the past succession of family generations. This sense of their living presence in the mind is inspired by "the relics of householdry" handed down through the generations, amid which glimpses of the "hands" of past owners are envisioned in the imagination:

> I see the hands of the generations
>   That owned each shiny familiar thing
> In play on its knobs and indentations,
>   And with its ancient fashioning
>   Still dallying:
>
> Hands behind hands, growing paler and paler,
>   As in a mirror a candle-flame
> Shows images of itself, each frailer
>   As it recedes, though the eye may frame
>   Its shape the same.

In this poem of mirrorings, it is the poetic imagination ("mirror") which is felt to be a medium for the sense of the living presence of the succession of family generations ("hands behind hands") in the mind, the "images" of which are paradoxically felt to be reflections of the self ("candle-flame"). The mirror is another recurrent image in Hardy's poetry, usually associated with the imagination. In the poem "Moments of Vision" the imagination is conceived as "That mirror / Which makes of men a transparency", and which "throws our mind back on us, and our heart, / Until we start". In "Old Furniture", the recursive poetic image of the candle-flame's receding "images of itself" in the "mirror" works on one level perhaps as a metaphor for the recursive and self-reflexive qualities of the mind.

The poem contains a succession of evanescent ghost-like yet living images: "On the clock's dull dial a foggy finger, / Moving to set the minutes right"; "On this old viol, too, fingers are dancing— / As whilom—just over the strings by the nut"; "And I see a face by that box for tinder, / Glowing forth in fits from the dark, / And fading again". There is a dream-like quality to the poem, suggestive of the workings of the unconscious in the activity of the imagination. There is also an air of reverence and sacredness (the "relics") which is perhaps an expression of what Harvey (1999), in his discussion of the poem, describes as "Hardy's identification with the past generations ... [and] his profound feeling for the continuity of human life" (p. 153). Harvey suggests that "As the generations live again, Hardy gives new meaning to their lives and they in turn bestow on him a surer sense of being" (*ibid*.). "Old Furniture" conveys a feeling of poetic inspiration derived from the impressions which "the hands of the generations" have left on the inherited "[f]urniture" of the mind. An important aspect of this is captured in Hardy's descriptions of movements or actions such as "in play", "dallying", "tentative touches that lift and linger", "receding, advancing", "Glowing forth … / And fading again", "Kindles to red"; the cumulative effect of these is a characteristic emotional quality of Hardy's poetry which has been described as his unique "note of tenderness" (Day Lewis, 1951, p. 158).

In "Old Furniture" I think this "note of tenderness" is fundamental to what Harvey referred to as Hardy's "surer sense of being" that is inspired by the living, haunting presence of the succession of past family generations in the mind. But as in the poem "In Front of the Landscape", such a sense of self based on internal value and meaning is felt to be at odds with the external world. Harvey comments on this when he observes that "Hardy wryly defines his own sense of alienation from the modern world, with its illusory promises of purpose, action and progress" (p. 152). This feeling of alienation is introduced in the last stanza and thus strikes the note of the poem's ending:

> Well, well. It is best to be up and doing,
>   The world has no use for one to-day
>   Who eyes things thus—no aim pursuing!

Here the modern world is felt to lack a "container" (Bion, 1962) for a sense of self and being in which the imagination plays a central role. Elsewhere in Hardy's poems—as for instance in the poem "In Front of the Landscape"—the self is experienced as having *internal* tensions and divisions which give rise to feelings of alienation, discontinuity, and displacement. This internal experience of the self, and a wish for the integration of what are felt to be disparate aspects of the self, form the subject of a group of poems to which I shall now turn.

The self in question: extern to thee nothing

The titles of poems such as "The Self-Unseeing" and "Self-Unconscious" highlight Hardy's preoccupation with the self and the capacity to be in touch with and aware of the self or aspects of the self. These poems are about a recognition of failure of self-awareness at a particular moment in time in the past—a failure which is not perceived at the time but only in retrospect, and is hence tinged with feelings of loss and regret. This failure is not one of intellectual understanding or insight, but rather a failure to be in touch with an internal emotional current or state. The retrospective sense of loss is therefore in relation to an emotional experience in the past that was missed but not felt to be missing. This sense of loss is associated with a lack of wholeness, or a compromise to the integrity of the self.

The poem "Self-Unconscious" pictures a remembered scene in which a solitary figure is walking along a road with the sea in the distance, his mind full of "the projects he mused upon" and "specious plans that came to his call"; in this state of absorbed contemplation of future endeavour and achievement he is oblivious to the wonders of "Earth's artistries" that surround him, and equally "himself he did not see at all":

> Along the way
> He walked that day,
> Watching shapes that reveries limn,
> And seldom he
> Had eyes to see
> The moment that encompassed him.

The exact nature of this missed "moment that encompassed him" remains a mystery to the reader—Barbara Hardy (2000, p. 187) points out how the impossibility of seeing "the whole" is thus mirrored in the reading of the poem; however, it appears to be characterized by the qualities of "Earth's artistries" that are impressionistically evoked in the poem. These consist of the vitality, exuberance, and industriousness of the nest-building yellowhammer birds "along the adjoining hedge", with their "mirthful clamours", "bustling air", soaring, swooping and looping, and "yellow flutter". The lively immediacy of these "Bright yellowhammers" in the foreground is balanced by the sense of perspective and distance linked with the more static and formal images of the sea in the background:

> The smooth sea-line
> With a metal shine,
> And flashes of white, and a sail thereon

The poem's stanzaic form embodies and amplifies this contrast of elements and dimensions of the self, in its repeated pattern of two compact short lines followed by one expansive long line, suggestive of abbreviation and elaboration.

Although "that self / As he was, and should have been shown, that day" is now known to the poet, it provides no consolation because the overriding feeling is of a missed opportunity:

> O it would have been good
> Could he then have stood
> At a clear-eyed distance, and conned the whole

Instead, the "vision" contained in the present knowledge of "the whole" self is felt to be "mere derision" which neither "soothes his body nor saves his soul". The poem ends with a rejection of "common-sense" false reassurance gained from deprecation of the missed experience of the self; rather, there is a facing up to the painful recognition that something of lasting emotional value—and integral to the self—is felt to have been lost:

> Not much, some may
> Incline to say
> To see therein, had it all been seen.
> Nay! He is aware
> A thing was there
> That loomed with an immortal mien.

The problem of the uneasy relationship between the present and past self is also the subject of the poem "Wessex Heights". The emotional tone of this poem is captured in Barbara Hardy's (2000) observation that "The feelings of acute anxiety and dread are Kafkalike in strength and kind" (p. 141), and in her reference to the poem's ending as a "release from the deep anxiety which marks the poem—touched by paranoia" (p. 142). The poem contrasts the "heights" of the title with the "towns" in the "great grey Plain", each characterizing a state of mind and also a mental space. The "heights" are associated with a sense of benign provision, release from persecutory feelings or experience, freedom of thought and spirit ("liberty"), and an awareness of one's true and false self—an imagined unbounded space of unfettered selfhood beyond the dimensions of time:

There are some heights in Wessex, shaped as if by a kindly hand
For thinking, dreaming, dying on, and at crises when I stand,
Say, on Ingpen Beacon eastward, or on Wylls-Neck westwardly,
I seem where I was before my birth, and after death may be.

The "lowlands" (and specifically the "towns"), in contrast, are associated with alienation, intellectual, and emotional isolation, mental encumbrances or intrusions, unreality, and a disturbing world of "[s]hadows" and haunting "forms now passed / For everybody but me"—a persecutory dream (or perhaps nightmare) space that is experienced as simultaneously constraining and inaccessible ("I cannot go to the tall-spired town, being barred"):

Down there they are dubious and askance; there nobody thinks as I,
But mind-chains do not clank where one's next neighbour is the sky.

In the towns I am tracked by phantoms having weird detective ways—
Shadows of beings who fellowed with myself of earlier days:

Hardy creates an unsettling and uncanny image of the past self ("my simple self") which is felt to be "watching" the present self ("strange continuator") with incomprehension at the connection between the two, and at how the latter developed from the former.

Down there I seem to be false to myself, my simple self that was,
And is not now, and I see him watching, wondering what crass cause
Can have merged him into such a strange continuator as this,
Who yet has something in common with himself, my chrysalis.

Here the feeling of dissonance and lack of direct connection between past and present selves is conveyed poetically through the half-rhyme of the endings of the first two lines of this verse ("was" / "cause"), the only pair of lines in the poem that do not have an identical rhyme. The poem evokes an intense atmosphere of dis-ease and depression—the internal "lowlands" of the spirit which are felt to have a specific, separate location and which, it is felt, can only be eschewed or kept at bay by withdrawal to the elevated and isolated "heights" of solitariness and freedom from tension and conflict, a kind of psychic retreat (Steiner, 1993) ultimately ending in expiry ("thinking" ... "dreaming" ... "dying"). In its surreal picturing of the uneasy mutual observation of past and present selves, the poem expresses a mood of self-alienation and division of the self that is typical of a number of Hardy's poems. Riquelme (1999) sees in this aspect of Hardy's poetry—and in what he refers to as its features of "ambiguity", "skepticism", "refusal to accept a deluded consolation" (p. 215), and "[Beckettian] tendencies towards silence" (p. 221)—the literary dawning of the spirit of modernism.

Self-doubt and depression, born of a sense of misattunement between self and other, are the keynotes of another poem of the self entitled "In Tenebris II". In this poem, the "other" takes the form of the presiding spirit of the times, a late-nineteenth century optimism that "all is for the best in the best of all possible worlds". The poem expresses how, for the individual who feels differently in such a climate, the sense of self can become distorted, giving rise to a melancholic feeling of being "one shaped awry". The fault is experienced as being in the self for not having "the vision ... to discern what to these is so clear", and "the blot seems straightway in me alone". In such a mood, the world is felt to be lacking in receptivity, and this is reflected partly in the poem's opening image of the "clouds' swollen bosoms" which "echo back the shouts of the many and strong / That things are all as they best may be, save a few to be right ere long". This echo, which is felt to negate the self, is mirrored in the poem in the echo of the endings of the verses: "one better he were not here", "one ... who has no calling here", "Why should such an one be here?", and "he disturbs the order here".

In its tone, the poem also wryly and sardonically characterizes the omnipotent belief underlying the unshakeable assurance and confident conviction that can be mustered through the collective assertion of "the many and strong": "And what the potent say so oft, can it fail to be somewhat true?". A sense of insistent repetition (what is said "so oft") is evoked poetically through the repetition, alliteration, and rhythmic echoes in the lines:

> Our times are blessed times, they cry; life shapes it as is most meet,
> And nothing is much the matter; there are many smiles to a tear;

Hardy brilliantly captures the emotional casualness and insubstantiality of such an outlook, in a single line that in its poetic expression and vision foreshadows the poetry of T. S. Eliot:

> Breezily go they, breezily come; their dust smokes around their career

There is a profound feeling of isolation and depersonalization in the poem, conveyed partly through the repetition of "one" and "he". The personal belief that "if way to the Better there be, it exacts a full look at the Worst", and the feeling "that delight is a delicate growth cramped by crookedness, custom, and fear", are felt to "disturb[] the order here". "In Tenebris II" painfully portrays the internalization of the negated self, and conveys the self-alienation of the individual whose emotional experience and personal "vision" do not accord with the basic assumption (Bion, 1961) that can operate at the level of the social.

Hardy's poems of the self that I have discussed so far focus on the tensions or divisions within the self, but Hardy also shows a poetic interest in the idea of the self as a whole. In the poem "Rome: The Vatican: Sala delle Muse" the sense of wholeness in relation to the self is bound up with creativity and creative inspiration, together with the notion of interiority. The latter is captured in the title which invokes a Russian doll image of containment and narrowed-down-focus (a "location within a location within a location", or "a room within a building within a city"). In the poem the "Sala delle Muse" is not just a physical location but also a metaphorical locus within the mind.

The scene of the poem is set, in the opening line, at the archetypal hour of midday—a liminal time that introduces an atmosphere of poise and balance. The poem's opening ("I sat ...") registers the physical position traditionally associated with thinking. The "action" itself is entirely internal—an imaginary dialogue between the self and the figure of an imagined "One" who "gleamed forth" at a suspended moment in time when the "Muses' Hall ... / ... seemed to grow still, and the people to pass away, / And the chiselled shapes to combine in a haze of sun". The contrasting elements of the immediate surroundings of the external world—the motion of people and solidity of stone—are temporarily and paradoxically frozen and dissolved, and a sanctuary of the mind, the place of poetic vision and thought, is entered into.

The imaginary "One" who "gleamed forth" is a symbol of wholeness and integration:

> She looked not this nor that of those beings divine,
> But each and the whole—an essence of all the Nine;

In her questioning about the poet's state of mind, she partly represents thoughtful inquiry about feeling and mood; she is felt to enshrine and encompass the disparate aspects of the self as they are expressed through the different elements of creative inspiration. In the dialogue between the self and the "One"—a poetic dramatiza-tion of the internal "dialogue" between self and object—the self expresses anxiety about "inconstancy" or infidelity due to shifting interest between a variety of artistic and formal elements ("Form", "Tune", "Story", "Dance", "Hymn"): "I worship each and each; in the morning one, / And then, alas! another at sink of sun". The benign figure provides assurance, affirmation and integration of the self through insight and understanding about the different parts of the self, and through steadiness of intent in the face of repeated doubt and questioning. In response to the anxious and agitated assertion that "The lover of all in a sun sweep is fool to whim— / Is swayed like a river-weed as the ripples run!", she replies:

> —"Nay, wooer, thou sway'st not. These are but phases of one;
> And that one is I; and I am projected from thee,
> One that out of thy brain and heart thou causest to be—
> Extern to thee nothing. Grieve not, nor thyself becall,
> Woo where thou wilt; and rejoice thou canst love at all!"

Thus she confers a sense of internal coherence, through a recognition of seemingly external diverse elements as in fact being "projected" from within ("out of thy brain and heart") and therefore having a common source ("I" / the self). The capacity to love, and for love to be the motivating factor in one's creative endeavours, is endorsed as the primary value. And the association between love and integra-tion is in part poetically rendered and emphasized through the final word of the poem ("all"), which echoes the earlier image of wholeness in "an essence of all the Nine".

A witty and humorous treatment of the theme of multiple parts of the self is found in the poem "So Various". The poem is in the form of an extended apostrophe to an imaginary person who has had a series of encounters, each with an individual of a particular character, each one delineated in a single verse. The verses alternate between characters of opposite traits (fiery/cold; staunch/fickle; ignorant/learned; sad/glad; unadventurous/enterprising; forget-ful/unforgetting). Each verse of five lines comprises two long lines followed by three short lines, re-inforcing the sense of contrast and discordance. The poem ends with the revelation that these were the different sides of one person:

> Now ... All these specimens of man,
> So various in their pith and plan,
>   Curious to say,
>   Were *one* man. Yea,
>   I was all they.

The poem plays on the reader's ignorance—until the disclosure at the end—of the fact that all the different descriptions are in fact of one person; a parallel is therefore set up between the reader and the imaginary addressee of the poem who has met all the people described. There is an implied or ascribed difficulty for each— confirmed in the reader's assumption that the descriptions *are* of different people—in recognizing, or being able to conceive of, such disparate and opposing characteristics as co-existing in one person. This sense of strain on credibility or comprehension is reflected in the grammatical incongruency of the closing line "I was all they".

I think that the poems "Rome: The Vatican: Sala delle Muse" and "So Various" illustrate a way of seeing Hardy's poetry, in terms of poetry as a medium functioning for Hardy as a *container* (Bion, 1962) for the disparate aspects of self and discordant emotional and psychic experiences. Poetry—part of the realm of literature and therefore of culture—perhaps served for Hardy as a "potential space" (Winnicott, 1971, p. 100) between self and society, one that offered a place for the creative exploration of the self and the relationship between self and other/society.

Shadows of the mind: a blankness looms, a curtain drops

A number of Hardy's poems are characterized by a strong sense of uncertainty about the location, identity, or status of certain persecutory thoughts or states of mind—states of mind that are felt to disturb the sense of self or to be a threat to the self. These "shadows of the mind", as I have called them, are felt and represented as "presences", "intrusions", "altered states" or "illusions". These poems express anxieties, doubts and ambiguities about what is "real" and what belongs in the mind; they often contrast the solidity and specificity of the physical world and its details, with the indeterminacy and instability of particular psychic states.

The poem "At the Royal Academy" is partly about doubts regarding the "reality" of the artistic or creative products of the imagination. It is concerned with the relationship between art and reality, and the illusory nature of realism or verisimilitude in art—in particular, in the artistic representation (or *re-presentation*) of the natural world. The poem contrasts the beguiling yet inspiring life-like images of nature in an exhibition of "summer landscapes" at the Royal Academy, with the fact that the "originals" in nature of these images of "grass and leafery" are actually from "Last year" and are therefore dead and "buried". In the poem it is merely stated as a fact that these living images of nature that "Seem caught from the immediate season's yield / I saw last noonday shining over the field" are "not this summer's though they feign to be" (i.e. neither living nor real), and the reader is left to draw his or her own conclusion.

Any "reading" of the poem turns on the themes of transience and the awareness of death. The poem expresses a consciousness of these that seems to cast a shadow over the creative and imaginative achievement of artistic representation and expression. What could potentially be a creative celebration and appreciation through painting of the beauty, freshness, abundance, and variety of "shining" nature, could equally constitute a denial or repudiation of time and death. And yet, ironically, Hardy himself paints in words a picture of nature—or rather, of the representation of nature in the paintings—that is every bit as lyrical, vivid, immediate, and credible as the paintings are:

> These summer landscapes—clump, and copse, and croft—
> Woodland and meadowland—here hung aloft,
> Gay with limp grass and leafery new and soft,
> ...
>
> ... these young foils so fresh upon each tree,
> Soft verdures spread in sprouting novelty,

Freud (1916[1915]) points out, in his discussion on the theme of transience, how "The proneness to decay of all that is beautiful and perfect can ... give rise to two different impulses in the mind" (p. 305), either "despondency" or increased appreciation. He links the former with "a revolt ... against mourning" (p. 306). Freud refers specifically to the way in which "the beauty and perfection of a work of art ... [can be felt to] lose its worth because of its temporal limitation" (*ibid.*); he also refers to our response to "the beauty of Nature" (p. 305), suggesting that the cycle of the seasons (what "is destroyed by winter ... comes again next year", (*ibid.*)) allows psychically for a sense of the "eternal".

Hardy's poem "At the Royal Academy" seems to encompass in its poetic expression the possibility of *both* sets of emotional responses—to the beautiful (whether in nature or art) and the ugly (in death and decay). The poem seems to suggest that, like past and present, each is always implicit in the other. Middleton Murry (1919) refers to this as a feature of Hardy's poetry when he writes that "the great poet remembers both rose and thorn; and it is beyond his power to remember them otherwise than together" (pp. 90–91). I think this feature of Hardy's poetry is a reflection of Hardy's interest in the theme of aesthetic experience. There is some similarity between Hardy's poetic conception of aesthetic experience and Segal's (1986, 1991b) psychoanalytic formulation to which I referred earlier.

Perhaps the poem "At the Royal Academy" is also partly a comment on the impulse to "capture" beauty in art—the scenes of nature "[s]eem caught" by "rapid snatch". Hardy's use of the word "foils" in reference to the leaves in the paintings invokes both the idea of nature's beauty being shown to advantage (set off) by art, and the idea of the paintings being frustrated or self-defeating (foiled) in their endeavour.

In the poem "Who's in the Next Room?" the shadow of the mind takes the form of a darkness of spirit linked with an ominous sense of something to come. The poem creates a tense, concentrated atmosphere of anxious and agitated apprehension—a persecutory mood of suspicion and fearful anticipation, related to a presence felt as menacing which inhabits an invisible but contiguous space, a psychic location poetically conceived as "the next room". A perceived danger remains undefined; although it has convention-ally been taken to be the figure of Death, the poem is not in fact so specific:

> "Who's in the next room?—who?
> I seem to hear
> Somebody muttering firm in a language new
> That chills the ear".
> "No: you catch not his tongue who has entered there".

The impression created is primarily of an overwhelming sense of impending *doom*. The poem dramatizes psychically the dimensions of the invisible, the state of not knowing, and the existence of a "next room". Britton (1998) links the "other room" of the imagination and "poetic space" with the "invisible" oedipal relationship between the parents. He suggests that the "other room" is "the location of the unwitnessed *primal scene*" (original italics) (p. 121). In this context, one way of thinking about the poem "Who's in the Next Room?" is that it is perhaps a metaphor for a more primitive, pre-oedipal psychic "other room". I see this as the location of primitive phantasy that is a *precursor* to imagination: in the poem this generates an intimation of doom—a potential depression (a "draught" from the "Polar Wheel") or associated state of mind—which is bound up with the felt presence of an "other" ("Somebody ... / Unknown") and with "a language new", and which later comes to be associated with the conception of death.

The poem is tightly structured, with four stanzas each containing two distinct "voices"—a child-like, nervous, urgent, and repetitive questioning voice, followed by a quietly assured, measured and authoritative (parental?) answering voice in the final line of each stanza. The insistent repetition of the first line of each verse ("Who's in the next room?—who?") conveys a feeling of mounting anxiety and urgency that remains uncontained. There is the consolation of one who knows (the answering voice) providing some reassurance, possibly in the promise of a future certain knowledge of something that for the present is only sensed:

> "Who's in the next room?—who?
> A figure wan
> With a message to one in there of something due?
> Shall I know him anon?"
> "Yea he; and he brought such; and you'll know him anon".

Gunn (1972) has pointed out that there is a quality of the "riddle" in the poem, linked with its particular form of question-and-enigmatic-answer. On another level, this applies also to the fact that the poem does not supply the missing term (e.g. "depression", "death", "fate") that would close or resolve its meaning; instead, it leaves open the "message" of the poem, which is therefore subject to a corresponding process of deferral.

Another poem with the theme of a threatening and dangerous "presence" is "The Interloper". It is possible to think of this poem as thematically linked with "Who's in the Next Room?", although it works in a very different way and achieves a different kind of effect. Originally the identity of "The Interloper" was similarly unspecified, but in response to the perplexity of contemporary readers Hardy felt compelled to add an epigram to the poem, which gives a particular identity to the figure: "And I see the figure and visage of Madness seeking for a home".

The poem takes the form of a succession of recollected scenes of intimate company, viewed in retrospect, and this creates a dual perspective: we see these scenes through the eyes of the person remembering them, who sees an additional figure undiscerned by those within the scenes at the time. We "see" more than was seen at the time, but less than is understood by the speaker, and our failure of imagination to conceive what the invisible "figure" represents is part of the poem's subject. The poem's air of mystery and suspense evokes a pervasive feeling of precariousness, which reflects a sense of the susceptibility of the mind, and of the security of ordinary intimate life, to an undermining force.

The opening scene of the poem conveys a precipitous feeling of danger, to which its participants seem oblivious:

> There are three folk driving in a quaint old chaise,
> And the cliff-side track looks green and fair,
> I view them talking in quiet glee
> As they drop down towards the puffins' lair
>   By the roughest of ways;
> But another with the three rides on, I see,
>   Whom I like not to be there!

The intimate groupings in the poem have a resonance in terms of their numberings: the poem moves from this initial scene of a threesome with an invisible fourth, to a scene of a twosome with an unnoticed third, followed by a group of "diners in a mansion place" where the presence of "a hollow voice" goes unperceived, and finally "Yet a goodlier scene" of "a crowd" on "a lawn" who "chatter and ramble as fancy leads" and who are unaware of the presence of "one mirthless, / Who ought not to be there".

The poem envisages, after each pictured scene, the reader's surmise about the "uninvited guest": "No; It's not anybody you think of", "No: not whom you knew and name", "No: It's not ... the stranger you met once", "Nay: It's not the pale Form your imaginings raise". This involvement of the reader in the psychic drama of failed imaginative perception is made all the more pertinent by the second verse:

> ... Next
> A dwelling appears by a slow sweet stream
> Where two sit happy and half in the dark:
> They read, helped out by a frail-wick'd gleam,
>   Some rhythmic text;
> But one sits with them whom they don't mark,
>   One I'm wishing could not be there.

The reference to reading a "rhythmic text" draws the reader into the frame, through its suggestion of a common experience, while the "frail-wick'd gleam" is suggestive of the faint light of the imagination that is insufficient to illuminate something real but not of the visible order. In the final verse it is revealed that the presence is not the "Fourth Figure" that "waits on us all at a destined time", but instead is "that under which best lives corrode". We might think of this as madness, or envy, or destructiveness. This insidious and corrosive undermining force seems to be experienced as something alien, an invisible and silent intruder—it is not felt to reside or to come from within, and remains to a large extent psychically unassimilated. The poem ends with an impassioned wish that such a force did not exist, though with an implied regretful acknowledgement that it inevitably does: "Would, would it could not be there!".

The mind's questioning of itself, and of what is "real" in the mind, is the subject of a dramatic short poem in three stanzas, "The Dream Is—Which?". The title denotes the theme of uncertainty related to an alternative state of consciousness, and the poem plays on the different meanings of the word "dream" (joy, the imaginary, the realm of the unconscious, illusion, and unreality). It is a poem of altered states, in which there is a succession of psychic transformations represented in alternations between joyful and lively romantic scenarios of a couple, and mournful, depleted scenes of solitariness and loss:

> I am laughing by the brook with her,
>   Splashed in its tumbling stir;
> And then it is a blankness looms
>   As if I walked not there,
> Nor she, but found me in haggard rooms,
>   And treading a lonely stair.

The experience portrayed is of something within the mind that is felt to intervene and to take over, described in the different stanzas as "a blankness looms", "a harsh change comes edging in", and "a curtain drops". This is embodied formally in the poem's rhyme scheme (a,a,b,c,b,c), in which union and closeness are reflected in the contiguous rhymes of the couplet at the beginning of each stanza (a,a), and interruption and separation are reflected in the alternating rhymes of the remaining four lines of each stanza (b,c,b,c). Union and separation are represented not as physical facts but rather as internal states of mind, mediated by the activity of the imagination and the unconscious, the latter containing shadows of the mind that give particular shape and emotional definition to psychic states.

Thomas Hardy tends to be associated with a focus on this darker side of the mind, and with an unbalanced bleak and pessimistic view of human nature—a criticism often levelled also at psychoanalysis!—and I therefore want to conclude with a look at some of Hardy's poems that express a very different outlook and sentiment.

Some blessed Hope: a glory through the gloom

In this final part of my exploration of Hardy's poetry, I shall consider a group of poems in which the theme of hope is prominent. In these poems musicality, rhythm, or benign conjunction (of time, place, and spirit) are often central to the experience and expression of hope; these elements are in turn bound up with qualities of vitality, passion, exuberance, freedom of spirit, and creativity, which find poetic expression partly through Hardy's innovative and original use of metre and stanzaic form. (Page [1999, p. 47] comments that there is "evidence that for Hardy a poem often began as a tune, or at least a rhythmic pattern, such musical elements being anterior to words and 'meaning'".)

A magical example of this is the poem "Lines", subtitled "TO A MOVEMENT IN MOZART'S E-FLAT SYMPHONY", with its explicit tribute to the inspiration of music. The poem is a beautiful poetic celebration of love and of amorous rapture remembered, but also of poetic expression and form itself:

> Show me again just this:
>   The moment of that kiss
> Away from the prancing folk, by the strawberry-tree!—
> Yea, to such rashness, ratheness, rareness, ripeness, richness,
>   Love lures life on.

The modulated cadences and rhythms evoke the sensation of musical expression and variation. The tone is affirmative, vitalizing, and uplifting, and the experience of reading the poem is partly one of renewal and optimism. The poem is not without intimations of the darker and more painful side of life and emotion—for instance in its reference to the intermingling of life's "bodings, broodings, beatings, blanchings, blessings". Similarly, the poem's refrain "Show me again ..." underscores the poignancy of loss implicit in the fact that the experience and the lived moment are gone. But this is balanced by the live memory of the feelings of love, feelings which can be enshrined and immortalized in poetic expression and form (I suspect the poem's title is partly a reference to Shakespeare's "eternal lines" in Sonnet XVIII—"When in eternal lines to time thou growest"—which plays on the contrast between the lines of ageing, leading to death, and the lines of poetry by which the writer's love and loved one are immortalized).

Hope is more explicitly the subject of "Snow in the Suburbs", though it makes its appearance unexpectedly only at the end of the poem. This marks a recurrent theme of hope appearing at an unexpected or unlikely time and place. "Snow in the Suburbs" works through a conjunction of richly impressionistic scenic description and emotionally symbolic poetic formulation. It opens with a marvellous poetic vision of transformation, in which an instinctive sensitivity to shape, form and motion finds expression:

> Every branch big with it,
> Bent every twig with it
> Every fork like a white web-foot;
> Every street and pavement mute:
> Some flakes have lost their way, and grope back upward, when
> Meeting those meandering down they turn and descend again.
> The palings are glued together like a wall
> And there is no waft of wind with the fleecy fall.

The snow obliterates angles and gaps ("Every fork like a white web foot"; "The palings are glued together like a wall"), spaces that are human markers of separateness and of differentiation, definition and order; but the observed scene is pregnant ("big") with the transformative power of imaginative significance and association, as all-encompassing as the snow.

Into this colourless scene, devoid of animate life but imbued with meaning for the observer by the life and forms of the imagination, comes a solitary sparrow that "enters the tree" and sets off a cascading chain reaction. Hardy humorously images a succession of cause-and-effect fallings that echo the movement of the falling snow—a "snow-lump thrice his own slight size / Descends on him and showers his head and eyes, / And overturns him, / And near inurns him", the sparrow falls onto a "nether twig", which in turn "Starts a volley of other lodging lumps with a rush". This indecorous fate of the sparrow shows Hardy having fun with a traditional symbol of poetry (the "poetic" bird is subject to the laws of gravity of the "real" world); but it represents also the frailty and fragility of life, as well as chance cause-and-effect and unexpected chains of events.

Finally, in a change of key and a modest, four-line concluding stanza:

> The steps are a blanched slope,
> Up which, with feeble hope,
> A black cat comes, wide-eyed and thin:
> And we take him in.

Taking in the cat is an empathic act based on recognition, through identification, of vulnerability, exposure, and need. The poem suggests the interconnectedness between the human capacities of observation and receptivity to impressions, the activity of the imagination, and the capacity for empathy and for hope. The "wide-eyed and thin" black cat symbolizes "feeble hope" itself, which needs internal protection and nurture if it is to survive and have the opportunity to flourish—in effect, to be taken in and given a psychic home.

In the poem "In a Waiting-Room", hope is inspired by the voice of a child and the child's spirit of optimism. The railway station waiting-room setting, contents, and atmosphere are both real and symbolic:

> On a morning sick as the day of doom
>   With the drizzling grey
>   Of an English May,
> There were few in the railway waiting-room.
> About its walls were framed and varnished
> Pictures of liners, fly-blown, tarnished.
> The table bore a Testament
> For travellers reading, if ouchwise bent.

The profound gloom of this "charmless scene" of waiting (literal and metaphorical) is compounded by the discovery of sums of accounts "scrawled" on the "printed page" of the bible—the most literal of "figures", suggestive of a gross failure of the imagination. Moreover, "To lend the hour's mean hue / A smear of tragedy too", there is the presence of a "soldier and wife" who are "parting as they believed for ever". Once again we see an "enkindling ardency"—in a scene of internal desolation and corresponding external impoverishment—associated with a sense of hope:

> But next there came
> Like the eastern flame
> Of some high altar, children—a pair—

The children laugh at the "fly-blown, tarnished" pictures on the wall, on to which they project not a depleted internal state that matches external circumstances or details, but instead a very different internal state shaped by their imaginative reveries: this takes the form of their anticipation of a destination ("Here are the lovely ships that we, / ... are going to see") and of a wonderful day out with their mother. The poem ends on a note of continued "waiting" which has, however, been transformed by a spirit that partakes of the sacred:

> It rained on the skylight with a din
> As we waited and still no train came in;
> But the words of the child in the squalid room
> Had spread a glory through the gloom.

The theme of hope is more complex in the poem "The Darkling Thrush" which I mentioned at the beginning. This much loved and probably best known of Hardy's poems counterbalances the states of depression and hope, and illustrates Hardy's poetic vision and expression. Harvey (1999) points out that the structure of the poem, in terms of its two halves, embodies this "duality of experience" (p. 150).

The Darkling Thrush

> I leant upon a coppice gate
>   When Frost was spectre-gray
> And Winter's dregs made desolate
>   The weakening eye of day.
> The tangled bine-stems scored the sky
>   Like strings of broken lyres,
> And all mankind that haunted nigh
>   Had sought their household fires.
>
> The land's sharp features seemed to be
>   The Century's corpse outleant
> His crypt the cloudy canopy,
>   His wind the death-lament.—
> The ancient pulse of germ and birth
>   Was shrunken hard and dry,
> And every spirit upon earth
>   Seemed fervourless as I.
>
> At once a voice arose among
>   The bleak twigs overhead
> In a full-hearted evensong
>   Of joy illimited.
> An aged thrush, frail, gaunt, and small,
>   In blast-beruffled plume,
> Had chosen thus to fling his soul
>   Upon the growing gloom.

> So little cause for carolings
>   Of such ecstatic sound
> Was written on terrestrial things
>   Afar or nigh around,
> That I could think there trembled through
>   His happy good-night air
> Some blessed Hope, whereof he knew
>   And I was unaware.

Barbara Hardy (2000) argues that in the poem "Hardy allows himself to imagine the romantic unity of being by insisting that the idea is not believed but merely entertained" (p. 105)—"I *could* think" [emphasis added]—and thus that "its pressure of wish-fulfilment is made clear" (p. 200). She suggests that the poem "articulates only the possibility of taking the bird as a symbol of optimism" (p. 200). This is an example of what she sees more generally as Hardy's literary traits of "uncertainty", "hesitation" and "provisionality" (like Riquelme [1999], she sees in Hardy's poetry precursors of literary modernity); the effect is to "check and destabilize imagination's tendency to idealize, systematize, blend and unify" (p. 217), and to "question the conventions of completion" (*ibid.*).

I take this to correspond to a form of "Negative Capability" (Keats, 1817, p. 43) in relation to the mind itself and to the products of the imagination. In "The Darkling Thrush"—a supreme and beautiful example of poetic expression and symbolism—"Hope" is linked with *the mind's capacity to generate symbols* (for Hardy this meant poetic symbols), but this also entails recognizing symbols as products of the imagination ("entertaining" them) and not as embodiments or tokens of reality ("believing" them).

I shall finish with a fitting quotation from Williams & Waddell (1991): "Poetry is in essence the symbolization of the spaces and tensions of mental life" (p. 184). I hope to have illustrated some of the ways in which this is true of Thomas Hardy's poems.

References

Bion, W. R. (1961). *Experiences in Groups*. London: Tavistock Publications.
Bion, W. R. (1962). *Learning from Experience*. London: Maresfield Library.

Britton, R. (1998). The other room and poetic space. In: *Belief and Imagination: Explorations in Psychoanalysis*. London and New York: Routledge.

Brooks, J. (1971). The homeliest of heart-stirrings: shorter lyrics. In: J. Gibson & T. Johnson (Eds.), *Thomas Hardy: Poems. A Selection of Critical Essays*. London: Macmillan, 1979.

Brown, D. (1954). Hardy's elegiac power. In: J. Gibson & T. Johnson (Eds.), *Thomas Hardy: Poems. A Selection of Critical Essays*. London: Macmillan, 1979.

Chandra, S. (1999). Thomas Hardy: Then and now. In: S. Chandra (Ed.), *Thomas Hardy: A Collection of Critical Essays*. London: Sangam Books.

Day Lewis, C. (1951). The lyrical poetry. In: J. Gibson & T. Johnson (Eds.), *Thomas Hardy: Poems. A Selection of Critical Essays*. London: Macmillan, 1979.

Freud, S. (1916 [1915]). On transience. *S.E.*, *14*.

Gunn, T. (1972). The influence of ballad forms. In: J. Gibson & T. Johnson (Eds.), *Thomas Hardy: Poems. A Selection of Critical Essays*. London: Macmillan, 1979.

Hardy, B. (2000). *Imagining Imagination in Hardy's Poetry and Prose*. London and New Brunswick, NJ: The Athlone Press.

Hardy, F. E. (1962). *The Life of Thomas Hardy*. London: Macmillan.

Hardy, T. (1922). Apology. In: *Late Lyrics and Earlier*.

Harris Williams, M. (1988). Holding the dream: the nature of aesthetic appreciation. In: D. Meltzer & M. H. Williams, *The Apprehension of Beauty*. Strath Tay: Clunie Press.

Harvey, G. (1999). Hardy's poetry of transcendence. In: S. Chandra (Ed.), *Thomas Hardy: A Collection of Critical Essays*. London: Sangam Books.

Keats, J. (1817). Letter to G. and T. Keats, 21, 27 December. In: R. Gittings (Ed.), *Letters of John Keats*. Oxford: Oxford University Press, 1987.

King, R. W. (1925). The lyrical poems of Thomas Hardy. In: J. Gibson & T. Johnson (Eds.), *Thomas Hardy: Poems. A Selection of Critical Essays*. London: Macmillan, 1979

MacDowall, A. S. (1928). Leading article in *Times Literary Supplement*, 26 January 1928. In: J. Gibson & T. Johnson (Eds.), *Thomas Hardy: Poems. A Selection of Critical Essays*. London: Macmillan, 1979.

MacDowall, A. S. (1931). An explorer of reality. In: J. Gibson & T. Johnson (Eds.), *Thomas Hardy: Poems. A Selection of Critical Essays*. London: Macmillan, 1979.

Maiello, S. (2000). "Song-and-dance" and its developments: the function of rhythm in the learning process of oral and written language. In: M. Cohen & A. Hahn (Eds.), *Exploring the Work of Donald Meltzer*. London and New York: Karnac Books.

Meltzer, D., & Harris Williams, M. (1988). *The Apprehension of Beauty*. Strath Tay: Clunie Press.

Middleton Murry, J. (1919). The poetry of Mr Hardy. In: J. Gibson & T. Johnson (Eds.), *Thomas Hardy: Poems. A Selection of Critical Essays*. London: Macmillan, 1979.

Page, N. (1999). Art and aesthetics. In: D. Kraemer (Ed.), *The Cambridge Companion to Thomas Hardy*. Cambridge: Cambridge University Press.

Riquelme, J. P. (1999). The modernity of Thomas Hardy's poetry. In: D. Kraemer (Ed.), *The Cambridge Companion to Thomas Hardy*. Cambridge: Cambridge University Press.

Segal, H. (1986). A psychoanalytic approach to aesthetics. In: *The Work of Hanna Segal*. London: Free Association Books/Maresfield Library.

Segal, H (1991a). Freud and art. In: *Dream, Phantasy and Art*. London: Routledge.

Segal, H. (1991b). Art and the depressive position. In: *Dream, Phantasy and Art*. London: Routledge.

Steiner, J. (1993). *Psychic Retreats*. London and New York: Routledge.

Williams, M. H., & Waddell, M. (1991). *The Chamber of Maiden Thought*. London and New York: Routledge.

Winnicott, D. W. (1971). The location of cultural experience. In: *Playing and Reality*. London: Tavistock.

Wright, D. (Ed.) (1978). *The Selected Poems of Thomas Hardy*. London: Penguin. [All quotations of Hardy's poetry are from this volume.]

CHAPTER EIGHT

The elusive pursuit of insight: three poems by W. B. Yeats and the human task

Judith Edwards

> He disappeared in the dead of winter
> The brooks were frozen, the airports almost deserted,
> The snow disfigured the public statues;
> The mercury sank in the mouth of the dying day,
> What instruments we have agree
> The day of his death was a dark cold day.
>
> W. H. Auden, "In Memory of W. B. Yeats", 1979, p. 80

I n his solemn elegy for Yeats Auden also says "You were silly like us; / Your gift survived it all". What I hope to do in this chapter is to take three poems from Yeats' prolific work and to suggest how like us all he was in his development. This will not then be an attempt to put either a poet or his poetry on the couch *per se*, except in so far as both partake of the human condition. Poetry survives the individual's death, says Auden, and is modified "in the guts of the living"—a digestive and assimilative process which one hopes produces growth. I hope to draw forth something from the large and varied output of one of the twentieth-century's greatest English-speaking poets that is representative of differing states of mind experienced within individuals struggling with the task of progressing towards a mature and realistic sense of self. This sense of self will inevitably be prone to instability and will be vulnerable to both internal and external attack, so that, in a sense, this developmental "line" is actually more of a loop—or even a spiral—much in the way that the Kleinian psychoanalyst Britton (1998, pp. 69–81) describes in the oscillation and either augmentation or diminution that occurs as a normal phenomenon in mental and emotional development in relation to the world inside the individual's mind. Britton talks of the important need to distinguish between these oscillations which result in positive psychic development following periods of turmoil, and more pathological regressions.

As Yeats himself described it in his journals (Foster, 1998) the ordinary man is "a bundle of accident and incoherence": however, the poet who emerges from the struggle with words and images in a finished work is "something intended, complete". (At least provisionally, we might add.) He talked of a pursuit of "radiance" being a central task, and I have paraphrased this to encompass something of the human task in the long and often painful journey on the path towards a more realistic sense of identity: what could be called "seeing the light" about the self.

I want to begin with one of Yeats' best-known poems, "The Lake Isle of Innisfree". He wrote it when he was a young man in London, and as he wandered despondently down the street he stopped to stare into a shop window (*ibid.*, p. 79). It was a poem which was to pursue him, often to his irritation, for the rest of his life, as he was asked many times to declaim it (which he did of course with relish.) (*ibid.*).

> I will arise and go now, and go to Innisfree,
> And a small cabin build there, of clay and wattles made:
> Nine bean-rows will I have there, a hive for the honey-bee,
> And live alone in the bee-loud glade.
>
> And I shall have some peace there, for peace comes dropping slow,
> Dropping from the veils of the morning to where the cricket sings;
> There midnight's all a glimmer, and noon a purple glow
> And evening full of the linnet's wings.
>
> I will arise and go now, for always night and day
> I hear lake water lapping with low sounds by the shore;
> While I stand on the roadway, or on the pavements grey,
> I hear it in the deep heart's core.
> (Yeats, 1995, p. 44)

"The deep heart's core" has some affinities, I think, with Wordsworth's "emotion recollected in tranquillity", and what Yeats is bringing into being for himself and his readers is an image which might also at one level be compared to Wordsworth's daffodils. But I think there are important differences in their internal inspiration. While Wordsworth's daffodils were "fluttering and dancing", and on show to everyone on the hills of the Lake District, Yeats' Lake Isle is for him alone. He has taken up residence in the small cabin, and his "nine bean rows" have a proprietorial ring to them— putting his seeds, as it were, on the land he has staked out—as I would like to suggest, some exclusive ownership of the land that may be compared to a very early experience and impulse to be in complete ownership of the mother, to the exclusion of father and siblings. In other words, the staking out of internal territory. The language and the way he deploys it has a sleepy, hypnotic effect, with the repetition of consonants and whole words emphasizing a slow contemplative rhythm that one might think could be related to the early infant's experience of the reassuring beat of mother's heart.

There is the idea of a protected space, which of course the small infant does indeed need in order gradually to be introduced to the external and internal stresses of the world via his mother's containment. She takes on his anxieties and fears, ponders on them in her own mind—what Bion (1962) called her "reverie"—and returns his thoughts to him in a less terrifying form.

Yeats' place of peace seems to describe an escape into the simple life from the complexity and conflict of relationships: his Lake Isle object is suffused with feelings of safety—there is no harsh light. He talks of the "veils" of the morning (which one could perhaps recast as mother's gentle lidded eyes), the glimmering of night (the dimmed light for the night-time feed), and the hushed feathery image of "the linnets' wings"; small murmurings at the edges of a soothing world. Again the rhythm is emphasized through allitera-tion with the low lapping of the lake water, and the whole picture has a soft-focus, almost "Vaseline on the lens" feel, which could be seen to represent one side of primary experience: what Freud (1927, pp. 66–72) called the "oceanic bliss" which observers of infants see when a baby is resting close to mother's breast after a satisfying feed, taking in the feed again in phantasy and recollection, with little mouthing movements, while his hands lie close to the breast itself. This vital experience provides the first way in which a baby takes in or introjects a good satisfying experience that then can act as a buffer when he is assailed by the internal monsters of hunger, pain, and loneliness.

There follows a good description of this, where after a period of being unsettled a baby finds some temporary peace:

> Mother is stretched out on the settee, and Pierre is lying on top of her, as if he wanted to encompass her whole body. His head is in the hollow of her left elbow, his body on her chest, his feet on her thighs with his left arm dangling, the other tucked behind her back. She offers him her left breast and he takes it instantly. At the beginning he seems to drink eagerly, then he sucks the milk with four or five movements of his lips—a pause—four or five more movements—another pause. Mother looks at him: he has his eyes shut and it seems as if he has fallen asleep, as he has fallen from the nipple. Then he moves his lips several times in the same sucking rhythm as before. He is breathing quite rapidly. His mother leaves him as he has fallen asleep, against her breast. When she moves a little, he moves; his mother dries his lips and he seems to wake up a little, repeating the same suck–pause rhythm, but more slowly now. His hand rests free, grazing the breast in a sort of caress. He is calm but not completely asleep; he begins to make a movement as if to let go of the breast, but takes the nipple again, and his mother helps him. [Sandri, 1999]

So, then, we have a picture in the Lake Isle of an ideal state, which can possibly be likened, as I have indicated, to the feelings a baby has when digesting a good experience or feed, close to the provider of the feed. These are experiences that need to be repeated for adequate introjection or location within the psyche to form the ego ideal. But there is also the possibility that this good experience can then turn from an ideal to an idealized state which defends against reality: Yeats' island could be seen to represent a turning away from difficulty and an image based on psychic retreat. While Steiner (1993) has powerfully delineated the pathological conse-quences of retreats based on grievance, there exists within any normal human being the impulse to retreat in the face of difficulty to a state of no suffering, an idealized fusion with a breast/nurturing object which provides refuge from frustration and the delusion that the infant self owns the breast (i.e. mother) exclusively. Britton (1998, p. 112) describes this as a "wishful psychosis ... a deficit is denied by hallucinating the missing object, or there is the delusion of *being it*". He emphasizes that this is a particular sort of non-pathological retreat. And we must remember the impulse of the poem, written on a grey, lonely day. "I will arise and go now" also possesses energy and resolve; a move from despondency. The ideal state is indeed "gone", and mourned in this poem. Remembering it in "the deep heart's core" is akin to mourning.

While I have mentioned not wishing to analyse Yeats as a particular individual, it might be worth pointing out that he had a mother who had, according to her husband, "never shown attention to me or to anyone". (Foster, 1997, p. 8) She was prone to depressive withdrawal, and would often fall asleep while reading to her children. For Yeats she was "the most beautiful woman in Sligo" and it is hardly surprising that he projected this idealization in the face of real difficulty on to the countryside of Sligo in general in his early poetry and on to the Lake Isle in particular. Grinberg & Grinberg (1999, p. 160) talk of the propensity for migrants to project on to the lost countryside all the human losses they have endured: "It is the non-human environment, especially the natural surroundings of the individual which have acquired an intense emotional meaning that usually persists unmodified as an object of longing and *a symbol of what is his own*" (my italics).

For the migrant, the loss of country represents one end of a continuum of losses. At the other end lie the ordinary losses originating with what psychoanalysts call "the absent breast" (O'Shaugnessy, 1964, pp. 36–43), and complicated further in the case of the breast/thinking experience offered by a mother preoccupied by her own distress and so not able to be "occupied" by the baby's feelings and emotional needs. (It is also important to note that since this "classical" formulation of the spur to first thought occurring in the space left by the absent breast, there has been more consideration (Alvarez, 1999, pp. 183–196) of the differential qualities of the *present* breast/object as a stimulus to thought.)

So here we have a primary state of mind represented by the Lake Isle, which has necessarily to be modified in order that the individual can move towards a fuller view. There is loss but also gain in this move, and it is essential to keep both in mind when considering any change in a previously-maintained psychic equilibrium (Joseph, 1989).

I want to move on to another short poem which sprang from a moment in time and then came to represent for the poet what seems like a pivotal developmental point, where there could be either a move forward or back.

It is no longer summer in "the bee-loud glade", but winter, on a day full of sunlight and harsh, brilliant contrasts, and the poet is taking a solitary walk.

The Cold Heaven

Suddenly I saw the cold and rook-delighting heaven
That seems as though ice burned and was but the more ice,
And thereupon imagination and heart were driven
So wild that every casual thought of that and this
Vanished, and left but memories, that should be out of season
With the hot blood of youth, of love crossed long ago;
And I took all the blame out of all sense and reason,
Until I cried and trembled and rocked to and fro,
Riddled with light. Ah! When the ghost begins to quicken,
Confusion of the death-bed over, is it sent
Out naked on the roads, as the books say, and stricken
By the injustice of the skies for punishment?
(Yeats, 1995, p. 140)

I think it would he hard to conceive of a more radically different tone in this poem from the previous one: gone is the soft, protected, and insular world of the Lake Isle. Instead the poet (and the reader) is exposed to a harsh and glittering sky, where opposites unite in a cruel discord, burning and freezing simultaneously. Foster (1997, p. 490) describes this poem in terms of a man looking back on his life and his failed loves, beset with queries about esoteric dilemmas he has puzzled over to do with death, ghosts and dreams.

The soft linnets have been replaced by the wheeling silhouettes of rooks, black against the steely sky. There is a powerful evocation of utter helplessness against the lightning flash of a new realization. The phrase "riddled with light" with its possible association to gun bullets and something irrevocably blown apart, holds within itself the paradox of the dark thoughts which accompany this attack of insight.

Heaney (1995, p. 148) describes the poem as a "spasm of

consciousness", where it is the poet's energetic engagement with his technical skills that succeeds in holding together a shattering moment. Heaney demonstrates this by his close textual analysis of the poem from the point of view of poetic technique:

> "The Cold Heaven" is a poem which suggests that there is an overall purpose to life; and it does so by the intrinsically poetic action of its rhymes, its rhythms and its exultant intonation. These create an energy and an order which promote the idea that there exists a much greater, circumambient energy and order within which we have our being. [Heaney, 1995, pp. 147–149]

Heaney's is one reading of the poem and, of course, a perfectly valid one. For my purposes in this chapter I want to focus more on the despair and the painful sense of guilt combined with a feeling of profound alone-ness. This is very different from the wished-for protected "alone-ness" in "The Lake Isle". What I want to suggest is that this represents an oscillating moment on "the threshold of the depressive position" where there can be either an evasion of the reality of the world as it is rather than as we would like it to be, and a retreat to the Lake Isle frame of mind, or a modifying cast of thought which mediates against the primeval terror of being responsible and thus culpable. In other words, a move from an idealized view of the blameless self to the acceptance of self-divisions, and a concern for the welfare of others in the face of one's more destructive impulses.

Yeats describes the force of the realization which makes him rock and reel with the pain of it. This would seem to be in the same imaginative terrain as Dante's ninth and last circle of Hell, where those who have betrayed their families, associates, and benefactors are buried in varying degrees of ice.

> Here the weeping puts an end to weeping,
> and the grief that finds no outlet from the eyes
> Turns inward to intensify the anguish
> [Musa, 1995, p. 183]

Although Yeats knows already by implication that something has happened which will then become modified by further thinking, at this moment "I took the blame out of all sense and reason". This brings thoughts of death, and then of infinite punishment. The unjust skies seem to represent a wrenching away from the gentle protecting maternal influence in the Lake Isle to the Jehovah-like paternal judgement which shows no mercy or ultimate forgiveness. At this moment, far from there being hope of redemption and faith in "an overall purpose", the poem can be read in the spirit of an individual mind which feels cast out forever, "naked on the roads", without compass or guide. It is a bitter expulsion from the Garden of Eden which is the Lake Isle.

This seems to me less about the exultation that Heaney suggests than about total despair. This is the agony rather than the ecstasy. The desperate rocking may put one in mind of the rocking rituals of autistic children, as they attempt to block out the pain of separation and loss by fervent self-comforting. This can result in the complete evacuation of the capacity to think; into a black hole where gravity and the space–time continuum collapse. I have talked of this phenomenon in autism elsewhere (Edwards, 1994). I would like here to see the poem rather in the light of more generalized anxieties activated by the bringing together of love and hate in both self and object, with the concomitant realization of responsibility for destructive impulses and the initial despair that this means as something more negative comes into the idealized picture of the self. There is fear that the attacked object will be lost, just at the moment when the whole picture can include the bad but alongside the undoubted good, which can be really appreciated. To put it at its earliest occurrence: the mother who made the baby wait is undoubtedly also the one that offers him goodness in terms of milk, thoughts, and feelings. As I have said, the phrase "riddled with light" could be construed as representing just such an epiphanic moment, where the realization itself, the light, forces an acknowledgement of hitherto unacknowledged internal darkness—the narcissistic self-image gives way to something which feels initially catastrophic, as Britton (1998, pp. 69–81) puts it, and the self, now feeling infinitely small rather than improbably large, occupying the whole of the island, has a sense of being ejected into the wilderness. What Britton then formulates is a state of affairs that will follow later ... "it is not a state of mind that is realised, but a hope, based on faith, that future developments will bring coherence and meaning". This hope is what Heaney seems to intuit as being a next step, although actually within the poem itself there seems to be the expression of despair in pure culture. Britton maintains that it is only later that a move forward occurs to something more manageable inside the mind.

> By the time this position (that of the promised land) is arrived at, we are back to the familiar depressive position; the promised land has become Israel and another struggle has begun. [*ibid.*]

In other words, there is a continual "looping" to-and-fro of states rather than stasis in an idealized "depressive position". In "The Cold Heaven" all responsibility is taken by the self, and the "burning ice" freezes this moment in time before the oscillation begins; the move towards real reparation of the damage and a more realistic and forgiving view of the self, which brings relief. The crucial point would seem to be, I think, to do with having enough strength to withstand being blinded by the "bullets" of realization, "riddled with light", without resorting to a bullet-proof vest which prevents any realization entering. Insight marks a pivotal point: there is then a choice about going forward, going back, or remaining in a stuck state, transfixed by "the light".

In work with children, in recent years there has been a predominance in our caseloads of deprived and borderline personalities who have not indeed experienced in a reliable way the kind of early foundational interactions between caretaker and infant that result in reliable introjections as a buffer against later difficulty. The oscillations between these "positions" may not be present at all. Months or even years may pass before discernible patterns may emerge, and there may be instant terrified returns to a "Lake Isle" position at the mere hint of the emergence of a different perspective. Dependence on an object and concern for its welfare could be seen as a kind of luxury to those children for whom defensive denial has actually been the only resort and comfort in situations of deficit and trauma.

For example, a ten-year-old boy I saw who had been severely abused in his family of origin had been a "late adoption" with his younger sister. Jim was referred to me because of his difficulties making a relationship with his adoptive family, particularly his adoptive mother.

He came to the first assessment meeting with his family, armed, it seemed burdened, by a huge "Life Story Book". One of my first thoughts was that at least part of my work would be to help him slowly relegate this to the past in order to free the present and create a less contaminated future. Therapy began, and while he railed against boundary setting (for instance that what he made in the room needed to stay there), he also seemed to appreciate firmness and my capacity to contain and think about his frustration. In the penultimate session of the first term he drew a flower rooted in a pot, which seemed to indicate his sense of being rooted in the therapeutic process. However, at times of breaks, or when Jim felt I thwarted him he would return to a more autonomous "Lake Isle" state, and he built a castle with huge defences which could only later include a drawbridge that sometimes opened to let me in ... "My parents look after me; I stay well away from you". It was clear that by my taking the role in the therapy of the one who had abandoned him, he was able more to appreciate the love of his adoptive parents.

Gradually, through a series of stories about a phoenix and a magic carpet he was able to sort out his defensive use of magic powers from an ordinary, healthy capacity to wish that things had been different. He was amazed when I endorsed his growing view that "life now" was more important, rather than his obsessive concentration on chronically difficult life history. This was after nine months of once-weekly meetings.

> After some "magic" play with characters who flew, I said sometimes he wished he lived in a magic world. "Yes I do", he said, "especially at bedtime, but then I have bad dreams. I dream about being Superman flying about, but then people shoot me down. I know it is bad for me to have these thoughts". I said it was so hard when he wanted to be the boss, but then he feared people like me would get cross and destroy him. But he also wanted people to think he's super too, a boy worth caring about. [He had been badly abused by his original parents.] He smiled, pleased. And I said it was hard to do what grown-ups said, like about bedtime or coming here when *I* said rather than when *he* wanted to. "Well I sometimes want to come", he said, "and sometimes I don't".

Jim needed me to help him overcome difficult experience and to foster growth, and I had to respect his retreats in the service of this, to the "Lake Island".

The third poem I want to focus on was one written when Yeats was in his late middle age, and the location has moved from an anonymous sky-filled space where the poet feels adrift in the universe to Coole Park in Ballylee, the beloved home of his friend and patron Lady Gregory. It represented many things to him, culturally and historically, but here I want to concentrate on its emotional significance as the locus for the moving on from implacable insight to something more reflective and philosophical.

The Wild Swans at Coole

The trees are in their autumn beauty,
The woodland paths are dry,
Under the October twilight the water
Mirrors a still sky;
Upon the brimming water among the stones
Are nine and fifty swans.

The nineteenth autumn has come upon me
Since I first made my count;
I saw, before I had well finished,
All suddenly mount
And scatter wheeling in great broken rings
Upon their clamorous wings.

I have looked upon these brilliant creatures.
And now my heart is sore.
All's changed since I, hearing at twilight,
The first time on this shore,
The bell-beat of their wings above my head,
Trod with a lighter tread.

Unwearied still, lover by lover,
They paddle in the cold
Companionable streams or climb the air;
Their hearts have not grown old;
Passion or conquest, wander where they will,
Attend upon them still.

But now they drift on the still water,
Mysterious, beautiful;
Among what rushes will they build,
By what lake's edge or pool

> Delight men's eyes when I awake some day
> To find they have flown away?
> (Yeats, 1995, p. 147)

Here the scene is set for late autumnal thoughts; a mature sort of beauty with its own quiet reflections as the water mirrors the sky. There is a dynamic tension in the poem between this stillness and the "clamorous wings" of the swan couples and in the whole poem with its free-flowing discipline of rhyme and rhythm a temporary acceptance of change, despite the "sore heart". This again has some resonances with Wordsworth, both in the idea of the return to a much loved place as Wordsworth returned to Tintern Abbey, and in the inevitable sadness attendant on life—the "still sad music of humanity", although Yeats' sadness seems more personally located rather projected into humanity as a whole. (Which in a sense can be seen as a more authentic working-though of sorrow: Britton (1998, pp. 129–132) postulates that Wordsworth's rather precocious poetic development gave way later in his life to a retreat to certainty rather than face the inevitable "loops" of psychological experience.)

We have moved in the bird imagery from the soft linnet and the cawing crows to the swans, with the emphasis on their wildness and their freedom to go where they will, as well as their uxoriousness (swans are known to mate for life). They are seen to "paddle" in the air: symbolically they represent the union of air and water (Cooper, 1978) and the swan is called "the bird of the poet". Here Yeats laments the passing of time "all's changed" ... and he seems to feel that his days of passion and conquest, which were causing him such agony of blame in "The Cold Heaven", are behind him, but embodied in the swans in their upwards passage from the stones by the lake. One could say that at this moment Yeats has projected his own lively engagement with life into these wild birds, and one could debate whether this might be a defensive exclusion of his own energies rather than an "integrated" perspective. There is the contrast between time passing in a human life and what he sees as the eternal timeless beauty of the birds.

These wild swans could be seen to represent a capacity to leave things in the moment without wishing to constrain them. They are also seen by Yeats as couples, so that the internal image of a parental couple who have their own autonomy has replaced the more primitive and passionate urge to control them. In the last stanza, as the swans drift quietly on the water after their clamorous flight, he wonders where they will go, when he wakes to see they have gone. We could see this as having something to do with an acceptance of his own mortality: that he too must at last "fly away"; and that he has developed the capacity to accept this and let go, in preparation for his own death. (Symbolically again the swan is seen as "the bird of death" and its dying song denotes resignation.) This could be seen as at least a temporary integration of opposites and the end of many struggles to come to terms with the finiteness of life. (This kind of integration, hard won, can nevertheless very easily fail under the pressure of fear, hatred of reality, or disbelief, and for Yeats himself there is strong evidence in his very last poems that this could only be achieved through a sort of distanced objectivity ... "Cast a cold eye / On life, on death, / Horseman, pass by!") By talking of himself in the third person in his very last published poem, "Under Ben Bulben"—'In Drumcliff churchyard Yeats is laid"—he objectifies himself perhaps as a way of dealing with the inevitability of the death we must all face. By locating energy and passion in the swans at Coole Park rather than himself, one could also think that the acceptance of death at this point means that Yeats may feel he has to be dead to the senses already. Is this mourning or melancholia?

Here there can be seen to be a contrast between what one might call the persecuting guilt of "The Cold Heaven", where despair and self-reproach all but annihilate the subject, and a more "depressive" approach, where there is a sense of nostalgia and feelings of responsibility. These feelings are the basis for the wish to repair the objects, to present them with a gift, which links more with Segal's ideas of the creative impulse as being firmly rooted in the depressive position (Segal, 1991). Or to go back to Freud's original work, we could see here the working through of "normal mourning" as opposed to the more pathological state of mourning where melancholia ensues (Freud, 1917, pp. 237–260).

And yet thinking has moved on since Segal's formulations about the creative impulse being firmly located in the depressive position, and the idea of a perpetual motion between states of mind over the life-span seems not only more akin to the internal lives human beings generally experience, in life as well as on the couch, but also to abandon the notion of morality in creativity, with a "depressive" cast of mind being a *sine qua non* for "good" creative work. Ehrenzweig's posthumously published book (1967, pp. 102–109) seems to have links with this notion of the free looping movement that is the hallmark of authentic creativity. An art education lecturer with a solid background knowledge of psychoanalytic principles, he talks of the three phases of the creative act.

Initially the artist (or poet, for the purposes of this chapter) projects what Ehrenzweig calls the schizoid parts of the fragmented self into the internal creative "womb" (much in the way that the baby, as I have already said, projects his terror and fear into his mother). There then occurs what he calls a "manic" scanning of these fragments, which begin to come together as the underlying structure of their nature is gradually revealed. I would like to suggest a link between this and the struggle between love, hate, and despair in "The Cold Heaven". The third phase is when the creator of the work of art re-introjects the hidden substructure into his ego, but at a higher mental level where the integrated work of art can be worked on by the tools and the technique of the creator. In the case of the poet this will be to do with the strength of poetic technique in terms of tone, structure, and use of language in a particular way. At which point the poem becomes a "thing-in-itself" with an independent existence.

Ehrenzweig observes that good art teaching, and creativity itself, is dependent on a great tolerance of anxiety, because of the need to work through the phase of chaos before the pattern emerges, and it requires, as he says, a more than average ego strength. This passage much illuminated for me a remark made by Eliot (1933, p. 140): "you cannot take heaven by magic, especially if you are, like Mr Yeats, a very sane person". It is this very management of the different elements in the personality which is the hallmark of the authentic creative act, rather than, I think, the notion of a purely "depressive position" state as an end-point.

It reminds me of an adolescent girl I saw with her family, where mother was complaining about (among other things) the mess in the kitchen when her daughter made cakes. We could return later in the work of disentangling their mutual negative projections to the metaphor of the cake: there has to be a mess out of which will ensue the finished product. I have talked to several artists and writers who readily identify with the tripartite nature of this process, akin I think also to what is at work in children's play. The process as described by Ehrenzweig has affinities, I think, with the concepts derived from chaos theory. Structure can emerge from chaos, and there ensues a rhythm of chaos, transition, and order before a new disequilibrium occurs (Gleick, 1987; Scharff & Scharff, 2000, p. 63)—this also links with Britton's ideas about development beyond the depressive position to a new area of struggle.

I think Ehrenzweig's formulation of the three phases of the creative process has links with the idea of a triangular internal space which develops when the individual leaves "The Lake Isle" and is able to tolerate separation and to acknowledge his debt to the objects he both loves and hates. This is the space where play is generated, and where later creative life is nourished.

So I would like to suggest that the wild swans can be understood in a number of ways. They represent the tolerance of the autonomy of the parental couple, an acceptance of departure and loss, and also an acceptance that provisional states of mind, hard won, may then be undermined, even necessarily will be so, in order for creativity to remain alive in the self, by the more anxious, angry and destructive parts of the self. As Yeats observes, he will wake one day to find the swans gone, along with his autumnal resignation. He, like the rest of us, will have to take back his projected passion and work with it in order not to become stuck in another form of retreat.

Since writing this chapter I have read Likierman's recent publication (2001) offering a fresh approach to Klein's work. I think her helpful delineation of two stages of depressive anxiety—what she calls "the tragic stage" and "the moral stage"—link with the ideas I have put forward about Yeats' persecuting guilt in "The Cold Heaven" and his eventual overcoming of it through toleration and an appreciation of reality.

There is, of course, the danger that any theory about the creative act or our understanding of it will become ossified. As Eliot (1933, p. 141) insisted:

> Even when two persons of taste like the same poetry, this poetry will be arranged in their minds in slightly different patterns; our individual taste in poetry bears the indelible traces of our individual lives with all their experience pleasurable and painful. We are apt either to shape a theory to cover the poetry that we find most

moving, or—what is less excusable—to choose the poetry which illustrates the theory.

I hope the reader will take the views expressed here as offering just one reading, from a psychoanalytic perspective, of the nature and shape of the creative act and the oscillating states of mind to which we are all prey, as seen in Yeats' three poems. I talked earlier of Yeats identifying "radiance" as something to which he aspired. I think my own appending of the word "pursuit", as well as "insight", conveys something of the chase to pin down, at least in a provisional way, often elusive ideas that do in any case get modified by subsequent thinking. In psychoanalytic culture these are underpinned by a fundamental understanding of the internal world as being prone to primitive mechanisms such as splitting, idealization and denigration, while the individual struggles towards integration or, rather, one might say management and tolerance of the flux.

I want to end by considering the image of the wild swans linked to a symbol produced by Jim in his therapy, thinking about these "transformative" images as being related to Bion's ideas about "O"—a state of mind which might be called "transcendent" without this necessarily meaning a return to an idealized state.

It is easier to speak of "O", the "thing-in-itself", "the ultimate reality" (Bion, 1970, p. 18) in poetry rather than psychoanalysis, because there hovers over such suggestions the fear of "wild analysis" and hallucination. Bion himself talks of the need to enter into a near-hallucinatory state without memory or desire. He maintained that verbal, musical, and artistic transformations are "transformations in O": "I shall use the sign O to denote that which is the ultimate reality represented by terms such as absolute truth . . . the thing-in-itself". These moments of "O" could then, he maintained, be translated into "K" or knowledge, but only when memory and desire have been renounced. These are complex and difficult ideas, not much debated because, I think, of the danger inherent within them for those practising psychoanalysis, but I believe that if the idea is approached through poetry it becomes more graspable.

The relationship between the poem and the reader lies in the space between them, which has links with the space between patient and analyst, containing not only the projections of the poet but the preconceptions of the reader; not only the projections of the patient but of the analyst. Just as no two sessions can be identical, so no two readings of a poem can be identical, because they occur at this interface. The symbols which arise in a poem, and in a session, have a particular meaning in relationship to both poet and reader, analyst and patient. In psychoanalysis, sometimes it may only be necessary to recognize the "O moment" rather than constrain it with words, even though words are our tools. This chapter is written in the spirit of this understanding: that one's meanings are ultimately one's own, but may also have relevance for others. The swans continue to fly away in each reader's imagination, and by so doing produce their own meanings. As Alvarez (1994, p. 124) puts it, in a chapter about the interpretation of dreams, "there are as many code-books as there are interpreters ... the discipline of psychoanalysis is based on the premise that dreams [and I would add, symbolism in poetry] are like the glittering fragments of a kaleido-scope, constantly shifting and rearranging themselves when the instrument is passed from hand to hand".

It was a year after work began with Jim that he was able to relax his defensive guard and a series of very moving sessions culminated in his producing a symbol which has, I think, affinities with the wild swans and Bion's formulation of "O". He was able to come out from his defensive hiding place and begin to believe that he could rework a difficult internal picture to make room for something new, and to turn to helpful external objects in the process.

He was drawing the cover for a book he planned to write. It was night-time in the picture, and a rabbit had come out to look around. Then he turned over the page and began again. He drew a tree which had roots but no leaves, and the roots were floating. Then he drew some breast-like hills, with one in the distance, and a straight path to the distant hill. There was a fence on the hill, and I asked about it. He said it was to stop people falling off the hill. The tree's roots were now within the nearer hill, and I talked about his feeling rooted here with a place to think. Perhaps we could think about sad things and happy things, without his falling off into space. [His growing awareness of being contained by thinking.] He was colouring the hills and then he drew a badger, saying "It's sunset [the whole sky was red] and he's waking up and coming out". I simply commented on the badger emerging into the quiet evening, and the beautiful sky. "Yes", he said, "and there's a young moon coming up", and he drew it on the right hand side of the page, a thin yellow crescent hanging over the hills.

I think this symbol of the "young moon" was a reworking of "Superman": a projected part of himself that could abandon omnipotence and begin a new cycle of growth and renewal. He had needed me to respect his working under cover of darkness for a long while before he could begin to emerge. This was a crucial turning point for Jim: not a flight from despair into idealization, but a movement towards something new. It is important in our work to recognize the difference (see Alvarez, 1992, p. 179). In this session there was a feeling of awe (on both our parts) that this had been achieved, and after the session he made eye contact with me and said goodbye simultaneously for the first time. In later occasions he was able to appreciate the idea that we made "stories about my feelings" and said he did his best work in therapy. He still had an enormous amount to work through and resistance was still a feature, but far less so. In a long series of sessions he built a "tent" in the room, and this could be explored as both a safe internal space for us to work together but also as a space where I had to stay outside with the humiliating wait before being "adopted" in the sessions by Jim. Within the therapeutic space he could dare more and experiment more in the way Ehrenzweig described with his art students; Jim would describe as an "art attack" (the name of a children's television programme) the fragments he brought and which we would then attempt to piece together to find out their possible meanings. This vital turning point was reached with the symbol of the young moon, the "thing-in-itself" an O symbol.

What I hope to have shown in this chapter is something of the ordinary life process which can be traced through three poems, where idealized states that are actually quite rigid under their apparent "soft-focus", as in "The Lake Isle of Innisfree", have to give way to notions of flexibility and experimentation which nevertheless depend on an internalized stability in order to unfold. While Yeats was a prolific poet who was important socially and politically, what I have been concentrating on is something which is common to us all. What the human task involves is to find a path between the two poles of Hell and Heaven in the psyche: this may involve occasional epiphanic moments which then need to be slowly built into understanding. Insight on its own is not enough: the uncertainty it brings is an opportunity, a necessity, to move forward and achieve change. While this can be formulated on the page it is extremely hard to live, and involves us all in psychic struggle throughout life, in what Hering (2002, personal communication) has called "the dialectic between defensiveness and openness".

Perhaps it is fitting to quote Yeats in his journals again (Foster, 1997) in order to conclude this exploration into what is involved in what I have called the elusive pursuit of insight.

> I suppose that I may learn at last to keep to my own [values and instincts] in every situation in life: to discover and create in myself as I grow old that thing which is to life what style is to letters: moral radiance, a personal quality of universal meaning in act and in thought.

Acknowledgements

Conversations with Al Alvarez, Andrew Baldwin and Christoph Hering have helped me enormously in writing this chapter.

Lines from the poem by W. H Auden are reproduced by kind permission of Faber & Faber.

Grateful thanks to *Contrappunto* and to Rosella Sandri for permission to translate and quote her baby observation.

References

Alvarez, Al (1994). *Night: An Exploration of Night Life, Night Language, Sleep and Dreams*. London: Jonathan Cape.

Alvarez, Anne (1992). *Live Company: Psychoanalytic Psychotherapy with Autistic, Borderline and Deprived Children*. London and New York: Routledge.

Alvarez, A. (1999). Frustration and separateness, delight and connectedness: reflections of the conditions under which bad and good surprises are conducive to learning. In: A. Alvarez, A. Harrison & E. O'Shaugnessy (Eds.), *Symposium on Frustration. Journal of Child Psychotherapy*, 25: 2.

Auden, W. H. (1939). *Selected Poems*, E. Mendelson (Ed.), 1979. London: Faber & Faber.

Bion, W. R. (1962). *Learning from Experience*. London: Karnac.

Bion, W. R. (1970). *Attention and Interpretation*. London: Karnac.

Britton, R. (1998). *Belief and Imagination: Explorations in Psychoanalysis*. London: Routledge.

Cooper, J. M. (1978). *An Illustrated Encyclopaedia of Traditional Symbols*. London: Thames and Hudson.

Edwards, J. (1994). Towards solid ground: the ongoing psychotherapeutic journey of an adolescent boy with autistic features. *Journal of Child Psychotherapy*, 21(1): 57–83.

Ehrenzweig, A. (1967). *The Hidden Order of Art*. London: Weidenfeld.

Eliot, T. S. (1933). *The Use of Poetry and the Use of Criticism*. London: Faber & Faber.

Foster, R. F. (1997). *W. B. Yeats: A Life, Volume 1: The Apprentice Mage*. Oxford and New York: Oxford University Press.

Freud, S. (1917). Mourning and Melancholia, *S.E.*, 14: 237–260. London: Hogarth.

Freud, S. (1927). The Future of an illusion, *S.E.*, 21: 66–72. London: Hogarth.

Gleick, J. (1987). *Chaos*. London and New York: Viking Penguin.

Grinberg, L., & Grinberg, R. (1999). Psychoanalytic perspectives on migration. In: *Psychoanalysis and Culture*. London: Duckworth.

Heaney, S. (1995). The Redress of Poetry. Oxford: Oxford University Press.

Joseph, B. (1989). *Psychic Equilibrium and Psychic Change*. London: Routledge.

Likierman, M. (2001). *Melanie Klein: Her Work in Context*. London: Quantum.

Musa, M. (Ed. & Trans.) (1995). *The Portable Dante*. London: Penguin.

O'Shaugnessy, E. (1964). The absent object. *Journal of Child Psychotherapy*, 1(2): 36–43.

Sandri, R. (1999). Il passagio dallo spazio del corpo allo spazio mentale. *Contrappunto*, 27: 7–25

Scharff, D. E., & Scharff, J. S. (2000). *Tuning the Therapeutic Instrument*. London and New Jersey: Aronson.
Segal, H. (1991). *Dream, Phantasy and Art*. London: Routledge.
Steiner, J. (1993). *Psychic Retreats*. London: Routledge.
Yeats, W. B. (1995). *Collected Poems*. London: Macmillan.

CHAPTER NINE

"Feeling into Words":
evocations of childhood in the poems
of Seamus Heaney

Hamish Canham

In the poem "In Memory of Sigmund Freud", W. H. Auden writes of Freud and the psychoanalytic method he developed:

> To us he is no more a person
> Now but a whole climate of opinion

> Under whom we conduct our differing lives:
> Like weather he can only hinder or help,
>   The proud can still be proud but find it
>   A little harder, and the tyrant tries

> To make him do but doesn't care for him much.
> He quietly surrounds all our habits of growth;
>   He extends, till the tired in even
>   The remotest most miserable duchy

> Have felt the change in their bones and are cheered;
> And the child unlucky in his little State,
>   Some hearth where freedom is excluded,
>   A hive whose honey is fear and worry,

> Feels calmer now and somehow assured of escape;
> While as they lie in the grass of our neglect,

So many long-forgotten objects
Revealed by his undiscouraged shining

Are returned to us and made precious again;
Games we had thought we must drop as we grew up,
Little noises we dared not laugh at,
Faces we made when no one was looking.
[Auden, 1966, pp. 168–169]

I start with this extract from Auden's poem because his phrase "So many long-forgotten objects / Revealed by his undiscouraged shining" applies so well to the focus of much of Seamus Heaney's poetry. That is, the way in which the detailed and honest observation and description of a moment, or a memory, can open it up and subjecting this moment or memory to such scrutiny can be both transforming and liberating.

In the essay from which I take the title of this chapter, "Feeling into Words" (Heaney, 1980, pp. 41–60), Heaney writes about the function of poetry as being "revelation of the self to the self", and he compares poems to being like archaeological finds. This, of course, is an early metaphor used by Freud for the process by which psychoanalysis uncovers what has been buried in the recesses of the mind and returns them to consciousness. This process is poetically expressed in Heaney's early poem "Personal Helicon":

As a child, they could not keep me from wells
And old pumps with buckets and windlasses.
I loved the dark drop, the trapped sky, the smells
Of waterweed, fungus and dank moss.

One in a brickyard, with a rotted board top.
I savoured the rich crash when a bucket
Plummeted down at the end of a rope.
So deep you saw no reflection in it.

A shallow one under a dry stone ditch
Fructified like any aquarium.
When you dragged out long roots from the soft mulch,
A white face hovered over the bottom.

Others had echoes, gave back your own call
With a clean new music in it. And one
Was scaresome for there, out of ferns and tall
Foxgloves, a rat slapped across my reflection.

> Now, to pry into roots, to finger slime,
> To stare, big-eyed Narcissus, into some spring
> Is beneath all adult dignity. I rhyme
> To see myself, to set the darkness echoing.
> [Heaney, 1966, p. 43]

This poem appeals to me because of the parallels that can be drawn between Heaney writing about the act of poetic expression—and indeed of reading poetry too—and the process that goes on between patient and therapist. When the process of reflection begins, the poet, reader, patient, therapist are shown pictures of themselves which do "set the darkness echoing". Some of these images will not necessarily be comfortable and may have, as it were, rats slapping across them; but Heaney seems to imply that they give the personality a "clean new music" or a truer version of who you really are.

What also comes out in this poem, is Heaney's ability to delve into his childhood experience and to bring it back for himself and for the reader as a source for understanding the present. The title "Personal Helicon", means source of poetic inspiration, and childhood experience here clearly provides for Heaney both a way into exploring himself and a link to the way he does this through poetry. For Heaney this process involves capturing the smells, sensations, and perhaps particularly the sounds of childhood. The smell of mint being cut over potatoes for Sunday lunch is the subject of one of his poems. A particular sensation from childhood is described in the poem "Wheels Within Wheels" from which I will quote the first stanza:

> The first real grip I ever got on things
> Was when I learned the art of pedalling
> (By hand) a bike turned upside down, and drove
> Its back wheel preternaturally fast.
> I loved the disappearance of the spokes,
> The way the space between the hub and rim
> Hummed with transparency. If you threw
> A potato into it, the hooped air
> Spun mush and drizzle back into your face;
> If you touched it with a straw, the straw frittered.
> Something about the way those pedal treads
> Worked very palpably at first against you

And then began to sweep your hand ahead
Into a new momentum—that all entered me
Like an access of free power, as if belief
Caught up and spun the objects of belief
In an orbit coterminous with longing.
[Heaney, 1991, p. 46]

This poem does indeed contain wheels within wheels. The Scottish poet, Douglas Dunn (2001), writes that in this poem, Heaney "studies his memory of an upturned bicycle . . . as if under a microscope". One might add to this that he is also studying a child's exploration of his internal and external worlds, the relationship between belief and longing, and through this the relationship of who he has become as an adult to how he was as a child. One feels that as an adult poet he is exploring the childhood sensation of the power of getting a grip on something and of entering so completely into an experience that it almost sweeps him away.

To return to the importance of the sounds of childhood. as one reads across Heaney's work, the sounds of the voices of the people close to him become very familiar. For example, his father's voice in the poem "The Errand":

"On you go now! Run, son, like the devil
And tell your mother to try
To find me a bubble for the spirit level
And a new knot for this tie".
[Heaney, 1996, p. 54]

And his mother's voice in the poem entitled "A Call":

"Hold on", she said, "I'll just run and get him.
The weather here's so good, he took the chance
To do a bit of weeding."
[Heaney, 1966, p. 53]

Heaney's own voice also becomes familiar, and is almost conversational in places. This is partly because it is familiar to us from his appearances on television and radio and from his readings of his work. However, it is also because his poetic voice is so close, I think, to his speaking voice and is imbued with the sounds of his childhood and where he comes from. But it is one of the features of Heaney's poetry that gives it its appeal and particular music. One feels intimately acquainted with what his childhood sounded like, as well as what it looked and smelled like. In a recent interview (with Karl Miller) Heaney says:

> The really valuable thing about my childhood was the verity of the life I lived within the house and the sense of trust that I had among the people on the ground. I am not away from that. And I'm not away, I don't think, from my first speech. I think of that speech as a kind of guttural bough—as opposed to a golden bough. It's a kind of passport through the perils of the fake speech you are bound to encounter, a register that stays reliable. It's not that I believe that you should confine yourself to the cultural or conceptual limits of that first language. Certainly not. In fact, it is precisely the experience of going beyond those limits that constitutes much of the luck of my life. But as a writer, I never want to get out of my phonetic depth, as it were. I like to feel that the line I am writing is being paid out from some old inner voice-reel, that is coming up from the place I re-enter every time I go back where I grew up. I still live a kind of den life when I go home, among my brothers and sisters in County Derry. [Miller, 2000]

Recent psychoanalytic writers have been interested to explore the nature of early auditory experience. For example Piontelli and Maeillo, child psychotherapists from Italy, have written convincingly of the foetus's auditory connection to the mother *in utero*. This early experience forms the basis of speech and gives each language its cadences, rhythms and its particular music. This can be heard with babies when they are lalling. T. S. Eliot made clear the connection he felt between music and poetry by calling his poem "Four Quartets". Eliot has written in "The Music of Poetry":

> I know that a poem, or a passage of a poem, may tend to realize itself first as a particular rhythm before it reaches expression in words, and that this rhythm may bring to birth the idea of the image ... [Eliot, 1957, p. 38]

Bringing together these converging ideas one might say that poetry reaches back beyond childhood to the earliest rhythms and interactions of the intra-uterine life. Certain passages of poetry may therefore move us mysteriously because they tap into these early rhythms. The way words, containing memory and feeling, have the capacity to reveal more than the most apparent meaning was, of course, one of Freud's main discoveries as a way into the unconscious of the patient. Heaney seems to be describing something similar in his essay called "Englands of the Mind":

> ... the cultural depth-charges latent in certain words and rhythms, that binding secret between words in poetry that delights not just the ear but the whole backward and abysm of mind and body; thinking of the energies beating in and between words that the poet brings into half-deliberate play; thinking of the relationship between the word as pure vocable, as articulate noise, and the word as etymological occurrence, a symptom of human history, memory and attachments. [Heaney, 1980, p. 150]

The psychoanalyst Meltzer (1997) has pointed out that while babies learn language and the music of language inside the womb, the conventions and limitations of the spoken word often make it hard to express adequately what you mean. He feels that adults are "rescued" by an ability to express what they feel in dreams and children through their play. In other words to find condensed symbolic expression for feelings. Heaney has also written about the problem for the poet of making a poem an authentic expression of a personal experience. This is the matter of putting "feeling into words". The other side of this is of putting *feelings* into words, and this can only be done, as it were, by feeling them—re-experiencing in the act of writing or reading the original sensation which led to the idea. Working as I do, predominantly with children, it is often their play rather than words or dreams with which I am working. It was one of Melanie Klein's great contributions to psychoanalysis that children's play could be read and understood in much the same way as adults' reports of dreams or free associations. Poetry and children's play both make use of certain images and symbols to give expression to, represent symbolically, and allow a chance for, extended exploration of events in the external world and unconscious internal phantasies.

Sometimes, the meaning behind a symbolic representation of a situation is easily recognizable, at other times the potential meaning of a symbol is worked on over a period of time in therapy. I want to give two examples to illustrate this point, taken from clinical encounters with two girls in the care system. It is a frequent experience for children "looked after" by the local authority to move many times from one placement to another for a variety of often complicated reasons. The impact of these moves on the internal worlds of children has been graphically illustrated to me by the ways these girls have symbolically, one might say poetically, represented how the situation has felt to them. I have felt that these representations of their situations, and feelings about them, have often been too painful for them to put into words, or that their level of linguistic skills was not up to the task, or that words are inadequate to describe what is going on. However, the symbols they have used have conveyed profoundly, succinctly, and movingly their plight.

The first example is taken from an assessment meeting with a girl of seven who had several placements from a young age before arriving in a more settled home. In her first assessment meeting with me I was very struck by the fact that when she came to sit down in the room, she continued to move her legs in a walking motion, as if she still felt constantly on the move. She began to explain to me who she had lived with, and who had been in the various family groupings, but my head was soon unable to organize the information and I was left feeling very confused. As this girl was telling me about her history, she decided to fold and cut out what she called gingerbread men—those paper cut-out figures that form a long line. However, when this girl fanned out the paper, she had cut them in such a way that they were not linked at all but formed separate figures which fell in a pile on the desk. She said resignedly, "sometimes they work, and sometimes they don't". In this way, she was able to convey her deep cynicism about whether relationships stick or not, her sense of life being a lucky dip, and her despair about possible future relationships. All of this, and possibly more, is contained in the image of the gingerbread men, an image that had stuck with me several years after I saw her and lasted in a way that her verbal descriptions of the situation have not.

The second example is taken from a case I have been supervising[1] where a ten-year-old girl, whom I shall call Mary, has been moving from one foster carer to another. Again this is the most recent of many moves. She has been able to explore and manage her feelings in relationship to this move in a quite remarkable way through an extended use of five pebbles, used mainly to play the game of Five Stones. These pebbles have come to represent her situation very clearly in the therapy, and have allowed Mary and her therapist to talk about the stones, the different games they play with them, her feelings about them and so on, which have given them a particularly high yield of meanings over time.

Shortly before the move, Mary began to bring to her sessions five pebbles which she had gathered. She carried these with her everywhere in a little bag and played with them in her sessions in a multitude of ways to represent her feelings and thoughts and state of mind in relation to the impending move. These stones gave Mary and her therapist a way into talking about her situation which, because it was a little removed from Mary herself, was generally acceptable to her. Because Mary continued to play with these stones outside her sessions, they also provided a constant link to her therapist and to what they had been discussing.

So, for example, on the day that Mary was due to meet her new foster carer for the first time, she came to her session beforehand and wanted to play a game she had made up with the stones. Mary wanted her therapist to try to balance one of the stones on one finger. As the therapist tried to do this, she said to Mary, "Maybe you feel a bit like this stone ...". Before she could complete her sentence, Mary interrupted to shout, "Stop it! Don't say your things". The therapist continued to try to balance the stone on her finger and while looking at it then said that she thought she understood something about her. Mary smiled at this and then pointed out how one of the stones had a crack in it. The therapist looked at it and said, "We don't want it to break, now". "No we don't", said Mary, and then, "Now I liked what you said."

It is clear that although Mary is under a huge strain because of having to move again, indeed, feels she could crack like the stone, she manages to let her therapist know that she wants to share her difficulty and she can only do this if her therapist talks about the stones while Mary and she both know it is really she who feels so off-balance. It is therefore Mary's capacity to express her internal situation via symbols that makes it bearable, and without the sensitive recognition of her need for this by her therapist one feels that Mary could, like so many children in the care system, become ill—really crack up, as it were, under the strain of repeated moves on top of the original trauma of being taken into care and the abuse that had preceded that.

As the time for moving from one placement to another came closer, Mary began to play the game of five stones but would count and say things relating to the game in Bengali. Mary is not Bangladeshi but goes to a school which has a large Bangladeshi population among whom the game is popular. One day, close to the move, when she was doing this, Mary told her therapist about a girl in school who had just come from Bangladesh and played the game in a "funny" way. It seemed that she just did things slightly differently—bouncing the stones on the ground before playing. Suddenly, Mary told her therapist that she said "Ama" to a friend of hers and asked the therapist if she knew what that meant. The therapist said she thinks it means "Mummy" and Mary said it did and then went on to tell her she also called a boy "Aba", which means "Dad".

Here I think we can see Mary getting ready for the move, using the stones once again. Perhaps starting to use another language to speak in is her way of preparing for the experience of entering a new family with the particular language all families have that give them their identity. Mary clearly identifies with the girl newly arrived from Bangladesh and perhaps, too, with the experience generally of a minority culture finding its place in a new land with different customs, food, religion, language, etc. In this respect there is something comforting, I think, for Mary in the constancy of these stones. Children play basically this same game in London and Bangladesh, and have probably done so for thousands of years. There are certainly depictions on Ancient Greek friezes of children playing this game. Mary here, too, clearly uses this idea of another language to tell her therapist about the difficulty of moving to someone new called "Mummy" and how in her current parentless state, she is so desperate to find a mother or father she finds herself splurting it out all over the place.

At around this time Mary says that her stones "feel alive" and her therapist is able to talk to her about the way in which she has invested them with her life and what is happening to her at the moment. Virtually every session is spent at least partially playing with the stones. On the day before Mary finally moves she is able to say how her black stone had fallen on to the floor and broken into many pieces. She tells her therapist that she liked that stone and is sad about losing it. She then plays a game with the stones in which her therapist has to pick one and then all the others are arranged leaning against it. Mary then has to try to remove all the other stones without dislodging the nominated one. Again, very clearly, Mary is representing her feelings of sadness at moving on by talking about the favourite black stone that has shattered. She also represents with the game where one stone is to be left unmoved, the impossibility of moving from one family to another without feelings being dislodged.

When Mary did move, the stones were quite quickly replaced by marbles, with which she played for a week or two, new games taught her by her new foster mother. But these marbles have not remained in her play for long. The five stones have served their function for Mary of being transitional objects, helping to get her across a gap and relinquished when no longer necessary. But they had been much more than this, too, as I hope I have conveyed—a way of giving expression symbolically to her circumstances, external and internal, which has very close parallels with the symbols used by poets. The achievement for Mary and in poems that work well is that, as Segal (1957) has pointed out, a communication with the external world has taken place and this capacity to use symbols is the basis for verbal thinking and the ability to communicate with oneself. It is therefore the means by which we are able to tolerate and make sense of our lives and what has happened and is happening in them.

Heaney's own childhood is described by himself in *Preoccupations* and in interviews with Corcoran and Miller, among others. He was born on a farm called Mossbawn in County Derry, in Northern Ireland. Heaney's aunt, Mary, was central to his upbringing as a constant figure in the Heaney household, where a second maternal figure was probably necessary as Heaney was the oldest of nine children. The sense that one gets of Heaney's childhood through his poems, prose, and interviews is of a lively, intimate time that has remained a source of inspiration to him. In his essay titled "Mossbawn", Heaney writes:

> All children want to crawl in their secret nests. I loved the fork of a beech tree at the head of our lane, the close thicket of a boxwood hedge in the front of the house, the soft, collapsing pile of hay in a back corner of the byre; but especially I spent time in the throat of an old willow tree at the end of the farmyard. It was a hollow tree

with gnarled, spreading roots, a soft, perishing bark and a pithy inside. Its mouth was like the fat and solid opening in a horse's collar, and, once you squeezed in through it, you were at the heart of a different life, looking out on the familiar yard as if it were suddenly behind a pane of strangeness. [Heaney, 1980, pp. 17–18]

This child's eye view of the world is something deeply inside Heaney. The poems about his childhood are most apparent in the earlier collections—*Death of a Naturalist* (1966) and *Door into the Dark* (1969)—and reappear strongly again in the later collections, *Seeing Things* (1991) and *The Spirit Level* (1996). In the collection *North* (1975), Heaney ventures into writing about the political troubles in Northern Ireland and draws heavily for inspiration on P. V. Glob's book, which describes the bodies of men and women found in the bogs of Jutland, naked, strangled, or with their throats cut, preserved under the peat since the Iron Age. Glob argues that these bodies were sacrifices to the mother goddess to ensure the fertility of the soil. The imagery of the sacrifices comes together in *North* with the bloodshed involved in the Irish struggles. For example, in the poem "Punishment", clear parallels are drawn between a young woman found strangled with a halter round her neck in a Jutland bog and the women who were tarred for sleeping with men across the sectarian divide. The book contains many poems about blood and violence, but Helen Vendler (1998) has pointed out that it begins with two poems of dedication to Heaney's aunt, "The Seed Cutters" and "Sunlight", collectively titled "Mossbawn", which serve to counter the accounts of the troubles in Northern Ireland by showing people living ordinary lives and the way in which the ability to draw on happy childhood memories fortifies the personality against difficulties encountered in adult life. I want to have a look at one of these poems, "Sunlight".

> There was a sunlit absence.
> The helmeted pump in the yard
> heated its iron,
> water honeyed
>
> in the slung bucket
> and the sun stood
> like a griddle cooling
> against the wall

of each long afternoon.
So, her hands scuffled
over the bakeboard,
the reddening stove

sent its plaque of heat
against her where she stood
in a floury apron
by the window.

Now she dusts the board
with a goose's wing,
now sits, broad-lapped
with whitened nails

and measling shins:
here is a space
again, the scone rising
to the tick of two clocks.

And here is love
like a tinsmith's scoop
sunk past its gleam
in the meal-bin.
[Heaney, 1975, pp. ix–x]

Several commentators (e.g. Corcoran, 1998; Vendler, 1998) have noted the resemblance of the poem to a Vermeer painting for the way it timelessly captures a domestic scene illuminated for a moment. This is the sunlight that Heaney shines on the scene but I think the sunlight of the title also refers to the childhood experience of a kind of indirect, diffuse attention, an easy pleasure in being in someone else's company, "like a tinsmith's scoop / sunk past its gleam". That is a kind of attention that allows space and freedom, "a sunlit absence", in other words. The unforced companionship described here is also the basis for another kitchen scene from a later poem, taken from the sequence "Clearances" (1987, pp. 24–32), written after Heaney's mother's death:

When all the others were away at mass
I was all hers as we peeled potatoes.

Heaney describes here again absent-minded companionship as the potatoes drop into the pan:

> Little pleasant splashes
> From each other's work would bring us to our senses.
> ...

And later:

> I remembered her head bent towards my head,
> Her breath in mine, our fluent dipping knives—
> Never closer the whole rest of our lives.

Perhaps this poem also reveals the absence in the earlier poem to be that of other siblings, at least for a while. In "Sunlight", Heaney manages to create an impression of timeless stillness. The pump in the yard, which Heaney has described as being the centre of life in "Mossbawn", is still. It is hot outside in the yard, it is hot inside, with the stove sending out its plaque of heat. At the centre of this stillness is Heaney's aunt, whose movements as she bakes seem to reinforce the surrounding quiet—"her hands scuffled", or dusting a board with a goose's wing.

While an idyllic childhood memory in "Sunlight" is deliberately set against and outside the troubles of Northern Ireland and the images inspired by P. V. Glob's book, *The Bog People*, a later poem in the collection *The Spirit Level* (1996), called "Two Lorries", brings these two elements together in one of Heaney's most moving and technically brilliant poems. This poem is written in the form of a sestina; a fixed poetic form comprising six stanzas, each of six lines, and a final three-line envoi. In place of rhyme, the same six line-ending words or syllables appear in each stanza, but in a shifting order. In the envoi, all six end-words are contained within the three lines (Steele, 1999):

> It's raining on black coal and warm wet ashes.
> There are tyre-marks in the yard, Agnew's old lorry
> Has all its cribs down and Agnew the coalman
> With his Belfast accent's sweet-talking my mother.
> Would she ever go to a film in Magherafelt?
> But it's raining and he still has half the load
>
> To deliver farther on. This time the lode
> Our coal came from was silk-black, so the ashes
> Will be the silkest white. The Magherafelt

(Via Toomebridge) bus goes by. The half-stripped lorry
With its emptied, folded coal-bags moves my mother:
The tasty ways of a leather-aproned coalman!

And films no less! The conceit of a coalman ...
She goes back in and gets out the black lead
And emery paper, this nineteen-forties mother,
All business round her stove, half-wiping ashes
With a backhand from her cheek as the bolted lorry
Gets revved and turned and heads for Magherafelt

And the last delivery. Oh, Magherafelt!
Oh, dream of red plush and a city coalman
As time fastforwards and a different lorry
Groans into shot, up Broad Street, with a payload
That will blow the bus station to dust and ashes ...
After that happened, I'd a vision of my mother,

A revenant on the bench where I would meet her
In that cold-floored waiting-room in Magherafelt,
Her shopping bags full up with shovelled ashes.
Death walked out past her like a dust-faced coalman
Refolding body-bags, plying his load
Empty upon empty, in a flurry

Of motes and engine-revs, but which lorry
Was it now? Young Agnew's or that other,
Heavier, deadlier one, set to explode
In a time beyond her time in Magherafelt ...
So tally bags and sweet-talk darkness, coalman.
Listen to the rain spit in new ashes

As you heft a load of dust that was Magherafelt,
Then reappear from your lorry as my mother's
Dreamboat coalman filmed in silk-white ashes.
[Heaney, 1996, pp. 13–14]

As you can see, the end-words here are "ashes", "lorry",
"coalman", "mother", "Magherafelt" and "load", although Heaney
beautifully and subtly changes these end-words, as with "load",
"lode", "lead", "payload" and "explode" most noticeably, but also
with "lorry" and "flurry", and "mother" and "other" and "meet
her". This gives the poem a feeling of an internal pressure that is
just contained by the formality of the poetic structure. As Corcoran

has noted, Heaney himself has commented on the use of the sestina in his book *The Redress of Poetry* (1995, p. 170), in reference to Elizabeth Bishop's poem simply entitled "Sestina". He writes:

> Like any sestina, this has a touch of virtuosity about it, but its virtuosity is not what engages one's attention. Its immediate effect is as emotionally direct as a fairytale. Just as Dylan Thomas's villanelle 'Do Not Go Gentle Into That Good Night' comes across as a dramatic cry rather than as a formal set-piece, so the narrative and dramatic interest of Bishop's sestina very quickly deflects attention from its master-class excellence as a technical performance. The poem circles unspoken sorrows, and, as it circles them, it manages to mesmerize them and make them obedient to creative will. [Heaney, 1995, p.]

Heaney's poem seems to circle time and memory, the sestina form reinforcing the poem's internal exploration of these themes, with its shifting end-lines, that juxtapose familiarity with change. The poem opens with a scene from the 1940s: Heaney describing a scene from his childhood, where the figure of Agnew, the coalman, enters to disrupt and plant thoughts in the mind of Heaney's mother and Heaney himself. It is the beginning of a time sequence which inevitably brings with it the recognition of death at the end of the poem. The two lorries of the title are that of Agnew the coalman who flirts with Heaney's mother and the other, separated in time by many years, is a lorry which drives into Magherafelt carrying a bomb. The fact that Magherafelt is also the place that Agnew has suggested to Heaney's mother for a trip to the pictures seems most significant. After the explosion Heaney asks, "But which lorry / Was it now? Young Agnew's or that other, / Heavier, deadlier one set to explode". The two lorries have merged in Heaney's mind so that they have become tangled and confused. By the end of the poem one is left unclear as to which image prompted the start of the poem—the explosion in Magherafelt or the scene in the yard several decades earlier. One reading of the merging of these two lorries into one is that the image contains within it a small boy's outrage at the flirtation between his mother and Agnew. Here is a boy disturbed by knowledge of his mother as a person with sexual desires, who is tempted by "red plush" and "leather aprons". It is a knowledge which creates a violent pressure in the mind of the boy, in the memory of the poet, and within the structure and narrative of the poem. Agnew's "load" shifts about to become "lode", then "lead", "payload", till finally it explodes.

The shattering of a child's world that this recognition brings is conveyed in the poem through the word "fastforwards", and associations to it, in the fourth stanza. It is a word that brings with it images of modern technology and video recorders—a world away from having to go to the cinema to see films and from coal lorries with their cribs, black lead, and emery paper. Of course, the image of a crib summons up images of babies asleep, not yet disturbed by knowledge of the adult world.

"Fastforwards" also emphasizes the poem's cinematic qualities—as if one is being shown a film that is playing inside Heaney's head. This effect is highlighted in several other ways in the poem, which give it a particular dream-like quality and adds to the fluid timeframe. Unless Heaney was in Magherafelt when the bomb went off, he must have seen reports of it on television. If not, he may have heard reports on the radio or read reports about it in the papers and visually constructed the scene in his mind. This has then been superimposed on to other images—Agnew's lorry, his mother in the waiting room of the bus station. The other way the poem is like an old film is the repeated black and white imagery, which starts in the opening line with the rain falling on the black coal and moves through the poem with the silk black lode giving ashes of the silkiest white, the black lead around the fireplace, to the final line of the "dreamboat coalman filmed in silk-white ashes". This imagery is undoubtedly intended in relation to the film that Agnew invited Heaney's mother to go to all those years ago. The black and white imagery is only interrupted by the "dream of red plush", which hints at the burgeoning sexual awareness in the poem and the accompanying feelings of smallness, exclusion, and anger the boy experiences in relation to this.

The end of "Two Lorries" seems to contain a complex set of feelings, for as well as the explosive rage I have described, the poem has a powerful restorative function in bringing back to life Heaney's mother and Agnew the coalman and allowing Heaney to re-examine his feelings in relation to them via his memory and the work he does on his feelings in the poem. In this way, poetry seems to offer a similar set of opportunities to psychotherapy for looking at old hurts, examining the roots of the feelings, and seeing how these can flood and distort the present. To give Heaney the last word, he writes:

> ... poetry holds attention for a space, functions not as a distraction but as pure concentration, a focus where our power to concentrate is concentrated back on ourselves. This is what gives poetry its governing power. [Heaney, 1988, p. 108]

Note

1.   I am grateful to Ariel Nathanson for permission to quote from his notes.

References

Auden, W. H. (1966). In Memory of Sigmund Freud. In: *Collected Shorter Poems*. London: Faber & Faber.

Corcoran, N. (1998). *The Poetry of Seamus Heaney: A Critical Study*. London: Faber & Faber.

Dunn, D. (2001). Quotidian miracles: seeing things. In: T. Curtis (Ed.), *The Art of Seamus Heaney*. Bridgend: Seren.

Eliot, T. S. (1957). *On Poetry and Poets*. London: Faber & Faber.

Glob, P. V. (1969). *The Bog People: Iron Age Man Preserved*. London: Faber & Faber.

Heaney, S. (1966). "Personal helicon". In: *Death of a Naturalist*. London: Faber & Faber.

Heaney, S. (1969). *Door into the Dark*. London: Faber & Faber.

Heaney, S. (1975). "Sunlight". In: *North*. London: Faber & Faber.

Heaney, S. (1980). *Preoccupations: Selected Prose 1968–1978*. London: Faber & Faber.

Heaney, S. (1987). "Clearances". In: *The Haw Lantern*. London: Faber & Faber.

Heaney, S. (1988). *The Government of the Tongue*. London: Faber & Faber.

Heaney, S. (1991). "Wheels within wheels". In: *Seeing Things*. London: Faber & Faber.

Heaney, S. (1995). *The Redress of Poetry*. London: Faber & Faber.

Heaney, S. (1996). "Two lorries", "The Errand" and "The Call". In: *The Spirit Level*. London: Faber & Faber.

Meltzer, D. (1997). Concerning signs & symbols. *British Journal of Psychotherapy*, 13(2): 60–66.

Miller, K. (2000). *Seamus Heaney in Conversation with Karl Miller*. London: Between the Lines.

Segal, H. (1957). Notes on symbol formation. *International Journal of Psycho-Analysis*, 38: 391–397.

Steele, T. (1999). *All the Fun's in How You Say a Thing: An Exploration of Meter & Versification*. Columbus: Ohio University Press.

Vendler, H. (1998). *Seamus Heaney*. London: Harper Collins.

INDEX